THE PROMISE FULFILLED:

A History of the
Modern Pentecostal Movement

This book is an outgrowth of a dissertation presented

to the Faculty of the Graduate School of

THE UNIVERSITY OF TEXAS

in partial fulfillment of the requirements for the

Degree of

DOCTOR OF PHILOSOPHY

IN HISTORY

Austin, Texas   August, 1959

THE PROMISE FULFILLED:

A HISTORY OF THE
MODERN PENTECOSTAL MOVEMENT

BY KLAUDE KENDRICK, Ph.D.

GOSPEL PUBLISHING HOUSE
Springfield, Missouri
2-578

[PRINTED
IN U.S.A.]

Foreword

THE CHARISMATIC sects of the twentieth century constitute what has been termed "the Pentecostal Movement", and that term has been applied realistically and accurately. Since 1906, the movement has spread to every continent and to nearly every country in the world. It has appeared in many forms, but with one common basic element, a belief in the supernatural of New Testament days, with special emphasis on the "glossolalia" or the speaking in "tongues" as an evidence of individuals having received in personal experience a baptism in the Holy Spirit.

Unlike revival movements of other days, the appeal of the Movement, in its beginnings, was not to the unconverted, but to earnest Christians, believers in Christ who had already received a crisis experience called the new birth. To these persons there came a hunger for spiritual reality which caused them to seek earnestly for a new experience which they envisioned as available to them according to the New Testament pattern. That an experience was received by them cannot be questioned, for there is no other explanation of the zeal which has inspired so many to devote themselves to the propagation of the Pentecostal message.

The author of this book has endeavored to lay a foundation for the beginnings of the Movement, to tell the story of its genesis in a small Bible school in a mid-western state, and then to describe the beginnings of the Assemblies of God the largest organized group of Pentecostal belief and practice. The evolution of the Assemblies of God, its rapid growth and development, its evangelism and missionary zeal are now a matter of record for all to read. The author has not stopped there, but has gone on to describe the beginnings and development of other Pentecostal organized groups. He has not attempted to tell the story of the independent missions or churches which are a part of the movement, concerning which there is little information available. The independent churches can never accomplish what has been accomplished through co-operative effort. It was this conviction which was responsible for the organizing of the Assemblies of God in the beginning. The author has described the growth of the service departments of a number of the larger organized Pentecostal groups, but has not attempted to tell in detail the results being obtained through these departments. That they are proving to be effective is evidenced by the continued growth of each of the groups he has described.

Books have appeared already telling the story of the rise and development of some of the organized Pentecostal groups, including the Church of God (Cleveland, Tenn.), the Pentecostal Holiness Church and the Assemblies of God. This is the first attempt, however, to present a documented treatise on the Pentecostal Movement as a whole in the U.S.A. The author has been very meticulous in his searching for and recording source material, and is to be commended for his effort.

Although a half century has witnessed the rise of the Pentecostal Movement, and movements normally have a tapering off in zeal and effort in the process of time, there is no evidence that this movement has reached this stage, In fact, the influence of the message of the movement is being felt in the ranks of the established churches to a degree hitherto unrealized. Should this treatise be used for the furtherance of the Pentecostal message, it will be most gratifying to the author, the publishers and all who have contributed to this worthy effort.

J. ROSWELL FLOWER, L.L.D.

Author's Preface

THE AUTHOR became interested in the study of the modern Pentecostal movement in the 1940's as a result of taking a position to teach history on the faculty of Southwestern Bible Institute, Waxahachie, Texas, a Bible College operated by the Assemblies of God. Among his other assignments he was asked to develop a course in Pentecostal history. This paper is the climax of the study started at that time.

The greatest problem involved in the project has been locating adequate sources. The early pioneers of the Pentecostal movement were not scholars, and published little historical material. To complicate the matter further, they attached so little importance to historical data that files of early papers were often destroyed after serving their original purpose. For the same reason few leaders kept personal journals or diaries. What is more surprising, very little material has been obtainable through personal correspondence except from the prominent officers of Pentecostal bodies; other "old-timers" seem to lack the inclination or stamina to write of their experiences. They display no such inhibitions about talking, however, thus a great deal of data has been obtained through interviews. Books of minutes, church manuals, and periodical files also furnish valuable aid in the study of various Pentecostal groups.

By design, the greater portion of this work is devoted to the beginnings of the Pentecostal revival and to the history of the Assemblies of God. The reasons for this emphasis are that no scholarly study of the early years has heretofore been made, that the author is a member of the Assemblies of God, that the Assemblies comprise the largest Pentecostal group, and that source materials relative to several of the other groups are comparatively scant. Extensive presentations of the Church of God and the Pentecostal Holiness Church have not been thought necessary, since excellent histories of these groups have been published in recent years.

Though the Pentecostal Movement went overseas in 1907 and strong organized Pentecostal bodies are found in many nations outside the continental United States, this work has chosen to ignore the history of the world movement, confining itself to the story of the rise and development of the movement in the United States of America.

The author gratefully acknowledges that the preparation of this work would not have been possible without the kind assistance of many persons. Of special help were those persons who took time from their busy schedules to provide materials by giving interviews, completing questionnaires, and writing letters.

The original manuscript, a dissertation prepared for the Graduate School of the University of Texas, was enhanced immeasurably by the direction and counsel of Dr. Barnes F. Lathrop, chairman of the author's graduate supervisory committee. Dr. J. Roswell Flower, for more than thirty years an Executive of the Assemblies of God, and Robert C. Cunningham, editor of THE PENTECOSTAL EVANGEL, gave valuable help in preparing the manuscript for publication.

Contents

TABLES

I
Introduction

JAMES MADISON stated that religious freedom

arises from that multiplicity of sects, which pervades America, and which is the best and only security for religious liberty in any society; for where there is such a variety of sects, there cannot be a majority of any one sect to oppress and persecute the rest.[1]

Probably he did not foresee just how safe, on the basis of this principle, American religious freedom would become. Literally scores of additional sects have joined the appreciable number of his day.

The present study is concerned with the modern Pentecostal revival, which developed at the beginning of the twentieth century and added more than two dozen to this array of sects in the United States. The only distinctive characteristic that this new revival movement contributed to the American religious tradition was the emphasis that it placed upon the incident found in the second chapter of Acts.

And when the day of Pentecost was fully come, they were all with one accord in one place. And suddenly there came a sound from heaven as of a rushing mighty wind, and it filled all the house where they were sitting. And there appeared unto them cloven tongues like as of fire, and it sat upon each of them. And they were all filled with the Holy Ghost, and began to speak with other tongues, as the Spirit gave them utterance.[2]

---

[1] Jonathan Elliot, The Debates in the Several State Conventions, on the Adoption of the Federal Constitution, as Recommended by the General Convention in Philadelphia, in 1787, together with the Journal of the Federal Convention, Luther Martin's letter, Yate's Minutes, Congressional Opinions, Virginia and Kentucky Resolutions of 1798-1799, and Other Illustrations of the Constitutions (second edition, 5 vols., Philadelphia: J. B. Lippincott, 1888), III, 330.

[2] Acts 2:1-4.

1

From this scripture are derived the name "Pentecost" and the peculiar religious experience that identify the movement. Pentecostal theology holds that every Christian believer may enjoy a similar "baptism of the Holy Spirit." A Pentecostal theologian describing this characteristic position stated that "in addition and subsequent to conversion, a believer may experience an enduement of power whose initial oncoming is signalized by a miraculous utterance in a language never learned by the speaker." [3] This tongues phenomenon as an evidence of the religious experience of the "baptism in the Holy Spirit" is the distinctive Pentecostal mark.

SCOPE OF THE MODERN PENTECOSTAL MOVEMENT

Detailed attention will be given here only to those Pentecostal groups that have figured prominently in the development of the movement, viz.: Assemblies of God; Pentecostal Church of God of America; International Church of the Foursquare Gospel; Open Bible Standard Churches; United Pentecostal Church; Pentecostal Holiness Church; Church of God; and Church of God in Christ. To show the comprehensiveness of the movement, however, the following names of other bodies in the Pentecostal family that appear in the yearbook [4] of the National Council of the Churches of Christ are given: Apostolic Overcoming Holy Church of God; Calvary Pentecostal Church; Christian Church of North America; Church of God of Prophecy; Church of God, World Headquarters; Church of our Lord Jesus Christ of the Apostolic Faith; Congregational Holiness Church; Emmanuel Holiness Church; Fire Baptized Holiness Church of God of the Americas; International Pentecostal Assemblies; National David Spiritual Temple of Christ Church Union; (Original) Church of God; Pentecostal Assemblies of the World; and Pentecostal Fire-Baptized Holiness Church. In addition to the bodies that have just been named, several smaller ones exist but are not

---

[3] Myer Pearlman, *Knowing the Doctrines of the Bible* (Springfield, Mo.: Gospel Publishing House, 1937), p. 310.

[4] Benson Y. Landis, ed., *Yearbook of American Churches, Information on all Faiths in the U.S.A.,* 1960 (New York: National Council of the Churches of Christ in the U.S.A., 1959).

reported in the *Yearbook of American Churches*. Among
them are sects that engage in bizarre practices, the most
prominent being snake handling. Though this radical fringe
has received attention through newspaper publicity because
of the novelty of its rites, it is by no means representative
of the Pentecostal movement and constitutes only a very
small minority of the total constituency.

The unusual growth of the Pentecostal movement is indicated by the figures in Table 1. During the twenty-four-
year period from 1936 to 1959 the number of churches
increased 407 per cent, the total membership, 582 per cent.
It should be pointed out that the statistics reported to the
National Council of Churches are not always current and
are sometimes questionable. For example, the National
David Spiritual Temple of Christ Church Union shows
an average local membership of 607, while the Assemblies
of God, the largest Pentecostal body, shows an average local
membership of only sixty-three. It is doubtful that such a
difference actually exists. The figures are the best available, however, and do indicate the general trends of the
movement.

THE PENTECOSTAL MOVEMENT'S RELATIONSHIP TO AMERICAN
CHRISTIANITY

How are the Pentecostal groups related to other Christian groups? What is the place of the Pentecostal movement on the American religious scene? These questions
can most rapidly be answered by a survey of American
religious bodies today. The classification of such bodies is
a difficult and debatable business, but for present purposes
they can be divided into churches, sects, and cults.

CHURCHES. The term *church* may be used to designate
a dignified, well-ordered body that has a long history and
stresses Christianity as an organization and a body of belief.

A number of characteristics are generally associated with
churches. They are confessional and place great emphasis
upon an official creed or confession of faith. They usually
practice infant baptism, which tends to make them all-
inclusive in their membership rather than exclusive. Elab-

TABLE 1

CHURCH AND MEMBERSHIP GROWTH OF PENTECOSTAL BODIES

	1936[1]		1959[3]	
	CHURCHES	MEMBERS	CHURCHES	MEMBERS
Assemblies of God	2,611	148,043	8,088	505,552
Church of God in Christ	772	31,564	3,800	380,428
United Pentecostal Church	413[2]	25,751[2]	1,595	160,000
Church of God	1,081	44,818	3,082	155,541
Pentecostal Church of God of America	81	4,296	900	103,500
International Church of the Foursquare Gospel	205	16,147	697	79,012
Apostolic Overcoming Holy Church of God	23	863	300	75,000
Church of God, World Headquarters	—	—	1,829	71,777
Pentecostal Assemblies of the World	87	5,713	600	50,000
Pentecostal Holiness Church	375	12,955	1,203	49,594
Church of our Lord Jesus Christ of Apostolic Faith	—	—	155	45,000
National David Spiritual Temple of Christ Church Union	11	1,880	67	40,701
Church of God of Prophecy	—	—	1,214	35,526
Open Bible Standard Churches	—	—	265	25,000
Calvary Pentecostal Church	16	1,046	35	20,000
Christian Church of North America	120[2]	11,114[2]	217	20,200
Fire Baptized Holiness Church	59	1,973	300	6,000
(Original) Church of God	—	—	75	6,000
International Pentecostal Assemblies	98	6,333	43	5,000
Congregational Holiness Church	56	2,167	138	4,121
Emmanuel Holiness Church	—	—	56	1,200
Pentecostal Fire-Baptized Holiness Church	55	1,348	42	615
	6,063	316,011	24,701	1,839,767

[1] Figures from U.S. Bureau of the Census, Religious Bodies: 1936 (2 vols., Washington:- Government Printing Office, 1941).
[2] This figure is a combination of those bodies that merged to form the group.
[3] Figures from Yearbook of American Churches, 1960.

orate church polity causes stress to be placed upon organization and ecclesiastical machinery.

In this survey the different communions will be grouped as Catholic Churches, Lutheran Churches, Reformed Churches, Arminian Churches, and Unionizing Churches.

Catholic Churches. In this category are the churches that antedate in tradition the Protestant reformation and that look either to Rome or to one of the Eastern Patriarchates as the original source of their authority. These bodies are highly developed hierarchical systems and doctrinally hold that man obtains grace through the sacraments.

The outstanding among them is the Roman Catholic Church, the largest single group of Christians in the United States. The Roman church was identified with much of the exploration of the New World and thus has a long history in American religion. The other churches connected with this family are related to the Eastern Orthodox Church, which is represented in America by over a dozen separate organizations, some bound in a measure to the authority of the homeland church, some completely autonomous.[5]

Lutheran Churches. Lutheran Churches trace their traditions back to the Protestant Reformation under Martin Luther. They have as a basis of their belief the particular creedal statements prepared and adopted during the period of 1528-1579 by Luther and his associates. These were collected and published in the *Book of Concord,* the Augsburg Confession being the basic Lutheran creed.

The Lutheran Church was first brought to America in the first half of the sixteenth century by the Dutch in their settlement of Albany and New Amsterdam. It was firmly established about fifty years later when many German Lutherans came to New York, Pennsylvania, Delaware, Maryland, and the Carolinas.

Though nineteen Lutheran bodies are listed in the *Yearbook of American Churches,* 1957, most of them are members of one of three groups: The United Lutheran Church, the Synodical Conference, and the American Lutheran

---

[5] F. E. Mayer, *The Religious Bodies of America* (St. Louis: Concordia Publishing House, 1956), pp. 9-121.

Church. The larger individual communions are the United
Lutheran Church, The Lutheran Church—Missouri Synod,
Evangelical Lutheran Church, American Lutheran Church,
Augustana Evangelical Lutheran Church, and the Evan-
gelical Lutheran Joint Synod of Wisconsin and Other
States.[6]

Reformed Churches. The American churches that adhere
to that system of theology generally associated with John
Calvin will be classified in this section. The name of John
Calvin figures prominently in this school of belief not because the doctrines were peculiar to him, but because he
first formed and systematized them.

Calvinism as a theological system can be summarized as
follows: (1) God is absolute sovereign in His Creation;
(2) God as sovereign both foreordains and foreknows all
things, including man's destiny; (3) originally man was
pure and made the image of God, but has fallen from this
state through his own volition; (4) man can only be saved
through the unmerited grace of God; and (5) those pre-
destined to salvation will be saved, since it is impossible
for the elect to fall away from grace. Though Calvin was
largely responsible for Presbyterian church government,
Calvinism has been associated with all types of church
polity. In fact, the system is so plastic that it has shown
the capacity of adjusting to many new situations and en-
vironments without abandoning its fundamental principles.[7]

Five "Reform" bodies with roots that reach back to the
European Reform churches of Calvin operate in America.
The Reformed Church in America, which was established
in 1628 by early Dutch settlers in New York, and its off-
shoot, the Christian Reformed Church are the only ones
of significant size. The remaining three are the free Magyar
Reformed Church in America, the Netherlands Reformed
Congregations, and the Protestant Reformed Churches of
America.[8]

The Presbyterian churches throughout the world com-

[6] *Ibid.,* 137-142, 180-189.
[7] James Hastings, ed., *Encyclopedia of Religion and Ethics* (12 vols., New
York: Charles Scribner's Sons, 1955), III, 146-155.
[8] Landis, *Yearbook of American Churches,* 1957, pp. 98-99.

prise more than 125 distinct denominations and constitute
the largest Protestant church group operating under a single
type of government. Only eleven of these bodies are found
in the United States. The largest is the Presbyterian Church
in the United States of America. Its first presbytery in the
western hemisphere was in 1706. The other Presbyterian
churches in order of numerical importance are the Presbyterian Church in the United States, United Presbyterian
Church of North America, Cumberland Presbyterian
Church, Colored Cumberland Presbyterian Church, Associate Reformed Presbyterian Church, Orthodox Presbyterian
Church, Reformed Presbyterian Church of North America
(Old School), Reformed Presbyterian Church in North
America (General Synod), Associate Presbyterian Church of
North America, and Bible Presbyterian Church.[9]

Calvinism provides the basic theology for Congregational
churches as well as Presbyterian, though this polity is much
different from that practiced by Calvin. The Congregational Christian Churches is the great Congregational body
in America today. This church resulted from a merger of
the Congregational Churches, whose history dated back to
the Pilgrim Fathers, and the Christian Church, which developed out of the revival movements at the end of the
eighteenth century.[10]

Baptist churches are included as Calvinistic bodies since
most of them have developed from this theological background. This is not the common bond, however, that unites
all Baptists.

The competency of the soul of man in matters religious is the
basic principle on which all Baptists are united and out of which
all Baptist beliefs grow. For want of a better term this principle
can best be defined as "theological individualism." For this reason
Baptists acknowledge no human founder, recognize no human authority, and subscribe to no human creed. Baptists have always
maintained that every believer has "absolute liberty under Christ,"
for as a member of Christ he has the right to interpret Christ's
will for himself.[11]

[9] *Ibid.*, pp 89-95; U. S. Bureau of Census, *Religious Bodies: 1936*, II, 1381-1476.
[10] Landis, *Yearbook of American Churches, 1957*, pp. 39-40.
[11] Mayer, *Religious Bodies*, p. 259.

Because of this individualism, and of roots that extend back to New England Congregationalism, almost all Baptists hold the Congregational type of church government.

There is some difference of opinion concerning the exact date that the first Baptist church was established in America. It is commonly agreed, however, that a local body existed as early as 1639.[12] Since that time Baptists have developed into the largest Protestant group in the United States. Twenty-seven different bodies worship in America. Those that have memberships of over 100,000 in the order of their numerical importance are as follows: Southern Baptist Convention, National Baptist Convention, U.S.A., National Baptist Convention of America, American Baptist Convention, American Baptist Association, North American Baptist Association, Conservative Baptist Association of America, Free Will Baptists, General Association of Regular Baptist Churches, and United Free Will Baptist Church.[13]

The Protestant Episcopal Church is difficult to place properly among the historic churches of America. Though it has definite Catholic and Lutheran characteristics, it is classified with the Reformed churches in this study because of the many communicants, possibly a majority, who are sympathetic with the Reformed position.[14] The mother body, the Anglican Church is noted for the theological variety that exists within the communion. It is held together, nevertheless, by a

common standard of worship and life in *The Book of Common Prayer*, a common post-Reformation historical tradition in which the Thirty-Nine Articles are a prominent milestone, a common espiscopal [sic] ministry, a common recognition of the pre-eminence of the primatial see of Canterbury, and such modern structural institutions as Lambeth Conference and the Anglican Congress.[15]

Arminian Churches. Arminian bodies hold a theological position that is directly opposite to Calvinism. The system was first strongly advocated by James Arminius (1560-

[12] *Ibid.*, p. 261.
[13] Landis, *Yearbook of American Churches*, 1957, pp. 16-27.
[14] Mayer, *Religious Bodies*, pp. 275-276.
[15] *Ibid.*, p. 276.

1609), a Dutch theologian. Arminius objected to a doctrinal development which made God the author of sin and of the condemnation of men. The Five Articles of the Remonstrance, addressed in 1610 to the States-General of Holland, expressed the Arminian tenets that rejected the beliefs of the five Calvinistic articles. This document teaches:

(1) God's knowledge of man's faith or unbelief the condition of election; (2) the universality of God's grace and Christ's redemptive work; (3) human freedom and responsibility under prevenient grace; (4) the resistibility of divine grace; (5) the possibility of final and total apostasy.[16]

Arminianism did much to soften the dogmatism that had developed in the Reformation from the influence of both Luther and Calvin. In the Wesleyan revival Arminianism became aggressive and passed swiftly across the Atlantic to the New World. It was an important factor in the American frontier revivals and became the basic theology for those sects that developed as a result of revivalism.[17]

The Methodist churches are the outstanding Arminian group in America. They have made a great impression on western religion with their message of universal redemption and personal godliness through "entire sanctification." Because of their appeal to the American frontiersman, the evangelical zeal inherited from John Wesley and his associates and an emotional "heart-felt" religious experience caused Methodism to flourish on the advancing frontier.[18] Methodism retained several vestiges of the Anglican Church, in which John Wesley was reared and ordained to the ministry. Most Methodist bodies are organized to the episcopal pattern and practice baptism by sprinkling.

Though more than twenty Methodist churches are listed among American religious bodies, only four have memberships in excess of one hundred thousand. The Methodist Church (so named following the union of the Methodist Episcopal Church with the Methodist Episcopal Church,

---

[16] *Ibid.*, p. 293.
[17] Hastings, *Encyclopaedia of Religion and Ethics*, I, 812-816
[18] *Ibid.*, VIII, 612.

South, in 1939) is the largest, having on its rolls approximately nine-tenths of all American Methodists. The other three are the African Methodist Episcopal Church, African Methodist Episcopal Zion Church, and the Christian Methodist Episcopal Church.[19]

Several Evangelical bodies belong to the Arminian family. The largest of these is the Evangelical United Church, which came into being as a result of a merger in 1946 of two bodies with backgrounds similar to that of Methodism—the United Brethren Church and the Evangelical Church. These churches were formed in Germany near the end of the eighteenth century, and patterned after Methodism both in theology and polity. The United Brethren in Christ, the United Christian Church, the Evangelical Congregational Church, the Evangelical Mission Covenant Church of America, and the Evangelical Free Church of America are smaller Evangelical, Arminian bodies.[20]

Unionizing Churches. A few churches can very conveniently be classified under this name because of their belief that Christendom should dispose of denominational creeds and unite in order to return to the Apostolic pattern. They do not agree concerning the means for accomplishing unity, but the unionizing factor is a common characteristic.

The Moravian Church is the oldest of these bodies. It originated in Europe in the late medieval period on the principle: "in essentials unity, in nonessentials liberty, in all things charity." Through its long history, the church has been noted for evangelical spirit. A small related body is the Evangelical Unity of the Czech-Moravian Brethren in North America.[21]

Another body of the unionizing variety is the Evangelical and Reformed Church, which was formed in 1934 by a merger of the Reformed Church in the United States and the Evangelical Synod of North America. Both of these churches had German backgrounds, the former beginning

[19] Landis, *Yearbook of American Churches,* 1957, pp. 75-84.
[20] Mayer, *Religious Bodies,* pp. 342-351.
[21] *Religious Bodies,* 1936, II, 1276-1288.

its American history in the early eighteenth century, the latter, in the mid-nineteenth."

The largest American indigenous body, the Disciples, also belongs to this division. Paradoxically, it has, instead of uniting Christians, been responsible for some additional schisms. The movement developed out of the frontier revivals at the beginning of the nineteenth century. The Christians, Christian Connection, General Convention of Christian Churches, Christian Union, Churches of Christ, and the Disciples of Christ are the bodies that belong to this family. None of them claims to be a denomination but rather a "movement to restore the sovereignty of the local congregation." For this reason only the loosest type of organization ties the churches together on a state or national basis."

Another unionizing body, quite small, is the Plymouth Brethren, which originated in England in the first half of the nineteenth century. It stresses anticreedalism and antidenominationalism and speaks of the "invisible membership in the church," maintaining that the Church is composed of all believers."

The Pentecostal Movement received many of its traditions from these American churches. All the Pentecostal bodies are Arminian in their doctrine. In regard to polity, all three types—episcopal, presbyterian, and congregational—are found among the groups. Baptism by immersion is generally practiced, just as it was in some of the former "poor man's" churches, the Baptists and Disciples. Salvation by a crisis experience and sanctification are doctrines of the Pentecostals that were once stressed by several churches, especially the Methodists before they established communions.

SECTS. An important part has been played in American religion by sects. This is pointed up by the fact that the bodies that now compose forty per cent of American Prot-

²² *Ibid.*, pp. 614-618.
²³ Mayer, *Religious Bodies*, pp. 371-386.
²⁴ *Ibid.*, pp 387-389.

estantism were despised dissenting minorities in the colonies less than two centuries ago.[25]

Though the term *sect* is generally used to designate an ignorant, highly emotional and fanatical group that is ephemeral in character, this study agrees with H. Richard Niebuhr that the sect constitutes an important phase in the process of religious denominational development.

In Protestant history the sect has ever been the child of an out-cast minority, taking its rise in the religious revolts of the poor, of those who were without effective representation in church or state and who formed their conventicles of dissent in the only way open to them, on the democratic, associational pattern. The sociological character of sectarianism, however, is almost always modified in the course of time by the natural processes of birth and death, and on this change in structure changes in doctrine and ethics inevitably follow.... Furthermore, wealth frequently increases when the sect subjects itself to the discipline of asceticism in work and expenditure; with the increase of wealth the possibilities for culture also become more numerous and involvement in economic life of the nation as a whole can less easily be limited. Compromise begins and the ethics of the sect approach the churchly type of morals. As with the ethics, so with the doctrine, so also with the administration of religion. An official clergy, theologically educated and schooled in the refinements of ritual, takes the place of lay leadership; easily imparted creeds are substituted for the difficult enthusiasms of the pioneers; children are born into the group and infant baptism or dedication becomes once more a means of grace. So the sect becomes a church.[26]

The sect possesses characteristics that are in contrast to those of the church. A church is a natural social group similar to a family or a nation. Members are born into the church, thus it is an inclusive institution and often national in scope and emphasizes the universalism of the Gospel. The sect, on the other hand, is a voluntary association because its members must join its ranks as a result of religious experience; it tends to be exclusive rather than inclusive, advocating baptism for believers only and completely rejecting infant baptism.

---

[25] John M. Mecklin, *The Story of American Dissent* (New York: Harcourt, Brace & Co., 1934), p. 3.

[26] H. Richard Niebuhr, *The Social Sources of Denominationalism* (New York: H. Holt & Co., 1929), pp. 19-20.

The church places importance upon its system of doctrine, the administration of its sacraments, and the teachings of an official clergy. The sect, conversely, opposes all creeds and confessions of faith, holding the Bible to be the only rule of faith and practice. It views sacraments as only symbols of fellowship, and frequently rejects an official clergy, favoring lay inspiration over theological or liturgical expertness.

Because the church is an inclusive social group and is generally closely tied to the national, economic, and cultural interests, its ethics must accommodate the morality of the respectable majority. The sect, however, is always activated by the ideal of the pure church, hence it emphasizes a strict discipline which results in separatism and often semiasceticism.[27]

The classification of sects here employed is taken from Elmer T. Clark's, *The Small Sects in America* (1949). Two categories that seem to fall more appropriately under cults have been omitted. Great difficulty is involved in attempting to distinguish between churches and sects. A number that are here called sects are considered by others to be churches, and some of the smaller bodies that have been listed as churches can be regarded as sects.

The Pessimistic or Adventist Sects. These groups have despaired of ever realizing the ends they seek through the means of social processes. They see only doom for the world, since it is bad and beyond hope of improvement. Through cosmic catastrophe the present world order will end with the casting down of the unbelievers and the elevating of the faithful to important places in the theocratic order that follows. The Seventh-day Adventists, Advent Christian Church, Church of God (Adventist), Church of God (Seventh Day), Primitive Advent Christian Church of God (Oregon, Illinois), Life and Advent Union, and Jehovah Witnesses are adventist sects. While Elmer T. Clark does not list the Pentecostals among the adventist sects, they are definitely adventist in doctrine and practice, even going so

[27] *Ibid.*, pp. 17-19.

far as to link the restoration of *pneumatika* (spiritual gifts) with the end of time and the return of Christ.

Perfectionist or Subjectivist Sects. These sects are similar in character to early Methodists. In fact, most of them are offshoots of Methodism. They seek holiness or personal perfection of life through the experience of sanctification. The outstanding bodies in this category are the Quakers, Church of the Nazarene, Pilgrim Holiness Church, Christian and Missionary Alliance, and the Church of God of Anderson, Indiana.

Charismatic or Pentecostal Sects. Since the Pentecostal sects have been considered at the beginning of this chapter, and will be dealt with in detail in the body of this study, they need no description here. Though Pentecostal bodies possess all the general characteristics of sects, some are approaching the phase in their development of becoming institutionalized so may shortly be entering the church classification.

Communistic Sects. These groups seek to realize their religious objectives by withdrawing from society and forming colonies. The common characteristic is community of goods. Very few can be considered successful in maintaining their communistic mark over a long period. The few remaining today are realizing at best only a struggling existence. The more prominent are the Shakers, Amana Church Society, House of David, and Church of God and Saints of Christ.

Legalistic or Objectivist Sects. Clark uses this designation to list those bodies that stress "rules, objective forms, observances, or 'things' which can be definitely performed as essential to true religion." Included in these would be groups that insist on such practices as foot washing as a religious rite and peculiarities of dress like the use of "hooks and eyes" instead of buttons. A few of the better known are the Mennonites, the Amish, and Dunkers, including the River Brethren and the Brethren in Christ.

CULTS. This term is used to designate those religious bodies that look outside the Christian tradition for their

TABLE 2

MEMBERSHIP OF CHRISTIAN BODIES[1]

CATHOLIC

Roman Catholic	39,509,508
Eastern	2,545,318
Old Catholic and Polish National Catholic Church of America	366,246
LUTHERAN	7,763,495

REFORMED

Reformed	459,869
Presbyterian	4,126,583
Congregational	1,381,124
Baptist	20,493,381
Protestant Episcopal	3,042,286

ARMINIAN

Methodist	12,213,097
Evangelical	887,392

UNIONIZING CHURCHES

Moravian	66,443
Evangelical & Reformed	806,365
Disciples	1,943,599
Christian Union	8,000
Churches of Christ	2,000,000

	97,612,706
SECTS AND CULTS	6,435,035
TOTAL CHRISTIAN CONSTITUENCY	104,057,741

[1] Statistics taken from *Yearbook of American Churches,* 1960.

basic and peculiar authority. They generally accept Christianity but only as a step on the path to greater "truth" coming from a new and additional authority beyond Christianity.

The largest and most important of the American cults is Mormonism. Its adherents embrace the Book of Mormon as a new revelation. Next in importance is Christian Science. *Science and Health* is its new discovery of truth and is considered absolutely necessary for a correct understanding of the Bible. Theosophy and New Thought represent a group of cults that are distinctive in that they combine influences from other world religions. Another group of cults stem from the teaching of P. P. Quimby, who stressed health, happiness and success. The Unity School of Christianity and Psychiana are of this type.[28]

The Pentecostal bodies, since they embrace only the Bible as their source of authority, do not possess cult characteristics.

An evaluation of Tables 1 and 2 produces the following comparisons:

	Per cent of total U.S. Christian population
Churches	93.8%
Sects and Cults	6.2%
Pentecostal bodies	1.8%

This study, then, will be concerned with a movement that in some fifty years has grown until it constitutes twenty-nine per cent of the total membership of the sects and cults and may, with its almost two million constituents, be considered a noticeable Protestant minority.

[28] Mayer, *Religious Bodies*, pp. 449-458, 525-557; Clark, *Small Sects in America*, pp. 232-235.

II
Tongues Phenomena Before the Modern Period

THE MODERN Pentecostal revival is the latest movement of a long succession of groups and individuals that have considered the tongues phenomenon to be of divine origin. Before considering the modern movement, these will be briefly identified.

TONGUES PHENOMENA IN THE NEW TESTAMENT

The first of this series is the New Testament church. Indeed, the Pentecostal bodies of today use Biblical incidents as the best justification for their unusual doctrinal position. The first of these occurrences, Acts 2:1-4, has already been mentioned [1] as the basic Biblical foundation for the Pentecostal belief in the "tongues experience." The second of the Bible events concerns the ministry of Philip in the city of Samaria. [2]

Though the account makes no mention of the tongues phenomenon, Pentecostal writers go to considerable lengths to show that it was one of the mystical manifestations evidenced there. [3] The third New Testament case, which is found in the ninth chapter of Acts, involves the Apostle Paul. Here again actual reference to "tongues" is absent from the narrative, but Pentecostal writers are convinced that Paul's experience included "speaking in tongues." [4] The

---

[1] See pp. 1-2.

[2] Acts 8.

[3] P. C. Nelson, *Bible Doctrines, A Handbook of Pentecostal Theology Based on the Scriptures and Following the Lines of the Statement of Fundamental Truths as Adopted by the General Council of the Assemblies of God* (rev. and enl. ed., Enid, Okla.: Southwestern Press, 1936), p. 95.

[4] Carl Brumback, *What Meaneth This? A Pentecostal Answer to a Pentecostal Question* (Springfield, Mo.: Gospel Publishing House, 1947), pp. 216-217. Though the historical account is missing from the New Testament narrative, (The Acts of the Apostles), Pentecostal believers also classify the Corinthian church as a "tongues" group because of the evidence found in I Corinthians 12 and 14.

17

fourth account relates the story of the Gentiles' receiving
the "Pentecostal experience."

> While Peter yet spake these words, the Holy Ghost fell on all
> them which heard the word. And they of the circumcision which be-
> lieved were astonished, as many as came with Peter, because that on
> the Gentiles also was poured out the gift of the Holy Ghost. For
> they heard them speak with tongues, and magnify God. Then
> answered Peter, Can any man forbid water, that these should not
> be baptized, which have received the Holy Ghost as well as we?[5]

The last scriptural event in which the "tongues experience" played a prominent role occurred some twenty years
later. This happened during the Apostle Paul's visit to
Ephesus. There a group of Christians "spake with tongues,
and prophesied"[6] after receiving instruction and prayer
from Paul.

TONGUES PHENOMENA IN THE ANCIENT CHURCH

There is a certain amount of evidence to indicate that
the tongues phenomenon continued to be displayed during
the entire period of the ancient Church. According to
Philip Schaff,

> speaking with tongues . . . was not confined to the day of Pentecost.
> Together with the other extraordinary spiritual gifts which distin-
> guished this age above the succeeding periods of more quiet and
> natural development, this gift, also, though to be sure in a modified
> form, perpetuated itself in the apostolic church. We find trace
> of it still in the second and third centuries, and . . . even later than
> this, though very seldom.[7]

A sect in the ancient Church that can be classed as
Pentecostal was that founded by Montanus of Phrygia, who
advocated strict church discipline and believed that the
Church was to receive a new Pentecostal baptism. Among
the disciples of Montanus ecstatic religious experiences became common. The group gained considerable prestige
when Tertullian, the noted Latin Father, embraced its
teachings. Tertullian describes the spiritual gifts, including

---

[5] Acts 10:44-47.
[6] Acts 19:6.
[7] Philip Schaff, *History of the Apostolic Church* (New York: Charles Scribner's,
1853), pp. 197-198.

the gift of tongues, demonstrated among the Montanists.[8] Eusebius writes that Montanus "was carried away in spirit, and wrought up into a certain kind of frenzy and irregular ecstasy, raving, and speaking, and uttering strange things." [9] Because of its unorthodox teachings and practices the group, which never enjoyed extensive popularity, was forced in time to withdraw from the Church, and its distinctive characteristics were ultimately branded as heresy.

The writings of Irenaeus (130-202) indicate that the tongues phenomenon existed in his day.

For this reason does the apostle declare, "speak wisdom among them that are perfect," terming those persons "perfect" who receive the Spirit of God, and who through the Spirit of God do speak in all languages, as he used himself also to speak. In like manner we do also hear many brethren in the Church, who possess prophetic gifts, and who through the Spirit speak all kinds of languages.[10]

TONGUES PHENOMENA IN THE MEDIEVAL CHURCH

A few instances of what may be regarded as the "gift of tongues" can be found among the saints of the medieval and early modern periods. With them the supposed phenomenon took the form of conversing in languages that they had never learned. A very early figure to whom this gift has been attributed was Pachomius (292-346).[11] Many biographers of Vincent Ferrer (1350-1419), a young Spaniard who became a Dominican, hold that he "was endowed with the gift of tongues, an opinion supported by Nicholas Clemangis, a doctor of the University of Paris, who had heard him preach." [12] The most colorful and famous of this group was the great Jesuit missionary, Francis Xavier (1506-1552). He was said to have been able to preach in

---

[8] Tertullian in *The Ante-Nicene Fathers* (10 vols., New York: Charles Scribner's Sons, 1885), III, 446-447; Philip Schaff, *History of the Christian Church* (reprint, 8 vols., Grand Rapids: Wm. B. Eerdmans Publishing Co., 1949-50), I, 236.

[9] Eusebius Pamphilus, *Ecclesiastical History*, Translated by C. F. Cruse (London: Bell and Daldy, 1870), p. 184.

[10] Irenaeus in *Ante-Nicene Fathers*, I, 531.

[11] George Barton Cutten, *Speaking with Tongues, Historically and Phychologically Considered* (New Haven: Yale University Press, 1927), p. 38.

[12] *The Catholic Encyclopedia, An International Work of Reference on the Constitution, Doctrine, Discipline, and History of the Catholic Church* (15 vols., New York: Robert Appleton Co., 1912), XV, 438.

many languages that he had never learned. Mackie, who
alludes to these accounts, questions their credibility.[13] Louis
Bertrand (1526-1581) was another believed to have mystical powers. The bull by which he was canonized for his
success among the Indians in western hemisphere "asserts
that to facilitate the work of converting the natives to God,
the apostle was miraculously endowed with the gift of
tongues." [14]

TONGUES PHENOMENA IN THE MODERN CHURCH

The infrequency of recorded manifestations of tongues
during medieval and early modern times seems to indicate
that the phenomenon was not then at all common. Mackie
says that

from patristic times until the power of the Reformation had made
itself distinctly felt the gift of tongues is an almost forgotten
phenomenon. The attention which the Reformation drew to the
Scriptures is the reason for the reappearance of the gift. Men do
not usually have the gift of tongues unless they know there is a
gift of tongues.[15]

This observation may be well founded, for after the sixteenth century the tongues phenomenon became more prev-
alent.

The first group in the modern era that exhibited Pentecostal behavior was the Jansenists. This French sect, which
rose in the Roman Catholic Church after the Council of
Trent, was subjected to persecution following the issuance
in 1705 of a bull condemning them. After persecution began,
mystical manifestations were reported among the group.
Cutten says that "speaking in tongues" was found among
them in 1731.[16] Knox records an account by Pere Lambert
of the behavior exhibited by this sect which includes the
phenomenon.[17] Newman considers some of the contemporary
accounts of the phenomena among the Jansenists exaggerat-

[13] Alexander Mackie, *The Gift of Tongues* (New York: George H. Doran Co.,
1921), p. 28.
[14] *Catholic Encyclopaedia*, IX, 377.
[15] Mackie, *Gift of Tongues*, p. 27.
[16] Cutten, *Speaking with Tongues*, p. 67.
[17] R. A. Knox, *Enthusiasm: A Chapter in the History of Religion, with Special
Reference to the Seventeenth Centuries* (New York: Oxford University Press,
1950), p. 372.

ed but accepts the main facts as being true.[18] The excesses of the party soon caused such a wave of criticism that even former sympathizers became hostile and the movement abated.

Another group in France exercising the tongues phenomenon appeared at about the same time as the Jansenists. These were Protestants who resorted to the Cevennes Mountains during the persecution that followed the revocation of the Edict of Nantes in 1685. They were called the Prophets of the Cevennes or Camisards. Among them a revival of religious enthusiasm occurred including phenomena as peculiar as those noted among the Jansenists.

Respecting the physical manifestations, there is little discrepancy between the accounts of friend and foe. The persons affected were men and women, the old and the young. Very many were children, boys and girls of nine or ten years of age. They were sprung from the people ... for the most part unable to read or write, and speaking in everyday life the *patois* of the province with which alone they were conversant. Such persons would suddenly fall backward, and, while extended at full length on the ground, undergo strange and apparently involuntary contortions; their chests would seem to heave, their stomachs inflate. On coming gradually out of this condition, they appeared instantly to regain the power of speech.... From the mouths of those that were little more than babes came texts of Scripture, and discourses in good and intelligible French such as they never used in their conscious hours.[19]

When some of the French Prophets emigrated to England and made converts, there, the tongues phenomenon was exercised among the British also.[20] The Camisard enthusiasm in France apparently did not last long. It is probable that their radical habits were eventually replaced by more orthodox ways and that they again merged with the traditional group of French Protestants.

A few sects receiving much of their inspiration from the Anabaptist movement and displaying Pentecostal characteristics developed in England during the seventeenth century. Outstanding among them were the Society of Friends; or

[18] Albert Henry Newman, *A Manual of Church History* (2 vols., Philadelphia: American Baptists Publication Society, 1903), II, 478.

[19] Henry M. Baird, *Huguenots and the Revocation of the Edit of Nantes* (2 vols., New York: Charles Scribner's Sons, 1895), II, 186-187.

[20] Cutten, *Speaking with Tongues*, p. 56.

Quakers. This group, it is true, did not carry its mystical tendencies to extremes. "Most mystic sects have sooner or later 'run out' (as Fox said of the Ranters) into absurdities, puerilities, fanaticism or immorality. Friends have [been] preserved in a large measure from such fate."[21] There is evidence, even so, that in the early years of the sect the exercise of "tongues" was present. Schaff lists the Quakers among those who were acquainted with the phenomenon.[22] However that may be, the Quakers' claim to prophecy, scorn of human learning, direct reliance upon inspiration and propagation of their beliefs by speaking rather than by writing, certainly lean in the Pentecostal direction. The preaching of youth and children and the involuntary movement from which Quakers receive their name are also closely related to practices and reactions that result in outbursts of spontaneous speech.

The Quakers were followed in the eighteenth century by a group that surpassed them in religious emotionalism. Because of the violent physical exercises that attended their worship, the sect became known as the Shakers. The roots of the group extend back into both the Quakers and the Camisards, the early leaders having been Quakers who accepted the teaching of the Camisards after they emigrated to England.[23] The Shakers inherited their religious enthusiasm, no doubt, from both of these bodies, and they carried it to great lengths.

Some who attended confessed their sins aloud, crying for mercy; some went into a trance-like state in which they saw visions and received prophecies of Christ's imminent second coming. Others shouted and danced for joy because they believed that the day was at hand for wars to cease and God's kingdom on earth to begin.[24]

Along with other spiritual phenomena "speaking in tongues" appears to have been prominent among the Shakers.[25]

[21] Elbert Russell, *The History of Quakerism* (New York: MacMillian Co., 1942), p. 56.

[22] Schaff, *History of the Christian Church*, I, 236.

[23] Marguerite Fellows Melcher, *The Shaker Adventure* (Princeton: Princeton University Press, 1941), pp. 5-6.

[24] *Ibid.*, pp. 21-22.

[25] Cutten, *Speaking with Tongues*, pp 76-81.

The eighteenth century should not be passed without a reference to the early Methodists. In the societies formed by John Wesley an atmosphere of informality, spiritual fervor, and religious enthusiasm became characteristic. Crying out with groans and sobs, shouting, and uttering of unintelligible sounds were common. Though the Methodist writers do not seem to make any mention of "tongues," some authors have attributed the exercise to the early Wesleyan period.[26] Wesley himself never described any "tongues" experiences in his works. He did take issue with a statement that after apostolic times no mention could be found in history of the exercising of the gift of tongues. By way of refutation Wesley cited the Camisards.[27] His argument does not, of course, necessarily mean that he accepted or approved the phenomenon.

Of all groups before the twentieth century showing Pentecostal characteristics, no other received as much notice as the Irvingites, a sect which developed in Great Britain about 1825. The momentous events of the late eighteenth and early nineteenth centuries aroused in the minds of many devout persons a conviction that Christ would soon return to earth. Since a number of pious persons felt the the church was in a state of unreadiness to meet Christ, they began to pray for a general revival of religion with the renewal of the spiritual gifts of apostolic days.[28] Edward Irving, a popular Presbyterian minister in London, played a prominent role in the movement. When various demonstrations of religious enthusiasm occurred, he accepted them as being of divine origin. His church at first did not become disturbed at these new developments. Confusion ensued, however, when the "gift of tongues" was exercised in his services. A strong faction formed that opposed the unorthodox religious expression, and ultimately Irving and his followers were turned out of the church.[29] This action resulted in the establishment of the Catholic Apostolic Church, often called "Irvingite" because of Irv-

---

[26] Schaff, *History of the Christian Church*, I, 237.
[27] Cutten, *Speaking with Tongues*, pp. 56-57.
[28] P. E. Shaw, *The Catholic Apostolic Church, Sometimes Called Irvingitee*, A *Historical Study* (New York: Kings' Crown Press, 1946), pp. 25-27.
[29] *Ibid.*, pp. 33-37.

ing's early leadership. This body wrote a "tongues" tenet in its theology.

In colonial America an unusual religious consciousness developed that was reproduced on every frontier as the nation expanded westward.[80] Each wave of revivalism connected with this religious consciousness had its share of excesses. Extreme physical exercises including groaning, shouting, weeping, dancing, the "barks," "holy laugh," and the "jerks," were characteristic.[81] One is not surprised to find "tongues" among such demonstrations.[82]

The last American body to be included in this catalog of "tongues groups" prior to the twentieth century is the Church of Jesus Christ of Latter-day Saints, commonly known as the Mormon Church, an indigenous American religious cult founded by Joseph Smith in 1830. The seventh Article of Faith of the Latter-day Saints states that they "believe in the gift of tongues, prophecy, revelation, visions, healing, interpretation of tongues, etc."[83] Heber Grant, the seventh President of the church, commented on this article of faith:

Now, we have had many men who have had the gift of tongues, out in the world, preach this gospel in a language of which they had no knowledge....

Unless the gift of tongues and the interpretation thereof are enjoyed by the Saints in our day, then we are lacking one of the evidences of the true faith.[84]

[80] W. W. Sweet, *Religion in the Development of American Culture*, 1760-1840 (New York: Charles Scribner's Sons, 1952), p. 146.

[81] Clark, *Small Sects*, pp. 89-93; W. W. Sweet, *The Story of Religion in America* (New York: Harper and Brothers, 1939), pp. 331-333.

[82] Melcher, *Shaker Adventure*, p. 60; Francis J. Curran, *Major Trends in American Church History* (New York: American Press, 1946), p. 72.

[83] Peter G. Mode, *Source Book and Bibliographical Guide for American Church History* (Menasha, Wisc.: George Banta Publishing Co., 1921), p. 491.

[84] Heber J. Grant, *Gospel Standards, Selection from Sermons and Writings of Heber J. Grant*, compiled by G. Homer Durham (Salt Lake City: Deseret News Press, 1941), pp. 10-12.

III
Background of the Modern Pentecostal Revival

THIS CHAPTER will undertake to show the movements and trends in the last part of the nineteenth century that contributed to the outbreak of the modern Pentecostal revival. The period was a critical one for American religion. As A. M. Schlesinger points out, the history of American Christianity

has been marked by recurrent conflicts between orthodoxy and heteredoxy, between fundamentalism and modernism, with every hard-won peace a truce and the battle line ever advancing to new fronts.... Perhaps at no time in its American development has the path of Christianity been so sorely beset with pitfalls and perils as in the last quarter of the nineteenth century.[1]

Conditions on the domestic scene and in the church following the Civil War resulted in a trend toward spiritual decay. There was so little interest in religion that churches were understaffed and church attendance was adversely affected. "In the period from 1865 to 1900 a large percentage of congregations in all Protestant denominations were without pastors." [2] By the end of the nineteenth century some of the larger churches were alarmed at the situation. In 1899 the Methodist Episcopal Church showed a loss in membership rather than a gain to break a century of growth.[3]

---

[1] A. M. Schlesinger, "A Critical Period in American Religion, 1875-1900", Massachusetts Historical Society, *Proceedings*, LXIV (1932), pp. 523-47.

[2] Aaron Ignatius Abell, *The Urban Impact on American Protestantism, 1865-1900* (Cambridge: Harvard University Press, 1943), p. 225.

[3] Frank Grenville Beardsley, *The History of Christianity in America* (New York: American Tract Society, 1938), p. 215.

MORAL, POLITICAL, AND BUSINESS CORRUPTION

This period was characterized by moral corruption. "Lowering of the standards of conduct in both public and private life was one of the unfortunate consequences of the Civil War." [4] It should be pointed out, however, that the Civil War was not the only cause for this moral decay. The rise of the city during this time contributed much to this condition. Slums became breeding places for delinquency while the concentration of wealth became a lure for crime, especially theft. Crime in the United States showed an alarming growth during the decade of 1880-90. [5] Gambling also flourished, especially in the frontier cities. One state operated a lottery. Prostitution operated openly in most cities. [6] The liquor evil became a formidable problem after the Civil War. The government's action in placing a tax on intoxicants to produce revenue for the war had given drinking a new respectability. The increase in the capital investment of the industry indicates its tremendous growth during this period. It expanded from $29,000,000 in 1860 to $193,000,000 in 1880. [7] The champions of traditional conduct and morals were alarmed at the appearance of the "concert-saloon" in the cities.

"The first of them opened on Broadway and the Bowery, and with their illuminated transparencies, jangling music and painted girls, made an instant success. They multiplied with astonishing rapidity; by 1869 it was said that New York had six hundred. The best of them, like the Louvre and Olympic, were gorgeously fitted up and maintained a certain decorum, but in Chatham Street and the Bowery were dens of a baser kind, which needed a better police supervision than they got." [8]

The lowering of conduct and morals was not limited to private life. The period was also characterized by its political corruption.

---

[4] W. W. Sweet, *The Story of Religion in America* (New York: Harper and Brothers, 1939), pp. 476-77.

[5] Arthur Meir Schlesinger, *The Rise of the City, 1878-1898* (New York: Macmillan Company, 1933), pp. 111-115.

[6] John D. Hicks, *The American Nation, A History of the United States from 1865 to the Present* (Second edition, Boston: Houghton Mifflin Company, 1949), p. 84; Allan Nevin, *The Emergence of Modern America, 1865-1878* (New York: Macmillan Company, 1927), pp. 325-26.

[7] Nevins, *Emergence of Modern America*, pp. 335-336.

[8] *Ibid.*, p. 93.

The war brought to prominence a class of rough unscrupulous men, with low standards of personal conduct, who too frequently were permitted to gain leadership in both business and politics. Out of such a general background came an era of wholesale corruption in politics which affected every section of the nation and every department of government.[9]

The situation was so bad that men of first rank purposely began to avoid political careers. Theodore Roosevelt received little encouragement when he decided to run for public office after graduating from Harvard in 1881. In fact, "his lawyer and business friends sought to dissuade him from a career which, they pointed out, was controlled not by 'gentlemen' but by saloon-keepers, horse-car conductors, and the like." [10]

Such a political stage made an excellent setting for the "boss" and the "machine" to rise to a place of dominance. New York fell prey to the Tweed Ring and later Tammany; Philadelphia had its Gas Ring, Minneapolis suffered under the corrupt "Doc" Alonzo Ames, while San Francisco had its "Blind Boss" Buckley. In fact, it was reported that there was not a city in the United States with a population of 200,000 that was not affected by such political corruption. Under such control cities were fleeced of millions through graft and manipulation. A glaring example of this was the success of the Tweed Ring in increasing New York City's debt in two and a half years by $70,000,000, the greater part of it going to individuals in the ring itself.[11]

This political rottenness also affected state and federal governments. In these areas of administration the power of wealth was significant.

A congressional investigating committee reported in 1873: 'The country is fast becoming filled with gigantic corporations wielding and controlling immense aggregations of money and thereby commanding great influence and power. It is notorious in many state legislatures that these influences are often controlling.' [12]

---

[9] Sweet, *Story of Religion*, p. 477.

[10] Schlesinger, *Rise of The City*, p. 388.

[11] Arthur Meir Schlesinger, *Political and Social Growth of the American People, 1865-1940* (Third edition, New York: Macmillan Company, 1941), pp. 71-72.

[12] *Ibid.*, p. 76.

Money was expended freely by big interests to buy votes
and offices and maintain powerful lobbyists.[13]

Business also was a victim of this moral perversion. In
fact, "probably no period in our history has seen our com-
mercial morality quite so widely debased as just after the
war." [14] This lack of business ethics was evidenced by a
wave of wildcat stock selling, defalcations, oil speculations
and fraudulent railroad projects. The business leaders
through their personal creative energy and drive realized
fabulous success. These were days of "steel kings", "coal
barons", "railroad magnates", and "Napoleons of finance".
Unfortunately, they did not often attain their successes
through scrupulous means.[15] "With nation-wide competition
at work only the ablest, the most selfish, and the most
unscrupulous of the competitors could survive." [16] Wealth
and fame were too often realized by trampling under foot
all rivals.

INCREASE OF NATIONAL WEALTH

American religious life was particularly affected by the
tremendous increase in the wealth of the nation.[17] The
prosperity of the times was revealed by changes in American
architecture and decoration and the demand for rich foods
and elaborate dress. This improved economy tended to
make the existing churches more and more concerned with
the middle and upper middle classes as their members
rose into these groups. The Baptist and Methodist communions, once the churches of the poor, even became interested in the welfare of the rich. The improvement of
the physical facilities of worship, plus the wide economic
gulf between rich and poor made the poor feel increasingly
ill at ease in the old established churches. Religion became more and more exclusive and the poor became more

[13] Nevins, *Emergence of Modern America*, pp. 178-190.
[14] *Ibid.*, p. 190.
[15] Sweet, *Story of Religion*, pp. 477-78.
[16] Hicks, *The American Nation*, p. 175.
[17] Schlesinger, *The Rise of the City*, p. 431; Carroll D. Wright, "Are the
Rich Growing Richer and the Poor Poorer?" *Atlantic Monthly*, LXXX (September,
1897), pp. 300-309.

and more neglected until the mass of them was largely unchurched.[18]

CHRISTIAN NURTURE THEORY

In addition to the tendencies induced by these worldly factors, considerable disturbance and controversy arose within American Christianity from the introduction of new theological and intellectual concepts. One of these involved the very nature of salvation itself. For a hundred years evangelical Christendom, and especially American revivalism, had taught that salvation involved a crisis experience. This belief was so basic that it might be said to be the foundation principle of American revivalism. But in the 1840's Horace Bushnell published a book entitled *Christian Nurture,* which appeared in its final form in 1861, that challenged this traditional position. Bushnell maintained that a child raised in the proper environment should grow up to be a Christian through the process of natural development.[19] Though Bushnell's position was sharply attacked, it steadily gained wider acceptance. In fact, by the time of his death in 1876 it had become so popular that he was acclaimed the leader of a new liberal movement in religion.[20]

The concept of gradual salvation naturally brought the technique of revivalism under fire. If a conversion experience was no longer necessary for salvation, the revival was an antiquated instrument. The extent of this criticism is indicated by the appearance of Davenport's *Primitive Traits in Religious Revivals.*[21] To be sure, the conservatives combatted this trend most violently.

SOCIAL GOSPEL

Bushnell's "nurture" theology also became the basis for the view that it was the duty of the church to attack elements of un-Christian nurture through social and political action. If Christian development was to be effective, the

[18] Abell, *Urban Impact,* pp. 1-6; Henry F. May, *Protestant Churches and Industrial America* (New York: Harper & Brothers, 1949), p. 119.
[19] Merrill Elmer Gaddis, "Christian Perfectionism in America" (unpublished Ph.D. dissertation, University of Chicago, 1929), pp. 456-457.
[20] Sweet, *Story of Religion in America,* pp. 476-477.
[21] *Ibid.,* p. 497.

American environment had to be reformed.[30] A series of
crises of poverty and violence on the domestic scene—the
railroad strike in the Hayes administration, the Pennsylvania coal mining disturbances with their "Molly Maguires,"
the activities of the Knights of Labor, the Haymarket bomb-
ing, the growth of the city with its slums, and the Home-
stead and Pullman strikes in the 1890's—further contributed
to a re-evaluation by American Protestantism of its attitude
toward society.[33] This interest in the sins of society produced the "social gospel."

The evangelical and conservative segment of American
Christianity continued to maintain that the best remedy
for the ills of society was to be found in the application
of the spiritual doctrines of the Bible. Sin was the cause
of the crises, thus individual regeneration was the solu-
tion.[34] This faction, therefore, opposed the social gospel and
devoted itself to the reformation of the individual through
conversion.

DARWINISM

The publication in 1859 of Charles Darwin's *Origin of
Species* became the cause of another controversy on the
American religious scene. What was popularly known as the
evolution issue continued into the twentieth century. Ap-
plying the principle of evolution to church doctrine, the
liberal wing of Protestantism favored allowing theology to
change and develop in order to adjust to new scientific
findings.[35] The champions of traditional orthodoxy, on the
other hand, resisted the theory passionately, defending their
literalistic interpretation of the Bible. To them

Darwin's theory seemed in flat contradiction to Biblical doctrine.
For example, the statement that God created man in His own
image appeared quite irreconcilable with the view that man had
descended from ape-like ancestors; and the Biblical account of crea-

[32] Charles Howard Hopkins, *The Rise of the Social Gospel in American
Protestantism,* 1865-1915 (New Haven: Yale University Press 1942), p. 5.
[33] Paul Allen Carter, *The Decline and Revival of the Social Gospel: Social and
Political Liberalism in American Protestant Churches, 1920-1940* (Ithaca, N. Y.:
Cornell University Press, 1956), p. 10.
[34] May, *Protestant Churches and Industrial America,* pp. 189-190.
[35] Stow Persons, "Evolution and Theology in America," *Evolutionary Thought in
America,* Stow Persons, ed. (New Haven: Yale University Press, 1950), pp. 425-433.

tion had been so completely identified with the scientific acceptance of permanent species that the whole Christian doctrine of creation, and with it the whole Christian doctrine of God's relation to the world seemed imperiled.[26]

HIGHER CRITICISM

Another blow to the fundamentalist faction in the church was the introduction from German universities of the "higher criticism" and studies in comparative religions. The former called into question the infallibility of the Bible and subjected the Scriptures to rigorous historical analysis. The sixty-six books, instead of constituting one volume of inspired literature, comprised rather a collection of history, folklore, discourses, poetry, and prophecy produced over a period of a thousand years. Studies in comparative religions, by demonstrating that all good was not monopolized by one faith, produced a new measuring rod for Christianity. One result of this new interest was the convening of the first World Parliament of Religions held in Chicago in 1893.[27] The conservatives continued, in contrast, to find solace in an unquestioning acceptance of the Bible and the belief that mankind could find the answer to its spiritual need only in Christ.

HOLINESS MOVEMENT

Since no existing church communion declared itself as a body against the religious laxness and innovations that disturbed the American church in the last half of the nineteenth century, the way was open for a new group to come forward as champions of traditional evangelical Protestantism. Under these circumstances the Holiness Movement came into existence. The people who united under this designation found their bond of union in the Wesleyan experience and doctrine of entire sanctification, commonly called the "second blessing." [28] In addition to reaffirming

[26] Robert Scoon, "The Rise and Impact of Evolutionary Ideals," *Evolutionary Thought in America*, pp. 30-31.

[27] Schlesinger, "Critical Period in American Religion," Massachusetts Historical Society, Proceedings, LXIV, pp. 525-527.

[28] Olive May Winchester, *Crisis Experience in the Greek New Testament; an Investigation of the Evidences for the Definite, Miraculous Experiences of Regeneration and Sanctification as found in the Greek New Testament, Especially in the Figures Emphasized and in the Uses of the Aorist Tense*, ed. with final chapter and appendix by Ross E. Price (Kansas City, Mo.: Nazarene Publishing House, 1953), pp. 1-3.

Wesleyan perfectionism, the movement also embraced a number of the characteristics of the frontier church. The "crisis experience" was considered the only means of realizing salvation, and revivalism the technique to be used in making converts. The group also entertained definitely "fundamentalist" views, opposing any position contrary to the verbal inspiration and literal interpretation of the Bible.[29]

Though the Holiness Movement started under Methodist leadership, it operated on an inter-denominational basis. Constituents of various churches professed the experience of sanctification.[30] Like the early Wesleyans, the Holiness people had in the beginning no intention of starting a new church. The primary purpose was to stimulate "holiness" and religious devotion among the members of existing churches. The camp-meeting was the means employed to accomplish this objective. The first general camp under Holiness auspices was held in 1867 at Vineland, New Jersey. Out of this first national meeting the "National Camp-meeting Association for the Promotion of Holiness" was organized. In a brief time local and area associations were operating camps all over America with the blessing of the national association. This development had a definite effect on those churches whose members were participating in the Holiness revival. Two parties began to assert themselves—one considering itself as the proponent of the new religious trends, the other regarding itself as the champion of heart-religion and primitive Christianity.[31]

The Holiness Movement continued to express itself for a number of years principally through bands, associations, and camp-meetings of a more or less extra-denominational character. Holiness groups were inter-related only by the loosest ties, to say the most. As the leaders of the established churches leaned further toward the new religious views, the Holiness factions became more and more uncom-

[29] William W. Sweet, *The American Churches, and Interpretation* (Nashville: Abingdon-Cokesbury Press, 1947), pp. 71-72; Clark, *Small Sects*, pp. 59-60.
[30] M. E. Redford, *The Rise of the Church of the Nazarene* (Kansas City, Mo.: Nazarene Publishing House, 1948), p. 38.
[31] Gaddis, "Perfectionism in America," pp. 443-448; Redford, *Church of the Nazarene*, p. 39.

fortable. "The inevitable result was that as these people felt increasingly ill at ease in their association with those who had no sympathy with their 'holiness' emphasis, they began to withdraw and form independent religious bodies." [32]

The Holiness Movement made two contributions that prepared fertile ground from which modern Pentecost could ultimately spring. First, it introduced to American religion a new interest in "spiritual experiences" subsequent to the "crisis-experience" of salvation, and, second, it produced another wave of motor phenomena which included "tongues."

The scriptural phrase "Baptism of the Holy Spirit", which was to have an important significance in the Pentecostal movement, was popularized as the name for the experience of sanctification, or "second blessing." All who came under the influence of the Holiness ministry became familiar with "spiritual baptism" with its emphasis upon cleansing from sin. Many claimed to receive such an experience and testified that it changed their entire Christian outlook. [33]

Certain persons connected with the movement went even further and advocated three "experiences" instead of two. The Rev. B. H. Irwin, while in the Holiness ministry, made a careful study of Methodist theology. In the works of John Fletcher, an early Wesleyan writer, he discovered the teaching of some sort of experience beyond sanctification which was described as a "baptism of burning love." Eventually Irwin sought for and claimed to have received this "third blessing." Subsequently Holiness circles became familiar through his preaching with the new doctrine of the "baptism of fire."

The Rev. Joseph H. King, who later became Bishop of the Pentecostal Holiness Church, related that he first met with this doctrine while he was serving the Simpson Cir-

[32] Sweet, *Story of Religion in America*, p. 506.
[33] Donald Gee, *The Pentecostal Movement, Including the Story of the War Years, 1940-47* (London: Elim Publishing Company, Ltd., 1949), pp. 4-5.
[34] Joseph E. Campbell, *The Pentecostal Holiness Church, 1898-1948* (Franklin Springs, Georgia: Pentecostal Holiness Church Publishing House, 1951), pp. 194-195.

cuit of the Methodist Episcopal Church in Georgia in the late 1890's. He there preached to a church that "had been taught that the baptism of the Holy Ghost and fire was received by faith after the grace of sanctification had been imparted, and as a result everyone that testified declared that they had been definitely baptized with the Holy Ghost and fire subsequent to sanctification." [35]

TONGUES PHENOMENA DURING LATE NINETEENTH CENTURY

In addition to these multiple "experiences," which laid a foundation for the later Pentecostal "experience," the Holiness Movement stimulated in its worship unusual motor phenomena that apparently contributed to a new interest in "tongues." Accounts of manifestations of "tongues" in the Holiness Movement are almost wholly reminiscent and come from persons associated with the later Pentecostal Movement, notably the Rev. Stanley H. Frodsham, who collected information on this subject from correspondence, printed statements, and interviews with participants or eye witnesses. Most of the instances that follow are taken from Frodsham's findings.

The Rev. R. B. Swan reported that "tongues" were manifested in his services in Providence, Rhode Island, as early as 1875. At least five persons who assisted him exercised the gift. These folk, known as the "Gift People," were not accepted by the established churches. Swan gave detailed descriptions of "speaking in tongues" by two individuals in his meetings.

W. Jethro Walthall also claimed a "tongues" experience as early as 1879 in Arkansas. Since his situation was undoubtedly similar to that of others who participated in the religious enthusiasm of that period, his statement merits quoting.

At the time I was filled with the Spirit, I could not say what I did, but I was carried out of myself for the time being. Sometimes in the services and sometimes when alone in prayer, I would fall prostrate under God's mighty power. Once, under a great spir-

[35] Joseph H. King and Blanche L. King, *Yet Speaketh, Memoirs of the Late Bishop Joseph H. King* (Franklin Springs, Georgia: Pentecostal Holiness Church Publishing House, 1949), p. 78.

itual agitation, I spoke in tongues. I knew nothing of the Bible teaching about the Baptism or speaking in tongues, and thought nothing of what had happened in my experience.[36]

This would indicate that "tongues" was merely incidental to the more general reaction. The recipient accepted such expression blindly with no scriptural or theological reason.[37]

Daniel Awrey affirmed that he spoke in an "unknown tongue" in 1890 while residing in Ohio and that his wife had a similar experience ten years later. He also stated that while he and his wife were ministering in Tennessee in 1899 about a dozen persons spoke in "tongues" in their services.[38] During the same year Evangelist Woodworth Etter encountered unusual phenomena in her services at "Kerry Patch" in St. Louis. Some of her converts, she later recalled, "received the gift of new tongues, and spake very intelligently in other languages." [39]

Similar motor demonstrations were noted about the same time in the Swedish Mission Church in Mooreland, Minnesota. A revival began there in 1892 and continued for several years; " 'very often as Pastor Thompson was preaching, the power of God would fall, people dropping to the floor and speaking in other tongues as the Spirit gave them utterance.' " [40] Prophecy and visions were also listed among the demonstrations.

Other witnesses testified to Pentecostal manifestations in some southern communities during practically the same years. R. G. Spurling, a Baptist minister who embraced the doctrine of Holiness, conducted meetings in Tennessee and North Carolina. Among the expressions of religious enthusiasm noted in his meetings were dancing, shouting and speaking in tongues. In 1896 W. F. Bryant and he

---

[36] Quoted by Stanley H. Frodsham, *With Signs Following, The Story of the Pentecostal Revival in the Twentieth Century* (Revised edition, Springfield, Missouri: Gospel Publishing House, 1941), pp. 11-12.

[37] Walthall later became associated with the Assemblies of God and served this communion as Superintendent of the Arkansas District for a number of years.

[38] When the Pentecostal movement began, Awrey became a part of it and enjoyed an international ministry until his death in 1913 in Liberia.

[39] Mrs. M. B. Woodworth Etter, *Signs and Wonders God Wrought in the Ministry for Forty Years* (Indianapolis: Author, 1916), p. 117.

[40] Frodsham, *With Signs Following*, p. 15.

conducted a meeting at Camp Creek, North Carolina, in which all of these demonstrations were present, including the speaking in "tongues."[41]

Frodsham lists several additional instances of the phenomenon occurring in the late 1890's. In the First Methodist Church, Greenfield, South Dakota, of which Rasmus Kristensen was pastor, persons spoke in "tongues" in 1896. C. M. Hanson of Dalton, Minnesota, alleged similar demonstrations in meetings he conducted in 1895 and 1897. And Sarah A. Smith claimed that she and forty others enjoyed the gift in a Holiness revival in Tennessee in 1900.[42]

These more or less isolated instances of "tongues" indicate that during the time of the Holiness revival this particular expression of religious enthusiasm once more made its appearance in widely scattered localities in America. For the most part this unusual manifestation (speaking in "tongues") passed unnoticed.

---

[41] Charles W. Conn, *Like a Mighty Army*, (Cleveland, Tenn.: Church of God Publishing House, 1955), pp. 25-26.

[42] Frodsham, *Signs Following*, pp. 16-17. Sarah A. Smith served on the staff of Lillian Trasher's orphanage in Egypt during the early years of that institution and until her demise.

IV

The Beginning of Modern Pentecost

A NARRATIVE of modern Pentecost should begin with Charles F. Parham, for he was the first leader of the revival and continued to hold a prominent place in it until his death in 1929. This distinction might entitle him to be called "the father of the modern Pentecostal movement." However, no such distinction has been given to him by the leaders of the larger Pentecostal groups.

PARHAM'S EARLY LIFE

Parham was born in Muscatine, Iowa, on June 4, 1873. His interest in religion began while he was very young.

The earliest recollection I have of a call to the ministry was when about nine years of age, and though unconverted, I realized as certainly as did Samuel that God had laid His hand on me, and for many years endured the feeling of Paul "Woe is me, if I preach not the gospel."[1]

He was converted in the Congregational Church when thirteen years of age and became an earnest student of the Bible. By the time he was fifteen he had enjoyed some success as a lay preacher.

At sixteen Parham entered Southwestern, a Kansas College, and it was here that he began to critically consider the ministry as a profession, and apparently lost all interest in the church.[2] In this frame of mind, he embraced the prospect of preparation to become a physician.

While in this irreligious condition, Parham was stricken with rheumatic fever. He failed to respond to treatment and ultimately became so ill that little hope was held for

---

[1] Sarah E. (Mrs. Charles F.) Parham, *The Life of Charles F. Parham, Founder of the Apostolic Faith Movement* (Joplin: Tri-State Printing Co., 1930), p. 2.
[2] *Ibid.*, p. 6.

his life. When very low, Parham got the impression that his physical condition was caused by his rebellion against God. Consequently, he reconsecrated his life to God and decided to enter the ministry if he recovered. He later testified that with this rededication "every joint in my body loosened and every organ in my body was healed." [*] To this incident he attributed his later becoming a proponent of faith healing.

PARHAM'S THEOLOGY

After leaving college, Parham became a minister in the Methodist Church. He seems, however, to have had difficulty in accepting the authority of the church, and was frequently in conflict with officials of the communion. This experience convinced him of the "narrowness of sectarian churchism." His difficulties finally resulted in open rupture, so that he withdrew from the Methodists and associated only with Holiness circles.

From this time forward Parham championed a position which he considered to be non-sectarian. "He told the people if they wanted to join the church they could join any one they desired, but it was not essential to salvation to belong to any denomination." [4] His preaching followed the general pattern of many ministers who were connected with the Holiness movement. Since his main tenets were carried over into our Pentecostal movement, it will be appropriate here to examine their history and meaning.

First and foremost, Parham held salvation to be a crisis experience. All persons were considered depraved by sin and thus separated from their Creator. Relationship with God could be restored only through regeneration provided by Christ through faith in His atoning death. [5] This belief differed little from the theology of most Protestant bodies, for it was the basic doctrinal position that had developed out of the Reformation.

Variance existed, however, in the matter of the means by which salvation was realized in a person's life. Until

---

[*] *Ibid.,* p. 8.
[4] *Ibid.,* p. 24.
[5] Nelson, *Bible Doctrines,* pp. 29-52.

the last half of the nineteenth century all of the non-sacramental Christian communions depended largely on re-vivalism to get people "saved." By this technique conver-sion was effected through "a sudden and violent paroxysm of exertion," and individuals were thought to have no "vital church relation until by conscious conversion, they came 'out of the world.' " [6] In other words, conversion was considered a definite, instantaneous religious experience. This position had been popularized by Wesley and his evangelical colleagues who were reputed to have succeeded in imposing upon Christianity a pattern which identified religion with an experience.[7] Because such conversions were generally characterized "by a struggle with sin and a con-scious self-renunciation," they have been called "crisis ex-periences" of salvation.

Most of the older revivalistic churches in the last quar-ter of the nineteenth century had a tendency to replace this concept with that of gradual conversion. Horace Bush-nell, who was the principal proponent of this belief, main-tained that a child should

grow up a Christian, and never know himself as being otherwise. In other words, the aim, effort, and expectation should be, not, as is commonly assumed, that the child is to grow up in sin, to be converted after he comes to a mature age; but that he is to open on the world as one that is spiritually renewed, not remembering the time when he went through a technical experience, but seem-ing rather to have loved what is good from his earliest years.[8]

Parham very definitely objected to the "nurture" con-cept and advocated only "crisis experience" conversion, one that he called a

"know-so" experience with God. This experience Mr. Parham taught all through his ministry, insisting that souls should "pray-through" with a godly sorrow for sin, till they really knew that they had the witness in themselves that they had passed from death unto life.[9]

---

[6] Lewis Bevens Schenck, *The Presbyterian Doctrine of Children in the Covenant, a Historical Study of the Significance of Infant Baptism in the Presbyterian Church in America* (New Haven: Yale University Press, 1940), p. 80.
[7] Knox, *Enthusiasm,* p. 547.
[8] Horace Bushnell, *Christian Nurture* (reprint, New Haven: Yale University Press, 1947), p. 4.
[9] Parham, *Parham,* p. 13.

Second, Parham taught that sanctification, like salvation, was a religious experience. Because it was realized subsequent to salvation, this experience was generally referred to as a "second definite work of grace." According to Parham this work of grace completely destroyed "inbred sin." [10]

This tenet was connected with the historical teaching of perfectionism which held that moral perfection in one's daily life and spiritual holiness resulting in the eradication of sinful desires were possible and should be the goal of all Christians. The early church contended for this position because of a literal interpretation of such scriptures as "be ye therefore perfect, even as your Father which is in heaven is perfect." [11] After the patristic period the concept was continued by the Pelagians. During the Middle Ages the monastic mystics, being influenced by the teaching of Thomas Aquinas, largely monopolized the experience. His theology became the basis for the later Catholic position which holds that perfection is attained by works of charity. In addition to its presence in the development of the recognized church, vital perfectionism was also found in a number of sects and heretical parties of which the Montanists, Fraticelli, Bogomiles, Euchites, Cathari, Bulari, and Albigenses were the most prominent.

The discounting of the tenet by the Reformation churches resulted in revolt movements. Some of the Anabaptist sects and the Pietists on the continent and the Quakers and Shakers in England rose to champion perfectionism. [12] "But the greatest impetus to the modern holiness movement was provided by the Wesleyan theology." [13] Though Wesleyan perfectionism did not remain vital in Methodism, it became permanently rooted in the numerous modern holiness bodies that developed from the Wesleyan movement. The tenet, as taught by Wesley and briefly summarized by Clark, contained the following features:

---

[10] Charles F. and Sarah E. Parham, *Selected Sermons of the Late Charles F. Parham and Sarah E. Parham*, compiled by Robert L. Parham (n. p.: [Published by the compiler], 1941), pp. 51-63.

[11] Matt. 5:48.

[12] Clark, *Small Sects*, pp. 52-54.

[13] Mayer, *Religious Bodies*, p. 320.

1. Christian perfection is the product of faith and means freedom from all sin, both outward and inner, including 'evil thoughts and temper,' though it does not insure against such human frailties as ignorance, mistakes, temptations, and the common infirmities of the flesh.

2. It is not the same as, nor does it ever accompany, justification, but is always subsequent thereto. "We do not know a single instance, in any place, of a person's receiving, in one and the same moment, remission of sins, the abiding witness of the Spirit, and a new, clean heart," Wesley wrote.

3. It is always an instantaneous experience though there may be gradual growth both previous and subsequent thereto. Wesley's statements to this effect are explicit, though his exact meaning is not entirely clear.

4. It may be at the moment of death, as Calvinists claimed; but Wesley combats this idea and holds that it might be attained long before death. While exhorting all persons to "press on" to the ideal, he seems to concede that the experience is relatively rare among Christians.

5. Once obtained, the blessing may be lost, in which case there is no insuperable obstacle to securing it again.[14]

Charles G. Finney popularized sanctification more than any other American revivalist. He maintained that

man inherits sin solely by his own free choice; that conversion is man's personal surrender, effected by his own choice and effort, usually under a great emotional strain; that entire sanctification includes complete freedom from evil thoughts and is an instantaneous act subsequent to conversion; and that this perfect liberation from sin is the normal experience of Christians.[15]

Parham was, of course, indebted to the Holiness movement for his introduction to the doctrine.

Parham's third distinctive doctrine concerned faith healing. He added this tenet to his personal theology at the time he was restored to health in college. Shortly afterwards, when two of his friends died, he determined to include it in his preaching. "As I knelt between the graves of my two loved friends, who might have lived if I had but told them of the power of Christ to heal, I made a vow that 'Live or Die' I would preach this gospel of healing."[16]

---

[14] Clark, *Small Sects*, pp. 55-56.
[15] Mayer, *Religious Bodies*, p. 316.
[16] Parham, *Parham*, p. 33.

The position most commonly held by modern believers in faith healing is contained in an outline entitled "Some Principles of Healing, As Taught in God's Word, Directly and Indirectly."

1. It is God's first will that men be pure in heart, spirit, poised in judgment, happy in circumstances, and strong and well in body.

2. God does not send disease. It comes through some disobedience to the natural laws of the body, conscious or unconscious, though rarely traceable in full. It may come from the Devil, or, because of the break of sin affecting all life. But always through that open door of disobedience to the laws of the body.

3. Christ heals men's bodies today by His own direct supernatural touch, sometimes through the physician and the use of means, sometimes without means, sometimes when means are confessedly powerless, and sometimes overcoming the unwise use of means. The Holy Spirit's leading is the touchstone.

4. In healing Christ is always reaching in for the far greater thing, the healing of the spirit, the life.

5. There is sometimes a waiting period, after the conditions are met, before the full healing comes. There is a disciplinary side in bodily suffering, but the healing comes as quickly as the lesson is learned. . . .

7. The conditions for Christ's healing are the same as for being saved. Trust Him fully as your Saviour and Master. Then go to Him for whatever you need, always seeking the Holy Spirit's guidance.[17]

Belief in faith healing has been present in every period of church history. The early church was familiar with the practice because of the healings performed by Christ and His apostles. The Fathers, notably Irenaeus, Justin Martyr, Tertullian, Origen, and Augustine, affirmed that divine healings were still taking place in their day. From the limited number of references, however, one can assume that the occurrences were not commonplace. An abundance of reports is available concerning healings in the lives of the medieval saints, but some scholars maintain these records are exaggerated. Though faith healing was embraced by none of the Reformation churches, the Moravians, Waldenses, Pietists, Quakers, Luther, and Wes-

---

[17] S. D. Gordon, *Quiet Talks about the Healing Christ* (New York: Fleming H. Revell Co. 1924), pp. 5-6. Gordon was an outstanding advocate of faith healing in the Holiness bodies.

ley were among the groups and individuals that were said to have practiced it.[18] Several of the Holiness bodies in America propounded the doctrine, the most prominent being the Christian and Missionary Alliance, which was founded by Dr. A. B. Simpson.

The final doctrine that Parham stressed was premillennialism. Millennial or chiliastic theology in general

has forecast the future transformation of the world by divine intervention and the establishment of the Kingdom of God on earth. The usual interpretation has been that this state of peace and blessedness will last a thousand years—the millennium—and will be followed by the final judgment.[19]

Millennialists hold that chiliastic beliefs were taught by the New Testament and the apostles, then "along with justification by faith and almost every other vital doctrine, chiliastic expectation was lost in the Dark Ages. That it was held by the early church Fathers is evident beyond doubt." [20] The doctrine was renounced during the Middle Ages by the Catholics, and replaced by the belief that the church was the Kingdom of God. After the Reformation, Protestantism revived interest in the subject to the extent that even persons like Isaac Newton became involved in its study. In the seventeenth century millennialism was brought to America by the Puritans and proceeded to take an important place in American Christianity.[21]

Millennial theology divided into three schools of thought after the Reformation. Postmillennialism holds that the second advent of Christ will follow a man-made millennium, amillennialism declares that the church is the Kingdom of God, and whatever millennium there may be is being experienced in the present age, and premillennialism avers that the second advent of Christ will occur prior to

---

[18] Hastings, *Encyclopaedia of Religion and Ethics*, IV, 698-699.

[19] Ira V. Brown, "Watchers for the Second Coming: the Millenarian Tradition in America," *Mississippi Valley Historical Review*, XXXIX (December, 1952), pp. 441-458.

[20] Lewis Sperry Chafer, *Systematic Theology* (Dallas: Dallas Seminary Press, 1947-48), IV, 270. Chafer is the only premillennialist that has produced a definitive systematic theology in the twentieth century.

[21] Brown, "Watchers for the Second Coming," *Mississippi Valley Historical Review*, XXXIX, 443-451.

the millennium.[22] This last concept was the one Parham expounded.

Parham also was influenced by the Holiness movement to value enthusiasm in his ministry, a practice later continued by the Pentecostals. Those who incorporate this into their systems hold that the emotions as well as the will are affected by religious experience. Wesley, in answering the critics of the practice, stated that it was

no other than heart-religion; in other words, righteousness, peace and joy in the Holy Ghost. These must be felt, or they have no being. All therefore who condemn inward feelings in the gross, leave no place either for joy or peace or love in religion, and consequently reduce it to a dry, dead carcase.[23]

Though enthusiasm was characterized in the early and medieval church periods by charismatic manifestations and ecstasies,[24] it

did not really begin to take shape until the moment when Luther shook up the whole pattern of European theology; did not . . . come out in the open till more than a century later. Not until the days of the Commonwealth can it be studied in its full context.[25]

Then it became for a century and a half a matter of religious importance in England, and even longer in America. The emotional expression of the Quakers, Pietists, Moravians, Camisards, and French Prophets first presented a rude challenge to the dignity of the institutional churches; then these were eclipsed in the middle of the eighteenth century by the enthusiasm in the Wesleyan movment.[26] In America, emotional expression adapted very well to frontier religion, and its physical demonstrations were common in outdoor revivalism.

In every revival of religion, excesses have been present in varying degrees of intensity. . . . The point at which tension, confusion, and strife between the old sinful ways and the new were overcome by the awesome sermons, prolonged prayers, and crowd pressures was often accompanied by strange bodily manifestations. Automatisms

---

[22] Chafer, *Systematic Theology*, IV, 280-284.
[23] Quoted in Knox, *Enthusiasm*, p. 537.
[24] Umphery Lee, *The Historical Backgrounds of Early Methodist Enthusiasm* (New York: Columbia University Press, 1931), pp. 13-37.
[25] Knox, *Enthusiasm*, p. 4.
[26] *Ibid.*, p. 4.

(bodily excitement, crying out, and hallucinations), while not considered positive evidence of conversion, were viewed as probable tokens of God's presence and attested to the power of preaching.[27]

The Holiness movement retained the use of enthusiasm when it had largely disappeared from the churches after the days of the outdoor camp meetings.

Most students of religious enthusiasm maintain that it is definitely affected by physical, social, and economic circumstances. "The tone of the forest revival was an accurate reflection of the population tide and level of social development of a particular region. As the environment of the pioneers grew less frustrating, so did the spirit of animal excitement at the camp meeting diminish." [28] One writer is of the opinion that excessive expressions of enthusiasm are a thing of the past.

The days of religious effervescence and passional unrestraint are dying. The days of intelligent, undemonstrative and self-sacrificing piety are dawning.... Religious experience is an evolution. We go on from the rudimentary and the primitive to the rational and the spiritual.[29]

In this connection one cannot help but observe that the fervor of the Holiness and Pentecostal movements cooled as the social and economic status of the participants improved.

Parham was indebted, then, to the Holiness Movement for four major doctrinal tenets—salvation, sanctification, faith healing and premillennialism—and for the practice of enthusiasm, all of which were to become fundamentals of the modern Pentecostal movement.

PARHAM'S MINISTRY IN TOPEKA, KANSAS

In 1898 the Parhams (he had married Sarah E. Thistlethwaite in 1896) opened the Bethel Healing Home in Topeka, Kansas. This establishment and others like it were

---

[27] Charles Albert Johnson, *The Frontier Camp Meeting: Religion's Harvest Time* (Dallas: Southern Methodist University Press, 1955), p. 173.

[28] *Ibid.*, p. 101.

[29] Frederick Morgan Davenport, *Primitive Traits in Religious Revivals, a Study in Mental and Social Evolution* (New York: Macmillan Company, 1917), p. 323.

inspired by the much publicized work of John Alexander Dowie [80] in Zion City, Illinois.

These "homes" sought to provide appropriate surroundings for infirm persons who desired a place of retreat where they could be prepared through instruction for faith healing. They were called "faith homes" not only because of faith healing, but also, for the most part, no charge was made for any services or entertainment, and they operated literally on "faith" that God would provide all material requirements through gifts of interested Christians. [81]

It was during this time that Parham began the publication of a periodical which he named *The Apostolic Faith*. It was published twice a month. "At first we had a subscription price, later we announced 'for subscription price see Isaiah 55:1,' and the Lord wonderfully provided." [82] The name of this periodical was used not only by Parham, but by others who perpetuated the name for similar, free-distribution papers, used for the propagation of the Pentecostal message.

PARHAM VISITS UNUSUAL MINISTRIES IN NORTH AND EAST

During the early part of 1900 several evangelists conducted services for the Parhams in a Topeka mission operated in connection with the faith home. From them Parham heard reports of unusual spiritual ministries in the North and East, and determined "to know more fully the latest truths restored by later day movements." Accordingly he left his work

in charge of two Holiness preachers and visited various movements such as Dowie's work who was then in Chicago, the Eye-Opener work of the same city; Malone's work in Cleveland, Dr. Simpson's

---

[80] Mayer, *Religious Bodies*, p. 446. Dowie established Zion City in 1899 under a communal, theocratic government. He was also the founder of the Christian Apostolic Church. He gained his greatest prominence through faith healing. Infirm persons from all over the world traveled to Zion, many of whom resided in his modest hotel, while they were prepared for divine healing. The Zion Hospice (hotel) was not considered a "faith home" in the full meaning of the term. Guests in the home (hotel) were charged for room and board. Dowie was a strong advocate of the tithing system, and his followers paid a tenth of their income into the church treasury.

[81] Parham, *Parham*, pp. 39-48.

[82] *Ibid.*, p. 39.

work in Nyack, New York, Sanford's "Holy Ghost and Us" work at Shiloah, Maine, and many others.[33]

The Bible school at Shiloah made a great impression upon Parham. It was characterized by a few singular policies and practices. Like the faith homes, the Bible school charged no tuition, depending rather upon "free-will" contributions to defray expenses. Prayer occupied a prominent place in the curriculum. Continuous supplication had been offered in a prayer tower on the campus for two years prior to Parham's visit. The only text used was the Bible. All of these features were to be incorporated by Parham in the school which he established soon afterward.[34]

Parham returned to Topeka "fully convinced that while many had obtained real experiences in sanctification and the anointing that abideth, there still remained a great outpouring of power for Christians." [35] This conviction was so real to him he began to pray and fast to determine how it should relate to his future. For some time friends had been urging him to open a school in conjunction with the faith home. He now decided to launch such a venture. Little did he realize that this school was to be the birthplace of the modern Pentecostal movement!

BETHEL BIBLE COLLEGE

Parham secured facilities for the school through what he called a "series of wonderful miracles." The property, located one mile west of Washburn College in Topeka, was known to the people of the area as the "Stone Mansion" or "Stone's Folly." Stone had planned to construct a castlelike building, but his funds ran out before construction was completed. As a result the first two floors had beautiful carved staircases and were finished in cedar of Lebanon, spotted pine, cherry wood, and bird's-eye maple, while the third floor was completed with cheap

---

[33] *Ibid.*, p. 48.
[34] "He Got Money," Topeka *State Journal*, October 20, 1900, clipping in Charles F. Parham's Scrapbook, p. 17. This scrapbook, which contains clippings, letters, and tracts relating to Parham's personal ministry, is held by his daughter-in-law, Mrs. Pauline Parham, Baxter Springs, Kansas.
[35] Parham, *Parham*, p. 48.

painted materials. The outside was in red brick on white
stone. An observatory occupied the highest part of the
front of the building, and the roof also supported a cupola
and two domes.[86]

According to later report, a friend of the Parhams al-
legedly saw just above the newly-acquired building "a vast
lake of fresh water about to overflow containing enough
to satisfy every thirsty soul." [87] Whatever the validity of
this apparition, it was in a measure symbolic of the influence the little school was soon to have upon the American church.

Parham opened his school in October, 1900, as the
Bethel Bible College with about forty students enrolling
for the first session. The only entrance requirement, seemingly, was an earnest desire to learn more about God and
His Word. Students, both men and women, came from
several walks of life. Quite a few were married, and children accompanied parents to the school. All necessary
household goods, and in some cases even horses and cows,
were brought by the students. The entire student body
lived in the building, rooms being assigned to single persons and apartments to families. The meals, eaten at a
common table, were described as pleasant experiences
where delightful fellowship prevailed.[88] Students came from
a number of denominations, though mostly from Holiness,
Methodist, and Friends communions. Twelve were ministers.[89]

One of the students who was to occupy a unique place
in the beginning of Modern Pentecost was Agnes N. Ozman. Agnes was born in Albany, Wisconsin, but her family
soon made Nebraska its permanent residence. She received
excellent religious training from earnest Christian parents.
After finishing her secular schooling, she attended C.

[86] "Wonderful History of the Latter Rain," *The Faithful Standard*, June, 1922,
p. 8; "He Got Money," Topeka *State Journal*, October 20, 1900, Parham's
Scrapbook, p. 17.
[87] "Wonderful History of the Latter Rain," *The Faithful Standard*, June, 1922,
p. 8.
[88] Mother Dobson, Houston, Texas, to Rev. E. N. Bell, Springfield, Missouri,
November 12, 1921, A. L. S., p. 6, Pentecostal File, Gospel Publishing House,
Springfield, Missouri.
[89] Parham, *Parham*, pp. 53, 63.

Horton's Bible school at St. Paul, Minnesota, in 1892-3. Though she had been raised in the Methodist Church, Agnes had become associated by this time with the Holiness movement. Following her work in St. Paul, she attended for one year A. B. Simpson's Bible school in New York. While on the East coast, she did considerable mission work in and around New York City. Before returning to Nebraska, she attended John Alexander Dowie's services in Zion City, Illinois. These experiences fired her with evangelical enthusiasm, so that she continued mission work in Nebraska and then in Kansas City. At this latter place she heard of the opening of Bethel Bible College and decided to join the student body.[40]

Parham managed the school on the "faith" basis employed at the healing home. Neither tuition, board, nor room was charged, yet the founder reported that "from day to day, week to week and month to month, with no sect or mission or known source of income back of us, God supplied our every need, and He was our all sufficiency in all things."[41]

The college had a distinctive curriculum. Since its primary purpose was "to fit men and women to go to the ends of the earth to preach 'This Gospel of the Kingdom' (Matthew 24) as a witness to all the world before the end of the age,"[42] Parham particularly stressed the spiritual development of his students. Considerable time was given to devotions and prayers. One of the domes was converted into a "Prayer Tower," where continuous prayer was made, corresponding to the practice of Shiloah, Maine. "Volunteers from among the students took their turns of three hours watch; so day and night prayer ascended unto God. Sometimes a student would desire to spend the night in waiting before the Lord and this privilege was allowed."[43]

Practical training in Christian work was also an important part of the curriculum. The students took part

[40] Agnes N. (Ozman) LaBerge, *What God Hath Wrought* (Chicago: Herald Publishing Co., [n.d.]), pp. 4-28.
[41] Parham, *Parham*, p. 51.
[42] *Ibid.*, p. 51.
[43] *The Faithful Standard*, June, 1922, p. 8.

regularly in the services of the mission that Parham operated in the city. This gave an opportunity for useful application of the things studied in class. Students also participated in a visitation program which took them into
many Topeka homes for practice in personal evangelism. "

As in the other faith schools of the period, the only
textbook used was the Bible. Several courses were offered, but the prerogative of election was not given, and
all students studied the same subjects simultaneously. The
faculty was quite limited, Parham being the only regular
teacher." Two methods of instruction were used. In one
the group was required to check all the references in the
Bible pertinent to an assigned subject, and then commit
the more important texts to memory. The other method
was a verse-by-verse study of chosen portions of Scripture."

"THE BAPTISM IN THE HOLY GHOST"

A few days previous to the Christmas holidays in 1900
Parham, who was preparing to leave on a trip to conduct
services in Kansas City, assigned the students "The Baptism in the Holy Ghost" as a subject. He introduced the
topic by reviewing the interest he had acquired in the
theme during his recent trip to the East.

Students, as I have studied the teachings in the various Bible
schools and full gospel movements, conviction, conversion, healing
and sanctification are taught virtually the same, but on the baptism
there is a difference among them. Some accept Steven Merrit's
teaching of baptism at sanctification, while others say this is only
the anointing and there is a baptism received through the "laying
on of hands" or the gift of the Holy Ghost, yet they agree on no
definite evidence. Some claim this fulfillment of promise "by faith"
without any special witness, while others, because of wonderful
blessings or demonstrations, such as shouting or jumping. Though
I honor the Holy Ghost in anointing power both in conversion and
in sanctification, yet I believe there is a greater revelation of His
power. The gifts are in the Holy Spirit and with the baptism
of the Holy Spirit the gifts, as well as the graces, should be manifested. Now, students, while I am gone, see if there is not some

---

[44] LaBerge, *What God Hath Wrought*, p. 28.
[45] Dobson to Bell, November 12, 1921.
[46] "Hindoo and Zulu, Both are Represented at Bethel School," Topeka *State Journal*, January 9, 1901, Parham's Scrapbook, p. 21.

evidence given of the baptism so there may be no doubt on the subject. "

Regular Bible lessons were discontinued during Parham's three-day absence, but the group did study in an informal manner. The instructor found on his return to the campus that the students had reached a startling conclusion from their investigation.

I returned to the school on the morning preceding Watch Night services in the year 1900.

At about 10 o'clock in the morning I rang the bell calling all the students into the Chapel to get their report on the matter in hand. To my astonishment they all had the same story, that while there were different things occured [sic] when the Pentecastal [sic] blessing fell, the indisputable proof on each occasion was that they spake with other tongues.[48]

J. Roswell Flower has written in reference to this incident:

This was a most momentous decision. There had been recorded many instances of persons speaking in tongues prior to the year 1900, but in each case the speaking in tongues was considered to be a spiritual phenomenon or at the most a "gift" of the Spirit, with the result that no particular emphasis had been given which would cause those seeking for the fullness of the Spirit to expect that they should speak in other tongues. But these students had deduced from God's Word that in apostolic times, the speaking in tongues was considered to be the initial physical evidence of a person's having received the baptism in the Holy Spirit. It was this decision which has made the Pentecostal Movement of the Twentieth Century.[49]

The group began to act upon the newly accepted "truth" immediately. A "baptism in the Holy Spirit" was sought which would be indicated by an ecstatic utterance in "tongues." The reaction of Agnes N. Ozman to the situation was probably characteristic of the entire student body:

At first and for a time I held to the experience I had in praises,

---

[47] Parham, *Parham,* p. 58.

[48] *Ibid.,* p. 52.

[49] J. Roswell Flower, "Birth of the Pentecostal Movement," *Pentecostal Evangel,* No. 1907 (November 26, 1950), p. 3.

joy and answers to prayer, in seeing the sick healed as the baptism
of the Spirit, but soon I was convinced of a need within. And...
my heart became hungry for the baptism of the Holy Ghost. I
wanted the promise of the Father more than ever I did food or
to sleep.[50]

An air of expectancy was on the campus during the
remaining hours of 1900. Miss Ozman related that "on
Watch Night we had a blessed service, praying that God's
blessing might rest upon us as the new year came in.
During the first day of 1901, the presence of the Lord
was with us in a marked way, stilling hearts to wait upon
him for greater things." [51]

THE BEGINNING OF MODERN PENTECOST

The first of the group received the Pentecostal "experience" on January 1, 1901. During the evening of that
day Parham and some of the students conducted a service
at the mission, while the rest of the student body continued prayer on the campus. About 7:00 p.m. when medi-
tating in her devotions, Agnes Ozman was reminded that
believers in the New Testament church were "baptized in
the Spirit" on several occasions when hands were laid on
them. Acting on an impulse when Parham returned from
the mission, she asked Parham to lay hands upon her in
Biblical fashion. Refusing the request at first, he finally
relented and said a short prayer as he laid his hands on
her. According to Miss Ozman's own testimony,

It was as his hands were laid upon my head that the Holy Spirit
fell upon me and I began to speak in tongues, glorifying God. I
talked several languages, and it was clearly manifest when a new dia-
lect was spoken. I had the added joy and glory my heart longed
for and a depth of the presence of the Lord within that I had never
known before. It was as if rivers of living waters were proceeding
from my innermost being. The following morning I was accosted
with questions about my experience of the night before. As I tried to
answer I was so full of glory that I pointed out to them the Bible
references, showing that I had received the baptism according to
Acts 2:4 and 19:1-6. I was the first one to speak in tongues in the

---

[50] LaBerge, *What God Hath Wrought*, pp. 28-29.
[51] Quoted in Parham, *Parham*, p. 66.

Bible school and it seemed to me that the rest were wanting to speak in tongues too. But I told them not to seek for tongues but to seek for the Holy Ghost. [52]

Although Agnes Ozman was not the first person in modern times to speak in "tongues", she was the first known person to have received such an experience as a result of specifically seeking a baptism in the Holy Spirit with the expectation of speaking in tongues. From this time Pentecostal believers were to teach that the "baptism in the Holy Spirit" should be sought and that it would be received with the evidence of "tongues." For this reason the experience of Agnes Ozman is designated as the beginning of the Modern Pentecostal Revival.

The manifestation of "tongues" by Agnes caused something of a sensation in the school, and the entire group began to pray earnestly for a similar experience. One of the larger upper areas in the building was converted into a prayer room, and there all the school continued in intercession for three days. [53] "Those three days of tarrying were wonderful days of blessing. We all got past any begging or pleading. We knew the blessing was ours with ever swelling tides of praise and thanksgiving and worship interspersed with singing we waited for the coming of the Holy Spirit." [54]

Many of the number received the Pentecostal Baptism on January 3. Parham gave an account of the incident.

On the night of January 3rd, I preached at the Free Methodist Church in the City of Topeka telling them what had already happened, and that I expected upon returning the entire school to be baptized in the Holy Spirit. On returning to the school with one of the students, we ascended to the second floor and passing down along the corridor in the upper room, heard most wonderful sounds. . . .

Twelve ministers, who were in the school of different denominations, were filled with the Holy Spirit and spoke with other tongues. [55]

---

[52] *Ibid.*, pp. 66-67; LaBerge, *What God Hath Wrought,* p. 29.

[53] Howard D. Stanley, Topeka, Kansas, to Rev. E. N. Bell, Springfield, Missouri, January 17, 1922, A. L. S., p. 3, Pentecostal File, Gospel Publishing House, Springfield, Mo.

[54] Parham, *Parham,* p. 53.

[55] Parham, *Selected Sermons,* p. 77.

Parham immediately joined the group in prayer and very shortly received a "tongues experience."[56]

No extremely violent physical exercises were noted, though some persons did tremble as they received the "experience." Concerted praying, praising, and singing were prominent in the services. An added mystical touch was furnished by the report of several present who claimed to see tongues of fire appear at one time in the improvised prayer room.[57]

The manifestation of tongues was so unorthodox and strange to contemporary religious practice that the phenomenon quickly received wide publicity. Newspapers in Topeka, Kansas City, and St. Louis ran a number of articles on the activities of the school, thereby stimulating a great deal of curiosity and resulting in many persons' visiting Stone's Folly. Some of the visitors were favorably impressed, others extremely and openly critical.[58]

Not all of the students in the school accepted the new doctrinal position. S. J. Riggins withdrew on January 8, 1901, and in an interview with the Topeka *State Journal* pronounced the institution a fake. He seems to have been the only student who was vocal in his opposition, although a few others left the college without receiving the "tongues" evidence.[59] Those who remained, on the other hand, were convinced of the genuineness of the "experience" and became enthusiastic evangels of the new doctrine.[60]

PARHAM'S FIRST KANSAS CITY REVIVAL

The Bethel group, obviously desiring to share its discovery at once with the world, immediately launched a project to proclaim the new message. A party led by Parham and including his wife, Lillian Thistlethwaite, his sister-in-law, Luella Moore, Agnes N. Ozman, Maude Stanley, Howard Stanley, and Albert Horr left Topeka

[56] Parham, Parham, p. 54.
[57] Ibid., pp. 53, 61; Stanley to Bell, January 17, 1922.
[58] "Parham's New Religion Practiced at 'Stone's Folly'," Kansas City Times, January 27, 1901, Parham's Scrapbook, p. 55.
[59] "Row at Bethel," Topeka State Journal, January 8, 1901, Parham's Scrapbook, p. 22.
[60] "Was a Pentecost," Kansas City Times, January 22, 1901, p. 1.

on January 21, 1901, to commence a missionary tour of the United States and Canada. The Topeka *State Journal* reported that the band planned to

go first to Kansas City where they will stop a few days to hold meetings among the believers.... It is the intention of these who are going on the missionary trip to visit all the principal cities and towns in the East. The company will also visit all the colleges and missionary schools of the faith type during the tour.[61]

This news release would seem to indicate that the group was quite optimistic and had elaborate plans. Actually the new message was not to be received as readily and kindly as the party probably anticipated.

The Kansas City *Times* gave the first meetings front page publicity. An extended article related the history of the Topeka revival and described in detail the first service in Kansas City.[62] The initial meetings were held in a small store building at 1675 Madison Avenue; in an effort to reach more people the Sunday services were conducted in the Academy of Music. The campaign lasted two weeks, and though some conversions were reported, no wide acceptance was given the new gospel. In fact, a reaction arose against the revival efforts. The established churches were not at all sympathetic, and very shortly the newspaper publicity became unfavorable.

Instead of continuing on the missionary tour, the party returned to Topeka when the Kansas City meeting ended. The cause for this change of plans is not definitely known, but the newspapers intimated that poor reception in Kansas City and lack of funds were the reasons.[63] This was probably the case, for Parham complained of being persecuted, and his remuneration for the meeting must have been small since, at his insistence, no public offerings were taken.[64] He was to find no wide acceptance of his new "experience" for several years.

[61] "Parham Leaves," Topeka *State Journal*, January 21, 1901, Parham's Scrapbook, p. 24.

[62] "Was a Pentecost," Kansas City *Times*, January 22, 1901, p. 1.

[63] "Parham Home, Bethel College Man Canceled His Eastern Tour," clipping in Parham's Scrapbook, p. 66.

[64] Parham, *Parham*, p. 73.

LAWRENCE, KANSAS REVIVAL

Shortly after returning to Topeka, Parham carried his message to Lawrence, Kansas. He took twenty of his students on this mission, the rest remaining at the school to pray for the success of the venture. The revival, begun February 15, 1901, was conducted in the Music Hall. Though the party worked hard, participating in service each evening, and canvassing the city by house-to-house visits during the day, the results of the revival were no better than those in Kansas City. Some conversions were reported and a few received the "Pentecostal Baptism."[65]

After the Lawrence meeting the group returned to Topeka, where Parham carried on the work of the Bible school for several months. Because Stone's Mansion was sold during the following summer, Parham was forced to close Bethel Bible College and to find a new location. He accordingly decided to establish his headquarters in Kansas City.[66]

SECOND KANSAS CITY MEETING

The attention now given by the Kansas City press was much different from that received on his preceding visit. Only brief references were made to his services, and these were either indifferent or hostile in character.[67] Parham remained in Kansas City long enough this time to conduct a four-months Bible school in facilities located at Eleventh and Oak Streets. These were the hardest days of Parham's Pentecostal ministry, for here he suffered both severe opposition and deprivation. He later recalled that

both the pulpit and the press sought to utterly destroy our place and prestige, until my wife, her sister and myself stood alone. Hated, despised, counted as naught, for weeks and weeks never knowing where our next meal would come from, yet feeling that we must maintain the faith once for all delivered to the saints. When we had car fare we rode, when we didn't we walked. When buildings were closed to us we preached on the street.[68]

---

[65] *Ibid.*, pp. 74-76; Parham's Scrapbook, p. 71.

[66] Parham, *Parham*, p. 80.

[67] Parham's Scrapbook, pp. 44, 46.

[68] Charles F. Parham, "The Latter Rain," *Apostolic Faith*, July, 1926, p. 3. The *Apostolic Faith*, a religious periodical, was published and edited by Parham until his death, and has since been continued by members of his family.

LAWRENCE, KANSAS; NEVADA, MISSOURI; AND EL DORADO SPRINGS, MISSOURI

During most of 1902, the Parhams resided in Lawrence, Kansas, and Parham conducted services in that city and vicinity. His success must not have been any greater than on his previous attempt, for Mrs. Parham in writing of this year says that "the people seemed slow to accept the truth." [69]

A change for the better finally came in the spring of 1903 when a Wesleyan minister, a woman who had accepted the Pentecostal message in the first meeting in Lawrence, invited the Parhams to conduct a meeting in her mission in Nevada, Missouri. The invitation was accepted, and the revival that followed was more successful than all previous ones. The Nevada meeting appears to have been the turning point in Parham's Pentecostal ministry. From this time forward his new message enjoyed a much wider acceptance. [70]

The Parhams went to El Dorado Springs, Missouri, to conduct a campaign during the summer following the Nevada revival. People with various infirmities came to this little city for the medicinal benefit of its spring water. Parham took advantage of this situation to emphasize his healing tenet. This innovation perhaps contributed to the unusual success of his ministry here. Parham related that his party regularly stood and preached

at the corner of the park where steps led down to the spring. People came by the hundreds to hear the message and hundreds were healed, bearing the message of God to all parts of the United States. Our home was continuously besieged with sick and suffering for prayer. [71]

Among those who professed to a healing attributed to Parham's prayers was Mrs. Mary A. Arthur of Galena, Kansas. She later wrote that she had suffered from a number of physical disorders, the most distressing being a condition of approaching blindness which after two operations had continued to grow worse. At the time she went

[69] Parham, *Parham*, p. 86.
[70] Parham, "Latter Rain," *Apostolic Faith*, July, 1926, p. 3.
[71] *Ibid.*, p. 3.

to El Dorado Springs, she had to depend upon one eye
for the little sight she had, and, owing to intense pain,
used it as little as possible. One day as she went to the
spring, she heard the Parhams preach and invite any persons desiring prayers for healing to visit the cottage meetings being held in their home near the park. On August
17, 1903, she attended one of these services and received
prayer for her physical condition. She claimed that within
a matter of minutes she could open her eyes in the light
and could even look toward a white awning and a cloud
without ill effects though brightness had previously made
her sick with pain.[72]

When Mrs. Arthur returned to Galena and reported her
alleged healing, one of her friends who was hopelessly
ill with what Parham called a "cancerous tumor" went
to El Dorado Springs to investigate this ministry. She
returned to her home also claiming a miraculous cure as
a result of Parham's prayers.[73]

GALENA, KANSAS REVIVAL

The healings of Mrs. Arthur and her friend created
so much interest in the new Pentecostal ministry that the
Parhams were approached to conduct a meeting in Galena.
Accordingly, services were started on October 20, 1903,
in the Arthurs' home.[74] After two days, the house could
not accommodate the crowds, and a tent was raised on
an adjoining lot; here the revival continued until Thanksgiving. At that time, because of cold weather and the need
for larger facilities, the Grand Leader building on Main
Street was secured for the services. The campaign continued until January 15, 1904.[75] This Galena revival proved
to be one of the greatest Parham ever conducted. The
influence of the services reached beyond the little city,
bringing in persons from surrounding areas to participate
in the meeting. The following special report by the Cin-

---

[72] Mary A. Arthur, Galena, Kansas, to E. N. Bell, Springfield, Missouri, December 7, 1921, A. L. S., 10 p., Pentecostal File, Gospel Publishing House, Springfield, Mo.
[73] Parham, "Latter Rain," *Apostolic Faith*, July, 1926, p. 4.
[74] Arthur to Bell, December 7, 1921.
[75] Charles F. Parham, "The First Shower of the Latter Rain," *Apostolic Faith*, June, 1927, pp. 6-7.

cinnati *Inquirer* under the date line of Galena, Kansas, January 27, 1904, enables one to realize the proportions of the revival:

It is doubtful whether in recent years anything has occurred that has awakened the interest, excited the comment or mystified the people of this region as have the religious meetings being held here by Rev. C. F. Parham, familiarly termed "The Divine Healer."

Almost three months have elapsed since this man came to Galena and during that time he has healed over a thousand people and converted more than 800. When Rev. Parham first began to attract attention he was holding services in a large tent, and soon the streets in that vicinity were crowded nightly with people who were anxious to see and hear the wonderful man who was healing the sick, the maimed and the blind without money and without price. When it was found that the tent was utterly inadequate to accommodate the crowd who assembled a large double storeroom that would shelter 2,000 people was procured, a platform was built at one end, stoves were set up, rough pine boards were installed to be used as seats. Here for the past six weeks Parham has preached to crowded houses, and the interest shows no sign of abatement. In this rude temple cures that are looked upon almost in the light of miracles have been performed. During the services there have been as many as 50 people at the altar at one time seeking to be restored in soul and body. Here people who have not walked for years without the aid of crutches have risen from the altar with their limbs so straightened that they were enabled to lay aside their crutches, to the astonishment of the audience.

These cures, they claim, are effected solely through prayer and faith. Nothing else is done, though Rev. Parham often lays his hands upon the afflicted one while the devotions are going on, with the result that some say it is due to his own magnetism that so much is accomplished. . . .

Here women who have formerly lived for society and gaiety kneel beside some fallen sister and endeavor to point her heavenward, and here the "followers" receive what they term "the Pentecost," and are enabled to speak in foreign tongues, languages which they are, when free from this power, utterly unfamiliar. This alone is considered one of the most remarkable things of the meetings. Last week a woman arose during the meeting and spoke for 10 minutes, not one apparently in the audience knowing what she said. An Indian, who had come from the Pawnee Reservation in the territory that day to attend the services, stated that she was speaking in the language of his tribe, and that he could understand every word of the testimony. . . . But of all the wonderful things which has [sic] transpired in connection with these meetings nothing has attracted the attention of the people as has [sic] the "healings," which have not been confined to an ignorant, uneducated class of people. On the contrary some of the most conservative, intelligent persons, not only here but within a radius of over 100 miles, have visited "the healer," with wonderful results.[76]

Parham estimated that 500 were "sanctified" and at least 250 were "baptized in the Holy Spirit" in the meeitng.[77] A. W. Webber, who was present at the Galena revival, wrote that some of the converts became evangelists of the Pentecostal message.[78] Their work no doubt accounts in part for the fact that the tri-state region around Galena became an early Pentecostal stronghold. "Spontaneously, meetings on these lines sprang up in all the mining camps around about. And as the need demanded, preachers like mushrooms developed over night and went out to fill the pulpits in these different meetings." [79]

BAXTER SPRINGS, KANSAS; MELROSE, KANSAS; AND JOPLIN, MISSOURI

Following the Galena revival, Parham conducted meetings in two neighboring small towns, Baxter Springs and Melrose. Though the results realized in these places were not as noticeable as in Galena, yet scores were attracted to the "full gospel," as Parham's theology was being called by this time. Parham was so impressed with Baxter Springs that he made it his permanent residence. As a consequence of the meeting in Melrose, the first Pentecostal chapel of the modern revival was erected at Keelville, a crossroads ten miles west of Baxter Springs.[80]

Parham held his next revival in Joplin, Missouri, in the fall of 1904. The results compared favorably with those at Galena. Many persons in an area from Carthage, Missouri, to Miami, Oklahoma, accepted the "full gospel," and numerous conversions and healings were reported in connection with the services.[81]

[76] Parham's Scrapbook, p. 72.

[77] Parham, "The Latter Rain," *Apostolic Faith*, July, 1926, p. 4.

[78] A. W. Webber, "Revival of 1903 in Galena, Kansas," *Apostolic Faith*, May, 1944, p. 11.

[78] Parham, "Latter Rain," *Apostolic Faith*, July, 1926, p. 4.

[80] *Ibid.*, p. 4; Parham, Parham, pp. 99-100.

[81] Parham, "The Latter Rain," *Apostolic Faith*, July, 1926, p. 4.

ORCHARD, TEXAS REVIVAL

While Parham was directing the Joplin revival, his health failed. This circumstance influenced him to accept an invitation to preach in Texas. Just prior to the Joplin meeting Walter Olyer and his wife, who were "baptized in the Holy Spirit" in the Galena meeting, had prevailed upon Mrs. Anna Hall, one of Parham's workers, to come to their home town, Orchard, Texas, to proclaim the new message. She had commenced her ministry there on March 21, 1905, but had met with so little success that she and the Oylers appealed to Parham for assistance. Their invitation came about the time his health failed, and he readily accepted the offer and immediately left for Texas, thinking that a change might speed his recovery.[82]

Parham preached his first sermon at Orchard on Easter Sunday, 1905. Because of the revival that followed, Orchard is generally considered the birthplace of the Pentecostal movement in Texas. According to a letter written by Parham to friends in Galena, only five or six persons believed in the Pentecostal message when he arrived in the town, but after two weeks the entire community had been impressed with the "full gospel," and persons were coming to the services in wagons for a distance of twenty miles.[83]

Among those in attendance at the Orchard meeting was Mrs. John C. Calhoun, who came from Houston to satisfy her curiosity about the new message. She became convinced that the "experience" was genuine and very shortly was "baptized in the Spirit." Returning to Houston, she carried the news of the "full gospel" to her home congregation, the Holiness Church of Brunner. Her report was received with interest, and the pastor, W. F. Carothers, began a study of the subject in his congregation.[84]

HOUSTON, TEXAS MEETING

On May 20, 1905, Parham returned to Kansas to fill previously scheduled appointments in missions that had been established as a result of his revivals. He held "rally"

---

[82] Parham, *Parham*, p. 107.
[83] *Ibid.*, pp. 108-109.
[84] Frodsham, *Signs Following*, pp. 27-28.

services in these places both to encourage the young congregations and to stimulate interest and support for a crusade that he planned for Houston, Texas.[85]

On July 10, 1905, Parham returned to Texas with a party of twenty-five persons to commence his revival in Houston. Bryan Hall was rented for the services. The workers preached the new message on the streets and from house to house during the day, and then met together to assist in the evening meetings at the hall. Pastor W. F. Carothers and his church at Brunner participated in the revival from the very beginning and embraced the Pentecostal doctrine without hesitation. The press gave some publicity to the services.[86] As a result of these contributing factors, the revival took on wide proportions. Not only was Houston affected, but surrounding towns as well. "Many scores were converted, sanctified and baptized with the Holy Spirit. Many were healed in answer to the prayer of faith, and others possessed with evil spirits were delivered." [87]

Unusual healings were reported in connection with the meeting. According to a Houston Heights newspaper, Mrs. J. M. Dulaney, who had been in a street car collision in 1902 and had since been unable to walk, attended the services in her invalid chair, was prayed for, and in a short time

arose from her chair and walked about the hall in a state of ecstatic joy, shouting, clapping her hands, and praising the Lord for restoration. The incident created much excitement. Mrs. Dulaney walked down the stairs from the hall, and went home. She has attended their meetings daily since, but not in the chair.[88]

Though the revival in Bryan Hall ended after five weeks, Houston continued to be the center of Parham's activity for some time. A strong Pentecostal work was developed in Brunner because of the influence of Carothers

[85] Parham, *Parham*, pp. 109-112.
[86] "Jews to Found Own Home," Houston *Chronicle*, July 18, 1905, p. 6; "Undenominational Meetings," Houston *Chronicle*, July 21, 1905, p. 6.
[87] Parham, *Parham*, p. 113; B. F. Lawrence, The *Apostolic Faith Restored* (St. Louis: Gospel Publishing House, 1916), p. 54. Lawrence was associated with the Pentecostal movement from its beginning.
[88] Houston *Suburbanite*, August 12, 1905, Parham's Scrapbook, p. 85.

and his congregation. Meetings were held by Parham's associates and converts in numerous other places including Richmond, Katy, Alvin, Angleton, Needville, and Crosby. The outstanding revival during the fall of 1905 was held in Galveston.[89] It was estimated that some 25,000 Pentecostal believers had come under Parham's influence by the winter of 1905.[90]

Scores of persons, married and single, were consecrating their lives to God, and volunteering for His service . . . to preach the gospel, but felt the need of Bible teaching. So Mr. Parham consented to go to Houston to spend the winter, not only to engage in training students but to firmly establish this great growing work in Texas.[91]

HOUSTON BIBLE SCHOOL

Accordingly Parham rented in December, 1905, a large house at 503 Rusk Street in Houston for the purpose of operating a Bible training school. The enterprise was conducted similarly to the Bethel Bible College in Topeka. Since it was considered a "faith" venture, no tuition nor fees were charged. The students were required, however, to share the domestic and maintenance work of the school. All study was confined to the Bible.

They took the subjects of conviction, repentance, conversion, consecration, sanctification, healing, the Holy Spirit in His different operations, prophecies, the book of Revelation and other practical subjects coming in for careful study in their due order. Everything that could be found in the Bible by the school on these subjects, was searched out, written down and discussed, and Mr. Parham gave a lesson each day.[92]

In connection with their studies, the students were provided opportunities to assist in services, hold street meetings, visit the sick, and engage in other types of practical Christian work.

It should be pointed out that during the years of the new movement Parham had retained the fears of eccle-

---

[89] "Apostolics at Alvin," Galveston *Daily News*, October 30, 1905, p. 5; "Apostolic Band and Their Creed," Galveston *Tribune*, November 17, 1905, p. 4; "The Apostolic Faith," Galveston *Daily News*, November 20, 1905, p. 8; "Apostolics Faith Meeting Today," Galveston *Daily News*, December 3, 1905, p. 10.

[90] Charles F. Parham, "The Story of the Origin of the Original Apostolic or Pentecostal Movements," *Apostolic Faith*, July, 1926, p. 5.

[91] Parham, *Parham*, p. 135.

[92] *Ibid.*, p. 140.

siasticism planted on him by his unpleasant experience
with the Methodists.[93] For this reason he advocated a
simple congregationalism in which individual churches were
administered by local elders amenable to no central authority. Parham was, nevertheless, the recognized leader
of the movement during its early years, and largely determined its direction. This place of prestige was more
or less automatically accorded him because of the important part he had played in the inception of the revival
and because of his unusual ability as a minister. After
1906, when the Pentecostal message had spread to California and from there to all parts of the country, no one
person was to hold such a place of primacy.

W. J. SEYMOUR AND HIS CALIFORNIA MEETING

Among those who attended the Houston school was
W. J. Seymour, a colored Holiness preacher. From his
study he became convinced of the veracity of the Pentecostal theology, though he never spoke in "tongues" while
he was in Houston. Seymour was to play a prominent role
in the transmitting of the Pentecostal message to other
parts of the United States.[94] During the time of the Bible
course a woman from Los Angeles visited Houston and
became impressed with his ministry and devotion. On returning home she warmly recommended the "very godly
man" in Texas to her friends, who agreed to invite him
to Los Angeles to preach in their small colored Holiness
church.[95]

Seymour's reception in California was, no doubt, different from what he expected. The very first Sunday
morning he chose for his text Acts 2:4 and proceeded
to preach a sermon on the new Pentecostal "experience."
He flatly stated that when a person was "baptized in the
Spirit" he would react as did the disciples on the day
of Pentecost and speak in "tongues." [96] The sermon probably was premature, since the congregation had heard little

[93] *Ibid.*, pp. 172-179.
[94] "Latter Rain History," *Apostolic Faith*, January, 1944, pp. 14-15.
[95] "When the Spirit Fell in Los Angeles," *Pentecostal Evangel*, No. 1613 (April 6, 1946), p. 6.
[96] Frodsham, *Signs Following*, p. 31.

of the new doctrine being preached in Kansas and Texas. The older members had claimed the "baptism of the Holy Spirit" for years, and here was a stranger telling them they were only "sanctified" and that there was yet another spiritual "experience." This was more than they could accept, and they rejected the new doctrine as heresy. When Seymour returned to the church for the afternoon service, he found himself locked out.[97]

Seymour was invited, nevertheless, into the home of one of the members both to reside and to hold prayer meetings. Then, a Baptist, who attended these cottage services, prevailed upon Seymour to conduct meetings in her home at 214 North Bonnie Brae. After a brief period of teaching, a number of persons became convinced that the new "experience" was scriptural. On April 9, 1906, seven were "baptized in the Holy Spirit" and spoke in "tongues." This service received wide notice.

They shouted three days and three nights. It was the Easter season. The people came from everywhere. By the next morning there was no way of getting near the house. As the people came in they would fall under God's Power; and the whole city was stirred. They shouted there until the foundation of the house gave way, but no one was hurt. During these three days, there were many people who received their baptism who had just come to see what it was. The sick were healed and sinners were saved just as they came in.[98]

It was no mere coincidence that Los Angeles was to have an outstanding spiritual awakening. According to Frank Bartleman, a minister who wrote an account of the revival, almost two years of preparation had developed an air of expectancy. In June, 1905, Joseph Smale, pastor of the First Baptist Church of Los Angeles, had returned from a trip to Wales, where he had witnessed the Welsh Revival and the ministry of Evan Roberts. In resuming his pastoral responsibilities, Smale contended that a similar revival should be expected for Los Angeles. His enthusiasm so impressed Bartleman and a few other Holiness and evangelical ministers in the area that they in turn

---

[97] "When the Spirit Fell," *Pentecostal Evangel*, April 6, 1946, p. 6.
[98] *Ibid.*, p. 7.

stimulated their people to expect a religious awakening.
As a consequence, many devout Christians were praying
for a great revival at the time Seymour came to the city.[99]

AZUSA REVIVAL

Because the happenings at 214 Bonnie Brae street attracted so much attention, larger quarters were soon needed.
An old frame building situated in the center of the city
at 312 Azusa street was rented. Formerly a Methodist
church, it had been unused for some time and had fallen
into a poor state of repair. Worthless construction materials had been stored in it, adding to its unattractiveness.
The new Pentecostal believers cleared space for an humble
sanctuary and equipped it with crude seats made of planks
laid on top of empty nail kegs. This place became famous
in Pentecostal circles as the "Azusa Mission." [100]

The services conducted at this new site continued to
attract crowds. A. W. Orwig, who first visited the meeting in September, 1906, recollected that he arrived at ten
o'clock in the morning and

at that early hour found the house practically full, with many more
coming later, some glad to secure standing room. . . .

One thing that somewhat surprised me at that first meeting I
attended, and also subsequently, was the presence of so many persons
from the different churches.[101]

Considering the nature of the services, this success was
quite remarkable. Seymour, the recognized leader in the
early months, was most unpretentious and humble. He
generally "sat behind two empty . . . boxes, one on top of
the other. He usually kept his head inside the top one
during the meeting, in prayer. There was no pride there." [102]
The speakers, sermons, and subjects were not scheduled
in advance and the meetings followed no formal program.
Those in attendance never knew what was coming, since
everything was seemingly done more or less spontaneously.

[99] Frank Bartleman, *How Pentecost Came to Los Angeles As It Was in the Beginning* (2nd Ed., Los Angeles: F. Bartleman, 1925), pp. 5-16.

[100] *Ibid.*, pp. 47-48.

[101] Quoted in Lawrence, *Apostolic Faith Restored*, pp. 77-78.

[102] Bartleman, *Pentecost to Los Angeles*, p. 58.

No choirs were used, nor offerings taken, and no advertising was purchased; yet the congregations grew.

A prominent place was given to prayer. The people customarily gathered for an undirected period of prayer before the services commenced. Seymour, upon finishing preaching, would fall on his knees and begin to pray. Without encouragement the congregation would follow for long periods of supplication.[103]

The Azusa services were accompanied by unusual religious exercises and manifestations. "Tongues" was emphasized and was regularly in evidence. Weeping and other emotional expression was common. An eye witness recorded in his diary an incident indicative of the uniqueness of some of the manifestations.

Today in the evening service a child, approximately ten or eleven years of age, arose to testify of her new found joy in Christ. After relating being baptized in the Holy Spirit the preceding day, she began to weep. Still weeping she went on in spiritual prophecy and exhortation, clearly beyond all natural ability. With tears still streaming down her heavenly illuminated face, having climbed atop her chair, delivered such a reverential, inspired, soul moving, judgment scene descriptive message, beseeching her hearers to humble themselves under the mighty hand of God.[104]

Another uncommon phenomenon reported was the "heavenly chorus," a demonstration in which persons broke forth in spontaneous song. The composition they sang was unknown to them, yet it was said not only that the music was harmonious but also, and even stranger, that persons participated who were normally unable to sing at all.

The revival in Los Angeles surpassed anything that had been accomplished previously in the modern Pentecostal movement. Eventually Seymour was superseded by men of greater natural ability, and after a while the races no longer mixed in services. "The meeting lasted for three years, going on day and night without a break." [105] The *Apostolic Faith*, a periodical published independently of the periodical

---

[103] A. G. Osterberg, "The Azusa Revival," *Voice of Healing*, July, 1954, p. 5. Osterberg was a pioneer of Pentecost in California and served as a superintendent of the Assemblies of God in that state.

[104] *Ibid.*, p. 5.

[105] "When the Spirit Fell," *Pentecostal Evangel*, April 6, 1946, p. 7.

of the same name in Texas, reported that during the Los
Angeles meetings hundreds were converted.[106]

During the course of the three years persons from every
continent visited the revival. Many of them were "baptized in the Holy Spirit" and returned home to propagate
the new doctrine in their own localities. For this reason
Azusa Mission is generally considered the center from
which Pentecostal influence spread not only to many places
in the United States but also to a number of other nations of the world.[107]

Available source materials are inadequate to permit a
systematic following of the spread of the Pentecostal movement from Los Angeles. A few accounts of meetings in
widely separated localities can be given, however, to show
the influence of Azusa street in the expansion that followed.

MODERN PENTECOST TO CHICAGO, CANADA, AND NEW YORK

News of the California revival had reached Chicago by
the summer of 1906. John C. Sinclair wrote that "the
saints at 328 West 63rd Street began to pray on the first
of July, 1906, that God would baptize us in the Holy
Ghost, as we had heard that the Saints at Los Angeles
had been baptized.[108] F. A. Sandgren, another minister in
Chicago, stated that he heard "speaking in tongues for the
first time in August, 1906, in a Holiness mission on West
Chicago Avenue by three persons from Los Angeles." [109]
A third minister wrote that "the mighty outpouring of the
Holy Spirit which visited Azusa St., Los Angeles, California, in 1906, accompanied by the speaking in other
tongues and other manifestations of the Spirit, soon spread
to Chicago." [110] Sinclair was the first person in Chicago
to claim the "tongues experience." He recounted that this

---

[106] Quoted in Frodsham, *Signs Following*, p. 35.

[107] Frodsham, *Signs Following*, pp. 35-40.

[108] John C. Sinclair, Portland, Oregon, to Rev. E. N. Bell, Springfield, Missouri,
January 3, 1922, L. S., 2 p., Pentecostal File, Gospel Publishing House, Springfield,
Mo.

[109] F. A. Sandgren, "One Sunday in August, 1906" (a sheet printed in 1917
by F. A Sandgren in Chicago for circulation in his church).

[110] W. C. Moody, Butler, Pennsylvania, to E. N. Bell, Springfield, Missouri,
November 17, 1921, A. L. S., 7 p., Pentecostal File, Gospel Publishing House,
Springfield, Mo.

occurred on November 19, 1906, and from that time a Pentecostal revival continued in his church for a number of months.[111]

W. H. Durham also had an important part in the Pentecostal revival in Chicago. Though he was quite skeptical of the new experience when he first heard of "tongues," Durham became convinced of its genuineness while visiting the Azusa meeting and was "baptized in the Spirit" on March 2, 1907. He then returned to his North Avenue Mission in Chicago and became active in preaching Pentecost.[112]

The Pentecostal Message reached Canada via Chicago. A. H. Argue, a minister of Winnipeg, Canada, heard of the revival, went to Chicago to investigate during the spring of 1907, was "baptized in the Holy Spirit," and returned to his home to become a Pentecostal pioneer. Soon the movement was spreading through his part of Canada.[113]

The Pentecostal testimony was also carried to the eastern part of the United States from Chicago. Marie Burgess, who had been connected with the Dowie work in Zion, Illinois, and had accepted the Pentecostal "baptism" in the Chicago revival, became an evangelist of the "full gospel," preaching first around Chicago and then in Toledo and Detroit. In 1907 she was prevailed upon to go to New York City. Several Holiness missions there had already heard of the Los Angeles and Chicago meetings from persons who had attended them and were returning to homes outside the continental United States. In New York Miss Burgess preached in missions and held cottage services, and a number of persons received the Pentecostal "baptism." By May, 1907, she had enough support to open Glad Tidings Hall at 416 West 42nd Street. Miss Burgess later married Robert A. Brown, and under their ministry Glad Tidings Tabernacle developed into and has

---

[111] Sinclair to Bell, January 3, 1922.
[112] Sandgren, "One Sunday."
[113] A. H. Argue, Winnipeg, Canada, to E. N. Bell, Springfield, Missouri, November 17, 1921, A. L. S., 4 p., Pentecostal File, Gospel Publishing House, Springfield, Mo.

remained the strongest Pentecostal church in New York.[114]

The influence of the revival in New York City was felt in other cities in New York State and New Jersey. A number of the Christian and Missionary Alliance people connected with the Nyack Bible Institute accepted the Pentecostal theology and became active in preaching the new message in that area.[115]

These specific instances of the beginning of Pentecostal works are typical of the manner in which the new doctrine was carried in many directions across America from the Los Angeles revival. Within a matter of months Pentecostal missions were springing up in all parts of the United States. Very shortly after 1906 the "full gospel" could be found on every continent. The story of the international aspects of the movement, which is outside the scope of this present study, has been sketched in books by Stanley H. Frodsham and Donald Gee.[116]

CHARACTERISTICS OF EARLY REVIVAL

What were the more prominent characteristics of the modern Pentecostal revival in its early years? Doctrinally, the tenets held by Parham [117] became the basis for most of the teaching and preaching of the movement. Besides these doctrinal beliefs, a number of unorthodox attitudes and practices characterized the revival. A strong feeling existed against having church membership rolls. "God has brought us out of old, dead ecclesiasticism and denominationalism. He has made us free people, and we are not going back into 'Babylon' any more." [118] Such an attitude was common in the Holiness movement, and may have come into Pentecostal thinking from that group. There was, nevertheless, definite if informal local organization.

[114] Mrs. Robert A. Brown, New York, N. Y., to E. N. Bell, Springfield, Missouri, April 5, 1922, A. L. S., 3 p., Pentecostal File, Gospel Publishing House, Springfield, Mo.; Gordon P. Gardiner, *The Origin of Glad Tidings Tabernacle* (New York: [n. p.], 1955), pp. 12-25.
[115] Harold H. Moss, North Bergen, New Jersey, to E. N. Bell, Springfield, Missouri, April 24, 1922, L. S., 5 p., Pentecostal File, Gospel Publishing House, Springfield, Mo.
[116] Frodsham, *Signs Following*; Gee, *Pentecostal Movement*.
[117] Above, pp. 38-45.
[118] E. S. Williams, "Forty-Five Years of Pentecostal Revival," *Pentecostal Evangel*, No. 1945 (August 19, 1951), pp. 3-4.

Though no church rolls were maintained, yet "the saints were unwritten members of the church. So we had organization in those days although in our simplicity we thought we were not organized." [119]

The churches had unusual musical programs. Congregational singing was not directed by any specially designated person. Anyone might start a song, then all joined in. Many of the missions had neither organ nor piano. There was no singing of pre-arranged rehearsed numbers, though any believer could sing if he wished. "No one asked him to do it—it was spontaneous, and God used to bless it. The thought was: 'Let's have everything move as God leads—let's keep away from that which is formal and mechanical.' " [120]

Another peculiarity of the early services was the practice of not designating a particular person to deliver the sermon. "If more than one minister were present, the leader would say, 'Now we will look to the Lord, and the person to whom the Lord gives the word, he is going to be the speaker.' " [121] This practice often resulted, unfortunately, in inferior ministry, for the more able preachers might not presume to push themselves to the front. Thus the less able and inhibited would preach more frequently.

Possibly even more unusual than the practices already mentioned was that of making no public solicitation for offerings. Ministers ordinarily depended for support upon contributions handed to them personally. To receive gifts to cover operational expenses, churches generally placed little offering boxes in the rear of the auditoriums. High-pressure drives for money, such as are common in present-day religious activities, would have been considered rank commercialism totally inconsistent with "faith" concepts. [122]

Religious enthusiasm was accepted as an important part of Pentecostal worship. Freedom of physical expression

---

[119] *Ibid.,* p. 4.
[120] E. S. Williams, "Forty-Five Years of Pentecostal Revival," *Pentecostal Evangel,* No. 1946 (August 26, 1951), p. 4.
[121] Williams, "Forty-Five Years," *Pentecostal Evangel,* No. 1945, p. 4.
[122] Williams, "Forty-Five Years," *Pentecostal Evangel,* No. 1946, p. 4.

was encouraged, with spontaneous praise, shouting, and weeping the rule rather than the exception in most meetings. Every service had its time for personal "testimonies," and all worshipers were given an opportunity to participate. Yet with this spontaneity and freedom of expression a very definite place was given to the Scriptures. "At the appropriate time someone would arise with the Word of God, and it was always the clincher of the service." [123] A kind of balance between physical demonstration and the Word seems to have been achieved. Direction was often needed, however, to prevent excesses of enthusiasm.

It should be noted, finally, that the movement was very evangelistic and missionary-minded. No hardships were too severe to be endured by the pioneers in publishing their message. At the price of much physical sacrifice they soon proclaimed the Pentecostal gospel in every part of the United States and throughout the world. [124]

---

[123] *Ibid.*, p. 5.
[124] Frodsham, *Signs Following*, pp. 50-51.

V

The Organization of the Assemblies of God

THE SUBSTANTIAL number of Pentecostal congregations formed in the years immediately following the Azusa street revival inevitably caused the new movement to be faced with the problem of formal organization. Because the early Pentecostal churches and missions were divided into two distinct categories, their development followed two courses. One course involved the congregations that had been formed by Pentecostal believers who had either withdrawn from or had never belonged to an established denomination. The other course was taken by those local churches associated with Holiness communions that embraced Pentecostal theology as a body after 1906. The formal organization of the unrelated groups of the first category will be considered in this and the immediate succeeding chapters, while the churches of the second classification will be the concern of later chapters.

CONDITIONS THAT INDICATED NEED OF ORGANIZATION

The independent churches and missions of the first type were operated on the loosest kind of congregational basis. Such a polity probably resulted from a concept of spiritual idealism. The constituents believed that the Holy Spirit had been "poured out" again upon the Church, and under His direction the Church should function in the way of truth. It became apparent very soon, however, that the Spirit could not lead those persons who would not submit to His administration. Many individuals followed their own inclinations, and as a consequence local groups were sometimes in a state of confusion—every person was an authority unto himself!

Such a condition often provided an occasion for un-scrupulous persons to take advantage of the local bodies. Opportunists having to answer to no governing authority found the new assemblies easy prey and frequently ex-ploited them. Funds were in many instances misappro-priated, and capital investments deeded to individual in-terests rather than those of the congregation. Congrega-tions had little protection against strange ministers coming into their services under the pretense of being loyal to the movement and then bringing schism over some strange doctrinal view.

Many of these abuses were corrected as better local government developed. Churches soon decided that the Holy Spirit could direct the functions of a congregation through human administration. With the recognition of lay boards and elected pastors came greater protection against imposition. But in spite of this improvement the thinking leaders of the movement felt that some type of central organization was still needed for other reasons.[1]

In the first place, there was a growing need for the promotion of Pentecostal fellowship on a broader basis than the local assemblies. Many who had entered the ranks of the new movement from Holiness bodies or other de-nominational communions desired the inspiration and stim-ulation of inter-group fellowship such as they had enjoyed in their former connections.[2]

Further, an urgent need existed for co-operative effort between the various churches in areas of mutual interest. This was especially true in connection with missionary enterprise. The movement seemingly produced an irre-pressible zeal for the spreading of the Gospel. "Consecra-tions were complete. Men and women sold out for God, left their occupations, and devoted themselves to the prop-agation of the Full Gospel message, under the conviction that the return of our Lord was at hand and what was

[1] Statement by the Rev. Hugh M. Cadwalder, Kerrville, Texas, 1954, personal interview. Cadwalder became connected with the Pentecostal movement in 1904 and has remained active in its ranks since.
[2] C. C. Burnett, "Forty Years Ago," *Pentecostal Evangel*, No. 2081 (March 28, 1954), p. 12.

done must be done quickly." [3] Many such persons departed to do missionary work in distant lands. Missionaries who had been under appointment of other communions found themselves without regular support as they were released by their boards when they accepted the Pentecostal "experience." A central agency was needed to supervise these widespread activities and to promote regular financial support for missions.

Doctrinal issues also arose to confuse the Pentecostal bodies because of the lack of any central voice. Theological differences were probably unavoidable since many who had entered the new ranks came from denominations with diverse doctrinal tenets. To illustrate, an early controversy known as the "finished work of Christ" concerned the Holiness experience of sanctification. All the early Pentecostal believers, influenced by their former Holiness connections, accepted sanctification as a "definite experience." As the revival spread, though, persons were attracted from those churches that held the baptistic view —that sanctification was provided in salvation. Pastor Durham of the old North Avenue Mission in Chicago spearheaded this position. The result of the issue is felt to this day; indeed, all contemporary Pentecostal groups can be classified by their view on this matter. Some persons felt that such controversies would be much less pronounced if a central authority existed to define doctrinal position. [4]

A fourth problem area involved communications. Though a number of publications sponsored either by individuals or by independent churches was making a definite contribution to the revival, they did not satisfy the demand for an organ to represent the movement. The need was for a periodical that could be read and accepted with confidence, one that emanated from a recognized authority. [5]

An adequate training program for ministerial recruits also posed an almost insurmountable difficulty for an un-

---

[3] J. Roswell Flower, "Why a General Council," *Pentecostal Evangel*, No. 1944 (August 12, 1951), p. 6.
[4] Burnett, "Forty Years Ago," *Pentecostal Evangel*, March 28, 1954, pp. 3, 12.
[5] Flower, "Why a General Council," *Pentecostal Evangel*, August 12, 1951, p. 6.

organized group. Short term Bible courses were conducted
by a number of the early leaders, but more extensive
training opportunities were needed for the young clergymen. To provide suitable instruction, established schools
would be required. Because of the costs involved, such
undertakings could only be realized through co-operative
effort.[6]

Finally, central organization was desired in order to
effect uniformity. In the early years of the revival a great
variety of practices and methods prevailed, and identification of the individual groups was often difficult. Especially troublesome was the diversity in church names together with the fact that the names employed seldom distinguished the bodies as Pentecostal.

Because of these conditions, then, many in the movement were convinced that action should be taken to
effect central organization, even in the face of the strong
sentiment that continued to exist against such a trend.

PARHAM AND CRAWFORD'S TREND TOWARD ORGANIZATION

Notwithstanding his outspoken opposition to any kind
of conventional ecclesiastical body, the first steps toward
formal organization should probably be credited to Parham.
In the first place, he gave a name that was widely used
by early Pentecostals—the Apostolic Faith. The title became popular because of the influence of his *The Apostolic Faith*, the only Pentecostal paper that had wide circulation during the first few years of the revival. The
bodies that accepted this nomenclature were generally
called Apostolic Faith missions. Parham also was responsible for the first large gatherings of Pentecostal believers.
These sessions were not organized on a formal basis, but
rather patterned somewhat after the old Holiness associations. They became annual affairs, starting in 1905, and
commanded interstate attendance. Parham was the recognized director of the meetings not by any kind of an
election but rather because of his prestige and ability as
a minister.[7]

---
[6] *Ibid.*
[7] Cadwalder, personal interview.

Another situation also involved Parham in a trend toward organization. All the early Pentecostal ministers were handicapped by not having any kind of ministerial certification. Not only were credentials important for identification purposes, but also for receiving many ministerial courtesies, the outstanding one being special railroad rates in a day when automobiles were still uncommon. In order to overcome this inconvenience, Parham commenced to issue clergy papers. The exact time the practice began is difficult to determine, but it was known to have been in use by 1906, when in that year Seymour wrote asking for credentials so that he could obtain clergy railroad rates.[8] Here again Parham was acting on assumed rather than delegated authority.

The tendency toward organization was accentuated by the influence of other leaders of the revival. Florence L. Crawford became associated with the Pentecostals at the Azusa Street revival. A short time afterwards she established a mission in Portland, Oregon, which was called the Apostolic Faith Mission, though she had no connection at all with Parham or his churches. This work grew and in time other missions were started by associates or converts of Mrs. Crawford. These looked to the mother church for direction and supervision. Members of the group volunteered for missionary work, and Mrs. Crawford sponsored them, encouraging missionary support from all the associated churches. A periodical was eventually published and distributed to all the branch missions. Here were all the components of an organized body, but the entire structure was held together by the personality and prestige of one individual. The advantages of concerted effort, nevertheless, were pointed up by these developments.[9]

STEPS TOWARD ORGANIZATION IN TEXAS AND SURROUNDING AREA

While persons like Parham and Crawford were developing their loose association of churches, other Pentecostal

---

[8] W. J. Seymour, Los Angeles, to Brother Carothers, Houston, Texas, L. S., July 12, 1906, 1 p., Parham's Scrapbook, p. 108.
[9] *A Brief Sketch of the Life and Labors of Florence L. Crawford* (Portland: Apostolic Faith Mission, [n. d.]).

believers moved further in the direction of formal organization. The foremost of these were concentrated in Texas
and surrounding states. They had become a part of the
Pentecostal movement largely through the influence of
Parham or Azusa and used the name "Apostolic Faith" [10]
though they operated independently of both the Kansas
and the West Coast groups. Leadership was developed in
the persons of E. N. Bell, H. A. Goss, Arch P. Collins,
D. C. O. Opperman and others. In spite of a great fear
of ecclesiasticism, these men were able to bring about
co-operative fellowship among independent Pentecostal
churches of several states. This association was not based
on a written instrument of any kind. Churches and ministers voluntarily participated because of the confidence
and esteem they held for leaders who promoted the undertaking. Annual camps became the outstanding vehicle
for holding the fellowship together. Participation in activities of mutual interest was stimulated by leaders who
in time became recognized as state directors.[11]

To illustrate the extent to which camp meetings were
featured for the promotion of co-operative fellowship, the
Word and Witness of June 20, 1913, listed the announce-
ments of no less than fifteen Pentecostal camp meetings
to which the public was invited. The list included The
Texas Annual Camp at Galveston; a camp in Indianapolis,
Ind.; a Pentecostal Holiness Camp at Memphis, Tenn.;
the Oklahoma State Camp at Tulsa; a local camp at Yell-
ville, Ark.; a camp near Mercer, Mo.; The North Alabama
Camp at Warrior; The East Texas Camp at Alto; The
Northwest Texas Camp at Olney; an Iowa-Missouri Camp
at Lineville, Iowa; a Pentecostal Camp at Cumberland,
Md.; camps at Topeka, Kans., and Winfrey, Ark.

The announcement of the Arkansas State Camp is of
particular interest:

To be held at Malvern, Ark. from Sept. 10-22. This is for the
whole state of Arkansas, the fourth annual camp, and brethren from

---

[10] Statement by W. B. McCafferty, Waxahachie, Texas, 1954, personal interview.
McCafferty was associated with this Apostolic Faith group, later became a charter
member of the Assemblies of God, and for years has been a professor in
Bible colleges operated by the Assemblies of God.
[11] *Ibid.*

everywhere are invited to come and be with us. We are expecting the Lord in the camp and a great time from heaven. Bring your own pillow, sheet, quilt, toilet articles, etc. *Meals and lodging free as the Lord provides.* Send the committee below all the Lord's money you have so we can get tents and cots beforehand. Note the change of place from Hot Springs to Malvern. Only 2 cents on the railroad and good connections, on the Iron Mountain railroad, forty miles south of Little Rock. Address H. A. Goss or E. N. Bell, Malvern, Ark. if you are coming.

This voluntary association of Pentecostal believers represented a successful step toward formal organization and accomplished much in spite of the loose basis of organization. Several periodicals were widely read because of group endorsement. One was a paper edited by E. N. Bell and called until 1913 the *Apostolic Faith*. The name was then changed to *Word and Witness* to escape the confusion that resulted from the publication of several papers under the title *Apostolic Faith*. Another periodical enjoying group endorsement was the *Christian Evangel* edited by J. Roswell Flower in Indiana.[12]

The quality of the ministry was improved within the group through attention to better training. Many short-term schools, generally lasting six weeks, were held among the local congregations, D. C. O. Opperman being most active in this type of work. After a time a few schools were established with more thorough curricula. D. Wesley Myland operated one of this kind in Plainfield, Indiana, and another was located at Hattiesburg, Mississippi.[13] Three schools in the East—Bethel Bible Institute, Newark, N. J.; Elim Bible Institute, Rochester N. Y.; and Beulah Heights, North Bergen, N. J.—also trained many Pentecostal ministers during this early period of the movement.

As in the case of Parham, necessity forced the group to issue ministerial credentials. During the Azusa street revival C. H. Mason, an overseer of a Negro Holiness church, went to Los Angeles and received his "Pentecostal baptism." As a consequence of this experience his denominational body, the Church of God in Christ, became the outstanding Pentecostal Negro church in America.

12 Burnett, "Forty Years Ago," *Pentecostal Evangel*, March 28, 1954, pp. 12-13.
13 *Ibid.*, p. 12.

When the need arose for credentials in the white group, Goss visited Mason and received papers from this recognized, incorporated Negro church, and at the same time received permission to issue credentials to the other ministers of his association in the name of the Church of God in Christ. This practice continued for several years though no association existed between the two bodies.[14]

STEPS TOWARD ORGANIZATION IN THE DEEP SOUTH

While this association of churches was developing in and around Texas, another federation formed in the lower Mississippi valley. G. B. Cashwell held a revival in Memphis, Tennessee, in 1907 soon after he had returned from attending the Azusa revival. In this meeting M. M. Pinson and H. G. Rodgers received the "Pentecostal experience," and they soon afterward evangelized with one of their converts, D. J. Dubose, in Mississippi and Alabama. As a result of their efforts a church was established at New Brockton, Alabama, and Pentecostal converts were made throughout the area.[15] As early as 1909 these believers were holding association meetings. In that year a three-day conference called by Rodgers at Dothan, Alabama, adopted the name "Church of God." The only test of fellowship imposed by the band was the "fruits of the Spirit." The group began to license and ordain ministers and took steps to secure recognition from the Southern Clergy Bureau.[16] By February, 1911, the association had developed into a definite though simple organization. In a convention then held at Providence, near Slocomb, Alabama, formal minutes were kept and officers were elected—Rodgers was chairman, and J. W. Ledbetter, secretary.[17]

TEXAS AND DEEP SOUTH GROUPS AMALGAMATE

In 1912 the name "Church of God," adopted in 1909, was regarded as undesirable when it was discovered that

---

[14] J. Roswell Flower, "A History of the Assemblies of God" (duplicated paper prepared for instructional purposes at Central Bible Institute, Springfield, Missouri, [n. d.]), p. 17. Flower was an early Pentecostal minister and a charter member of the Assemblies of God. He stated in an interview that a few credentials were issued under the name Church of God in Christ of Apostolic Faith.
[15] Burnett, "Forty Years Ago," *Pentecostal Evangel*, March 28, 1954, p. 12.
[16] Flower, "History of the Assemblies of God." p. 18.
[17] Burnett, "Forty Years Ago," *Pentecostal Evangel*, March 28, 1954, p. 12.

a Tennessee Pentecostal body was operating under the same title. Consequently in 1912 the Southern association worked out an agreement with the Texas group whereby it could assume the name Church of God in Christ. This was the beginning of a move to merge the two associations. While records of the negotiations between the groups are missing, it would appear that the consolidation was completed by June, 1913, when a convention meeting in Meridian, Mississippi, prepared a ministerial list of 352 names that included clergymen of both associations. Another phase of the merger was the combination of the *Word and Witness*, edited by Pinson for the Alabama-Mississippi body, and the *Apostolic Faith*, edited by Bell for the other group. The final arrangement was completed in the summer of 1913 at a camp meeting at Eureka Springs, Arkansas. As has been previously noted, Bell retained the editorship, and the periodical continued as the *Word and Witness*, a more distinctive name than *Apostolic Faith*.[18]

CALL FOR HOT SPRINGS, ARKANSAS, CONVENTION

Not long after the Eureka Springs camp meeting some of the leaders began to take active steps to effect organization on a more conventional basis. It is of interest to note that Parham took no part in this action because of his opposition to a formal ecclesiasticism. Goss and Bell were especially prominent in promoting the move. Enough interest had been stimulated by early 1914 to justify a meeting for the purpose of attempting formal organization.[19] Goss had leased the Grand Opera House in Hot Springs, Arkansas, where he held a pastorate, for a period of six months, and it was in this setting that a small convention was called to meet April 2-12, 1914.

The formal call for the convention, first published in the issue of *Word and Witness* for December 12, 1913, carried considerable prestige since it was signed by Pinson, Collins, and Opperman as well as Goss and Bell.[20]

[18] *Ibid.*, p. 13.

[19] Flower, "History of the Assemblies of God," p. 19.

[20] Word and Witness, IX (December 20, 1913), p. 1. Word and Witness was merged with the Pentecostal Evangel, official organ of the Assemblies of God, after 1915.

It was addressed to "all the Churches of God in Christ, to all Pentecostal or Apostolic Faith Assemblies who desire with united purpose to co-operate in love and peace to push interests of the kingdom of God everywhere." The convention would be "only for saints who believe in the baptism with the Holy Ghost with the signs following," and not "for any captious, contrary, divisive or contentious person." [21]

Five specific purposes were stated for the convention.

First—We come together that we may get a better understanding of what God would have us teach, that we may do away with so many divisions, both in doctrines and in the various names under which our Pentecostal people are working and incorporating. Let us come together as in Acts 14, to study the Word, and pray with and for each other—unity our chief aim.

Second—Again we come together that we may know how to conserve the work, that we may all build up and not tear down, both in home and foreign lands.

Third—We come together for another reason, that we may get a better understanding of the needs of each foreign field, and may know how to place our money in such a way that one mission or missionary shall not suffer, while another not any more worthy, lives in luxuries. Also that we may discourage wasting money on those who are running here and there accomplishing nothing, and may concentrate our support on those who mean business for our King.

Fourth—Many of the saints have felt the need of chartering the Churches of God in Christ, putting them on legal basis....

Fifth—We may also have a proposition to lay before the body for a general Bible Training School with a literary department for our people. [22]

The announcement caused an immediate flood of both favorable and hostile reaction. Some of the criticism published by opponents undoubtedly misinterpreted the objectives of the convention. As a consequence, a later edition of *Word and Witness* attempted further to clarify the involved issues and flatly charged that some of the censures contained misrepresentation. [23] Goss reported that

[21] *Ibid.*
[22] *Ibid.*
[23] *Word and Witness*, March 20, 1914, p. 2.

opposition to the convention was particularly strong among Pentecostal believers on the Pacific coast.[24]

The convening of the Hot Springs meeting was the result of the natural development of the Pentecostal movement. The introduction to the minutes of the convention indicates that the body was quite cognizant of this fact:

For a number of years, God has been leading men to seek for a full apostolic gospel standard of experience and doctrine. Some 14 years ago, in answer to prayer, the Lord began to pour out His Spirit in Kansas, then in Texas; and some eight years ago it reached Los Angeles, California, and from thence it soon became scattered over the civilized world. It has been so aggressive that almost every city and community in civilization has heard of the Latter Rain outpouring of the Holy Ghost, with many signs following, and not only has civilization been affected to more or less a degree, but hundreds of missionaries have consecrated themselves and gone forth until almost every country on the globe has heard the message and also the prophecy which has been predominant in all this great outpouring, which is "Jesus is coming soon" to this old world in the same manner as He left it to set up His Millennial kingdom and to reign over the earth in righteousness and peace for a thousand years.

As is true in all great religious awakenings, as evidenced by past history, all kinds of chaotic conditions have been manifested and as this great movement of God has no man nor set of men at the head of it but God to guide and mold it into clean-cut Scriptural paths by the Holy Spirit, individualism has been the human order of the day, every man being a law unto himself, and consequently that Scriptural co-operation and fellowship which go far to guarantee the presence and power of God have not been realized in the past in its fullest measure, but as we appropriate the divine order we shall experience the divine presence and power in this respect.

The Pentecostal saints in the United States and Canada especially have seen this great need of co-operation, fellowship and unity according to the Scriptures, and have felt such a great need of the same in the Home and Foreign Missions work that in different parts of the country brethren have undertaken, we believe in the name of Jesus, to accomplish this end, but seemingly God has a more Scriptural basis and method and a broader field and a greater work than has been accomplished.[25]

[24] Flower, "History of the Assemblies of God," p. 19.
[25] *Combined Minutes of the General Council of the Assemblies of God, April 2-12, November 15-29, 1914* (St. Louis: Gospel Publishing House, 1914), p. 2. Hereafter minutes of general council meetings of the Assemblies of God will be cited as *Minutes* followed by the year of the meeting.

When the organizational session duly convened the response proved most gratifying, for "between two and three hundred ministers and laymen attended. . . . Of this number, about 120 evangelists and pastors of established churches registered as delegates." [26] *Word and Witness* in reporting the assembly did not attempt to list the names of those in attendance who were connected with the Church of God in Christ association, but did give many names of prominent Pentecostal representatives from other areas. There were delegates from Buffalo, Baltimore, Findlay (Ohio), Chicago, Zion City (Illinois), Evansville (Indiana), Indianapolis, Memphis, and Portland.[27]

Though the convention opened on April 2, no business was conducted until April 6. The first days

> were given especially to reports, getting arranged, hearing messages calculated to draw us all nearer to God, and such other things as tended to unify the saints. Soon the most blessed spirit of fellowship prevailed throughout the gathered host. Hearts were blended together and a most blessed spirit of love, unity, and peace was manifested.[28]

These early days of conditioning may have contributed much to the ultimate success of the convention.

ASSEMBLIES OF GOD ESTABLISHED

This meeting formed the Assemblies of God by framing and adopting a document entitled "Preamble and Resolution on Constitution." This brief instrument set forth principles of equality, unity, and co-operation, guaranteed the sovereignty of each local affiliated church, and provided a basis of co-operative fellowship for both ministers and congregations. Since the declaration is very significant to the forming of this new group, the complete document follows:

> WHERAS, God, our Heavenly Father, sent His only begotten Son, the Lord Jesus Christ, into the World, Who purchased and redeemed fallen man with His own precious blood, and called out of the world and saved a people, of whom He built and established His church (Assembly of God. Matt. 16:18), upon the foundation

---

[26] Flower, "History of the Assemblies of God," p. 20.
[27] *Word and Witness*, April 20, 1914, p. 1.
[28] *Ibid.*

of the Apostles and Prophets, Jesus Christ Himself being the Head and Chief Cornerstone (Eph. 2:20), and organized and baptized it with the Holy Spirit, with its government upon His shoulders (Isaiah 9:6-7), said "the gates of hell shall not prevail against it" (Matt. 16:18); and

WHERAS, He gave the holy inspired Scriptures, (both old and new covenants, Heb. 8:6-13), as the all-sufficient rule for faith and practice (2 Tim. 3:16), as follows: "All Scripture is given by inspiration of God, and is profitable for doctrine, for reproof, for correction, for instruction in righteousness: That the man of God may be perfect, thoroughly furnished unto all good works," we therefore shall not add to nor take from it (Rev. 22:18); and

WHERAS, He commanded that there should be no schism (Division, sectarianism) in His body, the GENERAL ASSEMBLY (Church) of the first born, which are written in heaven (Heb. 12:23); and

WHEREAS, We recognize ourselves as members of said GENERAL ASSEMBLY OF GOD (which is God's organism), and do not believe in identifying ourselves as, or establishing ourselves into, a sect, that is a human organization that legislates or forms laws and articles of faith and has unscriptural jurisdiction over its members and creates unscriptural lines of fellowship and disfellowship and which separates itself from other members of the General Assembly (Church) of the first born, which is contrary to Christ's prayer in St. John 17, and Paul's teaching in Eph. 4:1-16, which we heartily endorse:

THEREFORE, BE IT RESOLVED, First, That we recognize ourselves as a GENERAL COUNCIL of Pentecostal (Spirit Baptized) saints from local Churches of God in Christ, Assemblies of God and various Apostolic Faith Missions and Churches, and Full Gospel Pentecostal Missions, and Assemblies of like faith in the United States of America, Canada, and Foreign Lands, whose purpose is neither to legislate laws of government, nor usurp authority over said various Assemblies of God, nor deprive them of their Scriptural and local rights and privileges, but to recognize Scriptural methods and order for worship, unity, fellowship, work and business for God, and to disapprove of all unscriptural methods, doctrine and conduct, and approve all Scriptural truth and conduct, endeavoring to keep the unity of the Spirit in the bonds of peace, until we all come into the unity of the faith, and of the knowledge of the Son of God, unto a perfect man, unto the measure of the stature of the fulness of Christ, and to walk accordingly, as recorded in Eph. 4:17-32, and to consider the five purposes announced in the Convention Call in the February, 1914, issue of "WORD AND WITNESS:"

RESOLVED, Second, That we recognize all the above said Assemblies of various names, and when speaking of them refer to them by the general Scriptural name "Assemblies of God;" and recommend that they all recognize themselves by the same name, that is, "Assembly of God" and adopt it as soon as practicable for the purpose of being more Scriptural and also legal in transacting business, owning property, and executing missionary work in home and foreign lands, and for general convenience, unity and fellowship.[29]

Two very difficult matters facing the convention were the establishment of an acceptable system or organization, and the formulation of a doctrinal statement to which the delegates could and would subscribe. What made these formidable problems was the fact that the delegates came from many religious backgrounds with wide differences in theology and polity.

The two problems were solved by the general nature of the legislation passed. In the matter of organization, a very simple kind of polity was adopted. It was not patterned closely upon any of the traditional church polities, though it did include features of several. The relationship of the local churches to the organization was placed on a purely congregational basis. Flower states, in referring to the first council, that "there was no desire or purpose to establish an ecclesiastical body to assume jurisdiction over the free Pentecostal churches." [30] This was unquestionably true, since it is affirmed in the Constitutional Declaration. Through the years the sovereignty of the local church was to be maintained.

With these congregational tendencies were combined certain Presbyterian characteristics in the provision of a central administration to facilitate missionary and evangelistic activities as well as to guarantee the preservation of high ministerial standards. A general chairman and a secretary-treasurer were to serve as the officers of the group, and a board of twelve men, called the "Executive Presbytery," was "to act in all necessary matters on behalf of this General Council, as a Home and Foreign Missionary and Executive Presbytery, during the ensuing year, or until

[29] *Minutes,* April 2-12, 1914, pp. 4-5.
[30] J. Roswell Flower, *The Origin and Development of the Assemblies of God* (Springfield, Missouri: Gospel Publishing House, 1947), p. 7.

their successors are appointed." [81] This completed the basic polity established by the organizing body.

In formulating a doctrinal position the Constitutional Declaration did not define any specific tenets. The convention felt it sufficient merely to state that the Holy Inspired Scriptures were the all-sufficient rule for faith and practice. No matter what their background, all those present could subscribe to such a broad creed. This legislation was "adopted amid great joy and shouting," [82] which would seem to indicate a spirit of unanimity.

Several other important actions were taken in this first council. The body voted to be incorporated under the name "General Council of the Assemblies of God." The papers of incorporation were finally executed on October 13, 1914. [83] *Word and Witness* and *Christian Evangel* were recognized as the official organs of the Assemblies of God. Local assemblies were authorized to form district councils in harmony with the principles and purposes of the General Council. Ministerial credentials were denied all persons who were divorced and remarried (this provision has been maintained through the years). Before adjourning, the assembly authorized the executive presbytery to plan and call succeeding councils. [84]

GENERAL COUNCIL

The simple organization provided by the first council has been expanded and developed through the years to meet the new demands of the growing church. The General Council has remained the highest constitutional authority and continued primarily as a legislative and policy making body. It is a representative assembly composed of all ordained ministers of the Assemblies of God and one delegate from each recognized church. [85] During the early years frequent meetings were necessary to care for the many problems connected with the establishment of the infant group. Two general councils in the first year

[81] *Minutes*, April 2-12, 1914, p. 5.
[82] *Word and Witness*, April 20, 1914, p. 1.
[83] *Pentecostal Evangel*, No. 2082 (April 4, 1954), p. 9.
[84] *Minutes*, April 2-12, 1914, pp. 6-8.
[85] *Minutes*, 1953, p. 44.

were followed by annual councils until 1921, at which time the body voted for future sessions to convene biennially. The councils have had no regular meeting place, convention cities being chosen generally for the convenience of their geographical location and facilities to accommodate the meetings.[86]

DISTRICT COUNCILS

District Councils developed apace with the General Council. Constitutional provision for these area administrations was made by the first general convention. Their function was to supervise and expedite the activities of the Assemblies of God within their prescribed geographical limits. A district council "being the creature of the General Council and subordinate thereto, cannot be authorized, in any way, to violate the principles of the General Council constitutional agreements or bylaws." [87] District council boundaries generally follow those of states, though in areas of unusually sparse constituencies more than one state sometime constitutes a district, while in those of unusual density a state may be divided into several districts. The district councils elect their own officers and arrange for their own conventions. Though the structures of the different district organizations may vary somewhat within the framework prescribed by the central body, they are largely patterned after that of the General Council itself.[88]

GENERAL PRESBYTERY

The central administrative body next in order of authority to the General Council was provided by the council in 1916 and is called the General Presbytery. This committee exercises important executive and judicial powers clearly stated in the constitution.

The General Presbytery shall be empowered to act in all matters pertaining to foreign missionary and ministerial relationships, and all matters which pertain to the proper functioning of the departments and institutions in the fellowship. It shall constitute an advisory body to the Executive Presbytery. All decisions pertaining

---

[86] *Minutes,* 1921, pp. 50-51.
[87] *Minutes,* 1955, p. 60.
[88] *Minutes,* 1955, pp. 59-60, 66.

to constitutional order or fundamental doctrines shall be referred
by it to the General Council for ratification. . . .

The General Presbytery shall also act as a Court of Appeal for
the reviewing of testimony given in missionary and ministerial trials.
Its decisions shall be final.[39]

For a number of years men of prestige were nominated
and elected from the floor of the General Council to
serve in the General Presbytery. The council held in 1933,
in order to assure wider area representation, provided that
each district council should be represented in the General
Presbytery by the district superintendent and two other
persons to be nominated by the districts but still elected
by the General Council.[40] It was found, however, that the
district councils had become so numerous that considerable
difficulty was encountered in trying to elect the membership of the General Presbytery at the general conventions.
For this reason the council of 1935 authorized the district
councils not merely to nominate but actually to elect their
general presbyters.[41]

EXECUTIVE PRESBYTERY

The first council set up an Executive Presbytery to
serve as the executive committee of the Assemblies of God.
Its functions have remained substantially the same throughout the years, but its composition has varied a good deal
in what has apparently been a trial and error effort to
develop the best administration. The initial council provided for an Executive Presbytery of twelve persons, the
second increased this number to sixteen, the council of
1916 reduced it to five and the council of 1919 raised it
to seven. In 1925 the structure was further changed when
provision was made for the general officers and four
elected persons (these eventually became representatives
of four geographical areas of the United States) to constitute the committee. The council of 1959 increased the
number again by providing for four additional geographical
representatives.[42]

---

[39] *Minutes*, 1953, p. 51.
[40] *Minutes*, 1933, p. 99.
[41] *Minutes*, 1935, p. 93.
[42] *Minutes*, April 2-12, 1914, p. 5; *Minutes*, November 15-29, 1914, p. 10;
Minutes, 1916, p. 6; *Minutes*, 1919, p. 17; *Minutes*, 1925, pp. 68-69; *Minutes*,
1947, p. 8; *Minutes*, 1959, pp. 25-27.

OFFICERS OF THE ASSEMBLIES OF GOD

While the organization of the Assemblies of God was in its infancy, administration was simple and required few officers. The first council provided for only two, a chairman and a secretary. As the church grew and its organization became more complex, other officers were established to furnish adequate administrative leadership. The chairman's title was changed in 1927 to general superintendent, a designation that has been perpetuated.[43] This executive heads the general office and supervises all the work of the Assemblies of God in the interim between general councils. He presides at general council, general presbytery, and executive presbytery meetings. Two of his important duties are the signing of all credentials and the appointing of directors to head the various departments of the church.[44]

The office of assistant chairman (the title was changed to assistant superintendent in 1927) was established by the general council of November 15-29, 1914.[45] Apparently the position did not have much prestige until 1923, for during the years between 1914 and 1923 it was at times not even filled. Since the council of 1923 the office has always been staffed, a fact which probably indicates that the post took on increasing importance. In 1945 the superintendent reported concerning the existing executive arrangements:

The growth of the General Council of the Assemblies of God in the past few years has so enlarged the responsibilities and increased the activities of the executive officers that it has become physically impossible for them to meet the demands of their offices, and the constant requests for field ministry requires them to be absent from the office to such an extent that it renders them unfamiliar with the current affairs at headquarters.[46]

Accordingly provision was made that year for four assistant superintendents to be elected to help the general superintendent in the administration of the central office. The next general council made their responsibilities more

---

[43] *Minutes*, 1927, p. 80.
[44] *Minutes*, 1953, pp. 48-49.
[45] *Minutes*, November 15-29, 1914, p. 8.
[46] *Minutes*, 1945, p. 7.

specific by stipulating that they should serve as directors of departments and do field work under the direction of the general superintendent.[47] Following the council of 1947 the missions department continued to be directed by the foreign missions secretary. In order to adjust the structure of this area to comply with that of the other departments, the general council in 1959 elevated the office of foreign missions secretary to the status of assistant superintendent bringing the total number of five.[48]

The secretary provided for by the first council served for a number of years as both secretary and treasurer, though this latter office was not officially established until 1925.[49] At that time, the Executive Presbytery was authorized to select the treasurer and it continued to assign the function to the secretary until 1947, when the convention voted to fill the offices with two individuals. After this action the treasurer was nominated by the General Presbytery and elected by the General Council.[50] The secretary has the responsibility of keeping records of all the proceedings of general meetings, is custodian of the official seal, issues credentials on the recommendation of the proper authorities, and keeps accurate lists of ministers and churches. The treasurer is responsible for all General Council funds and is required not only to keep accurate fiscal records but also to submit regular financial reports to the General Council and the Executive Presbytery.[51]

DEPARTMENTAL ORGANIZATION OF THE ASSEMBLIES OF GOD

The different enterprises of the denomination are administered as departments. This organizational pattern developed slowly, departmental status being given to the various functions only when they had grown to a place of importance in the church program. To illustrate, missionary work was begun at the first council. For a number of years the chairman and secretary directed this ac-

[47] *Minutes,* 1947, p. 75.
[48] *Minutes,* 1959, p. 24.
[49] *Minutes,* 1925, p. 65.
[50] *Minutes,* 1947, pp. 10, 57.
[51] *Minutes,* 1955, pp. 63-64.

tivity. By the time of the council in 1919, interest and participation in the missionary program had become so great that a Missions Department was established.[52] Again, youth work attracted the official attention of the General Council as early as 1927 but did not grow large enough to become a department until 1943.[53]

The main interests of the Assemblies of God had so increased in number and prominence by 1953 that the council of that year reorganized all the work into fifteen departments, each supervised by an executive director and a secretary.[54] The development of the more important departments will be considered in greater detail in subsequent chapters.

FISCAL POLICY OF THE GENERAL COUNCIL

The fiscal policy of the central office has been changed several times. In the early years the entire church program was financed on the free-will offering plan. Officers were guaranteed no salary and received only that which was voluntarily contributed for their services.[55] This arrangement was altered in 1916 by the requirement that all ordained ministers contribute at least one dollar per month for the support of central headquarters. The council of 1949 increased the levy to $1.50 per month, and in 1955 the amount was raised to two dollars and all licentiates were assessed one dollar per month.[56] This financial support from clergymen has been supplemented through the years by voluntary contributions from churches and profits from the auxiliary enterprises of the church. As the fiscal condition of the group improved, financial administration became much more carefully supervised. Today expenditures are controlled by a detailed budget, and all fiscal records are subjected to rigid audits.

ASSEMBLIES OF GOD CLERGY

The General Council through the years has retained as one of its principal functions the supervision of its clergy.

[52] *Minutes*, 1919, p. 12.
[53] *Minutes*, 1927, pp. 73-75; *Minutes*, 1943, pp. 24-26.
[54] *Minutes*, 1953, p. 16.
[55] *Minutes*, November 15-29, 1914, p. 12.
[56] *Minutes*, 1949, p. 19; *Minutes*, 1955, pp. 12-14.

Though no professional training is required for the ministry, high standards are encouraged. Three classifications of ministers are recognized: An Exhorter certificate is granted to the novice who has training or demonstrated ability but not experience; a License to the young clergyman with limited experience; and Ordination to the mature, experienced minister.[57] Much of the detailed supervision of the clergy is now delegated to the district councils, but the Executive Presbytery and the General Presbytery of the central organization remain the courts of final appeal in all matters relating to the ministry.[58]

DOCTRINAL POSITION OF THE ASSEMBLIES OF GOD

As already noted, the Assemblies of God was organized in 1914 with little said about a formal doctrinal statement. The first convention simply took the position that the Bible was the all-sufficient rule for faith and practice. Because the Pentecostal movement was disturbed shortly afterward by a controversy over the doctrine of the Trinity, the council in order to preserve unity drafted and adopted in 1916 a declaration of beliefs. This document, entitled, "Statement of Fundamental Truths," contained sixteen basic tenets. It seems somewhat surprising that through the years the necessity has never arisen for any modification of this doctrinal statement.[59]

The second tenet of the "Statement of Fundamental Truths" indicates that the denomination is Trinitarian; the third and fourth uphold Arminian theology; the fifth and sixth recognize only water baptism by immersion and the Lord's Supper as Church ordinances; the ninth advocates sanctification of the baptistic type (a progressive rather than a definite experience) ; while the fourteenth supports premillennialism. These positions classify the Assemblies of God in regard to the more controversial points of Protestant theology.

---

[57] *Minutes*, 1917, pp. 20-21.
[58] *Minutes*, 1955, pp. 67-74.
[59] *Minutes*, 1916, pp. 10-13. The council of 1959 named a committee to study the Statement of Fundamental Truths; thus a revision may be pending.

VI
The Departments of Propagation of the Assemblies of God

THE Assemblies of God has realized a healthy growth during the years since organization. On the first printed ministerial roster the names of 531 ordained clergymen were listed.[1] This number had grown to 1,641 in 1929, 3,592 in 1939, 6,225 in 1949, and 9,227 in 1959. Churches and church membership increased proportionately. The following table shows expansion in these areas:

Year	Churches	Membership
1929	1,612	91,981
1939	3,496	184,022
1949	5,950	275,000
1959	8,094	505,552[2]

An article in *Time* dealing with the growth of American church bodies credited the Assemblies of God with an increase of 474 per cent during the period of 1926-1949.[3]

The work of the departments of propagation and training contributed much to this rapid expansion. For this reason the present chapter and the next one will be devoted to a survey of the development of these agencies.

FOREIGN MISSIONS DEPARTMENT

As was noticed in the preceding chapter, a very important reason for organizing the Pentecostal movement was to facilitate missions, a function that had characterized the revival since its inception.[4] This activity has continued

---

[1] *Minutes*, November 15-29, 1914, pp. 13-16.
[2] *Reports*, 1959, p. 9.
[3] *Time*, LVII (April 2, 1951), p. 81.
[4] Frodsham, *With Signs Following*, p. 50.

to hold a place of importance in the Assemblies of God, being one of the programs in the church that is most emphasized today.

IMPORTANCE ATTACHED TO MISSIONS

The Assemblies of God must stress missions if its practice is to be consistent with its doctrinal position. According to Pentecostal theology the purpose of the "Baptism in the Holy Spirit," the distinctive Pentecostal experience, is to provide power for the believers to "be witnesses in Jerusalem, and in all Judea, and in Samaria and unto the uttermost parts of the earth." [5] A communion holding both such a concept and a belief in the premillennial second coming of Christ, as the Assemblies of God does, must of necessity emphasize missionary enterprise.

DEVELOPMENT OF A FOREIGN MISSIONS PROGRAM

The early missionaries of the modern Pentecostal movement courageously "went out . . . by faith, with no church board back of them, and no promise of financial support apart from such promises which may have been made by their home assemblies." [6] They soon found that a clearing agency was needed—one that could receive and forward funds, make appeals, and publicize the work of missions. The Assemblies of God became just such an agency. The first council directed the chairman to serve as a "missionary secretary" and to administer all missionary contributions. The Executive Presbytery was also considered a "missionary presbytery" and as such assisted the chairman with the missionary problems of the new group. [7]

By the time of the third council in 1915 a definite missionary policy was desired. Accordingly, the following written plan was adopted as the basis of the missionary practices of the church:

Resolved, That this Council exert all its powers to promote the evangelization of heathen lands according to New Testament methods, viz:

---

[5] Acts 1:8.

[6] Flower, *Origin and Development of the Assemblies of God*, p. 9.

[7] *Word and Witness*, May 20, 1914, p. 1.

First. In the proper testing of those who claim to be called to the foreign work. Rev. 2:2; Acts 13:1-4.

A. As to a personal experience of full New Testament salvation.

B. As to a definite call to foreign work.

C. As to physical, mental and spiritual fitness for the work.

Second. In the proper sending, supporting and supervising of those approved.

A. Every Assembly ought to have a definite part in it, either sending and maintaining one or more missionaries of its own, or sharing the burden of one or more missionaries with one or more other assemblies.

B. Missionaries receiving the baptism on the field ought to be brought in touch and supported by the assemblies having no missionaries of their own.

C. Missionaries who fail on the field ought to be brought home by assemblies concerned.

D. Missionaries are responsible to the assemblies supporting them for all funds entrusted to them and should give a periodical report.

E. No missionary should return home without the approval of his or her supporting assemblies except in extreme circumstances.

Third. Missionaries home on furlough should be maintained and supervised by their assemblies the same as while on the field. Every opportunity should be afforded them to present the needs of their field and of mission work in general, not only to their own assemblies, but the Assemblies of God everywhere.[8]

This statement has gone through several modifications and revisions since the council of 1915. Today the basic policy runs to nine pages in the bylaws,[9] and the manual that regulates the practices resulting from the application of the missionary policy contains ninety-seven pages.[10]

ADMINISTRATION OF FOREIGN MISSIONS

The administration of missions has also been altered from time to time to meet the demands of a growing program. During the first years no distinct officers were required, since the general officers and the Executive Presbytery were able to supervise missionary activities as

[8] *Minutes,* 1915, pp. 9-10.

[9] *Minutes,* 1955, pp. 22-31.

[10] Foreign Missions Department, *Missionary Manual* (revised to 1956, Springfield, Missouri: Gospel Publishing House, 1956).

well as the other affairs of the infant church. By 1919, however, the responsibilities had grown to such proportions that the General Council established a foreign missions department directed by a missions secretary. The Executive Presbytery continued under this arrangement to serve as a missions committee.[11]

The foreign missions department has, as it happens, had very few secretaries. J. Roswell Flower was selected as the first in 1919 and held the office until 1923, when he was succeeded by William M. Faux.[12] In 1926 the office was filled by Noel Perkin, who retained the position until his retirement in 1959. The council of 1959 provided for different persons to hold the offices of executive director of foreign missions and foreign missions secretary, thus bringing the department into conformity with the departmental structure of the General Council.

In the early 1940's the foreign missions secretary was given administrative assistance by the installation of field secretaries. These subordinate officers were provided to represent the interests of large geographical areas in which missionaries worked—Africa, Europe, Latin America, Far East, and Near East.[13]

When the responsibilities of the Executive Presbytery became so heavy it could not devote sufficient time to missionary problems, a foreign missions board was established to direct the function. This board is composed of the foreign missions director, two executive presbyters, the department secretary, four field secretaries, and six pastors of Assemblies of God churches. Formulation of departmental policy within the framework of the constitution, and appointment of missionaries, are its principal duties. The general administration of the department is under the supervision of a foreign missions committee, made up of the foreign missions director, the department secretary, all the field secretaries, and the heads of the

[11] *Minutes*, 1919, p. 12.
[12] Elizabeth A. Galley Wilson, *Making Many Rich* (Springfield, Missouri: Gospel Publishing House, 1955), p. 12; *Facts and Figures* (Springfield, Missouri: Foreign Missions Department, Assemblies of God, [1953]), p. 2.
[13] *Minutes*, 1943, pp. 44-45; *Missionary Manual*, pp. 17-18.

major divisions of the department.[14] For the handling of
detailed work, divisions of finance, promotions, transpor-
tation, and Spanish publications, and sub-divisions for
bookkeeping, correspondence, filing, and deputational work
were organized as they were needed.[15]

INDIGENOUS METHODS ADVOCATED

The missionary practices of the organization have followed proven concepts and methods. A late book published
by the Assemblies of God on missionary technique states
that "the purpose of missions must be to build up churches
which would be 'self-supporting, self-governing, and self-
propagating.' In other words, the purpose of missionary
endeavor is to establish indigenous churches." [16]

The principle of indigenous missions is embraced by
the Assemblies of God and is clearly expressed in the
Missionary Manual.

In all fields occupied by Assemblies of God missionaries, every
effort shall be exerted to establish autonomous Assemblies of God
organizations, composed of co-operating, sovereign assemblies. It is
realized that no fixed organizational pattern is possible. Every organization should take on a form fully consonant with local conditions, manner of life and thought patterns. Missionaries should
studiously avoid the practice of proposing a western type of organization, but should encourage a type readily understood and easily operated by the nationals of the country in question.[17]

How this principle is actually applied in the development of Assemblies of God works in foreign areas may
be illustrated by a brief account of the establishment of
the French West African mission. The first Assemblies
of God missionaries entered this region in the early 1920's.
Since few of the nationals spoke either English or French,
the workers first concerned themselves with language study,
so that they could communicate the gospel in the native

---

[14] *Minutes*, 1959, pp. 113-115.

[15] "Foreign Missions Department Report to General Presbyters, September 5-7,
1956" (prepared and duplicated by Missions Department, Assemblies of God,
Springfield, Missouri, 1956), p. 3; hereafter cited as "Foreign Missions Report."

[16] Melvin L. Hodges, *The Indigenous Church* (Springfield, Missouri: Gospel
Publishing House, 1953), p. 3.

[17] *Missionary Manual*, p. 71.

tongue. With this accomplishment the missionaries were able to make their first converts to Christianity.[18]

In keeping with the indigenous principle, a program was then launched to prepare the early converts to assume the responsibility of propagating Christianity. This involved three initial major steps: first, the language had to be reduced to written form; second, the Scriptures and other necessary tools had to be translated into the vernacular; and third, the converts had to be trained to read and proclaim the gospel intelligently.[19]

The translation work was a slow, difficult process. By the end of the first decade a few books of the New Testament, duplicated in the vernacular by multigraph, were being used by native Christians. As time passed other portions of the Scriptures were translated, and finally in 1940 the New Testament was completed and soon afterward published and made available for general distribution by the American Bible Society.[20]

Since the converts could not read, the training program included both a general education course, which had teaching of reading and basic Bible as its main objectives, and a more formal Bible curriculum for the training of prospective ministers. When a native worker's training was completed, he was sent into villages surrounding the mission station to preach. In this way churches were established through a region. It was found that the native minister, not handicapped by language difficulties, ignorance of local customs, or native suspicions, was often more effective in making converts than the missionaries themselves.[21]

Another objective of the indigenous principle realized by the west African mission was the development of a self-supporting native church. Though in the early years

---

[18] Wilson, *Making Many Rich*, pp. 112-115.

[19] *Ibid.*, p. 118.

[20] John F. Hall, "An Emperor Receives the New Testament," *Bible Society Record*, XCII (September, 1947), pp. 100-101; John F. Hall, "The New Testament in Mossi," *Missionary Challenge*, V (July, August, September, 1955), pp. 14-15.

[21] Arthur E. Wilson, "Developing Native Evangelism in Mossi Land," *Pentecostal Evangel*, No. 1057 (July 14, 1934), pp. 11, 14.

the missionaries had to subsidize native ministers, by 1947 they were entirely supported by the local churches.[22]

PROMOTION OF MISSIONS

The missionary activities of the church are kept before its constituency through the carefully co-ordinated program of the promotional division of the missions department. Missionaries on furlough are scheduled for deputation work in such a way that congregations have occasion periodically to hear representatives of all the major mission fields. The circulation of missionary films is another means of stimulating interest in the work of missions.

The department published a twenty-page monthly missionary magazine, *World Challenge* (it was first issued as *The Missionary Challenge*), from 1943 to 1959. When it was discontinued, *The Pentecostal Evangel,* which had carried a weekly missions feature for years, began in addition to devote one weekly edition each month to world missions. All facets of the missionary program have in this way been brought regularly to the attention of the church.[23]

MISSIONARY FINANCE, STAFF, AND FIELDS

The financing of the missionary program has not followed any set pattern. Each individual congregation is left to determine its own policy and practice. A great many take one offering a month in their Sunday schools, while others raise funds periodically in other services. Special contributions are usually requested when churches are visited by missionary personnel. Surprisingly, this basis of voluntary giving has proven quite effective in raising funds, for the contributions have increased through the years. In 1916 only $4,879.50 was given to missions, while four years later the amount had increased to $63,548.59,[24] and comparable growth has continued to be realized. The present proportions of the missionary budget are shown by

---

[22] Wilson, *Making Many Rich,* pp. 130-131.

[23] "Foreign Missions Report," 1956, pp. 4-9; *Minutes,* 1945, p. 60; *Reports,* 1959, p. 87.

[24] *Minutes,* 1919, p. 7.

the receipt of $7,041,748.86 during the twenty-one month period ending March 31, 1959.[25]

The growth of the missionary staff has kept pace with the giving. The following data show this development:

Year	Number of Missionaries
1923	222
1933	259
1941	394
1956	743
1959	758 [26]

The missionary corps has extended its bases until today stations are located in the following seventy-one countries or geographical divisions: Basutoland, Belgian Congo, Dahomey, Ghana, Liberia, Nigeria, Nyasaland, Senegal, Sierra Leone, Southern Rhodesia, Tanganyika, Togoland, Union of South Africa, Upper Volta, China, Fiji, Formosa, Hong Kong, Indonesia, Japan, Korea, Malaya, Philippines, Samoa, Burma, Ceylon, North India, Pakistan, South India, Egypt, Israel, Lebanon, Iran, Hashemite, Jordan Kingdom, Syria, Austria, Belgium, Bulgaria, Denmark, France, Russia, Germany, Greece, Hungary, Italy, Yugoslavia, Poland, Spain, British Honduras, Costa Rica, El Salvador, Guatemala, Honduras, Mexico, Nicaragua, Argentina, Bolivia, Brazil, Chile, Columbia, British Guiana, Paraguay, Peru, Uruguay, Venezuela, Bahamas, Cuba, Dominican Republic, Haiti, Jamaica, and Hawaii.[27]

HOME MISSIONS DEPARTMENT

For a number of years the central organization concerned itself little with the work of home missions. The matter of establishing new churches in America was left largely to individual ministers and existing assemblies. Eventually, however, certain types of home ministry came to need supervision, and the foreign missions department

---

[25] *Reports*, 1959, p. 77.
[26] *Minutes*, 1925, p. 48; *Minutes*, 1933, p. 53; *Minutes*, 1941, p. 88; *Reports*, 1959, p. 76.
[27] *Reports*, 1959, p. 76; Serena M. Hodges, *Look on the Fields*, a Missionary Survey (Springfield, Missouri: Gospel Publishing House, 1956), pp. 192-201.

undertook this service. Excellent progress was made under this arrangement among foreign-language groups and the American Indians.

DEVELOPMENT OF DEPARTMENTAL STATUS

The council of 1937 separated home missions from the foreign missions department and consolidated it with education to form a new department to be administered under a newly elected Assistant General Superintendent.[28] This move resulted in greater impetus for the activity, and the work of the new department was sufficiently great by 1945 to warrant dividing home missions and education into separate departments.[29] This constitutional change and later minor modifications stipulated that the department should be administered by an executive director, a national secretary, and such other personnel as might be needed to care for the assigned duties. A home missions committee composed of the director, secretary, and four other members appointed by the general superintendent became the policy-making group of the department.[30]

The scope and purpose of home missions were clearly stated so that there would be no overlapping with the work of foreign missions. To it was "delegated the responsibility of doing all within its power to spread the gospel within the United States and Alaska." [31] Assistance and supervision is given by the department to eight different ministries, viz.: the establishment of new Assemblies of God churches, ministry to Jews, prison evangelism, ministry to the deaf, work in Alaska, ministry to the American Indians, ministry to foreign language groups in the United States, and industrial chaplaincy program.[32]

Outstanding success has been achieved in the work of

---

[28] *Minutes,* 1937, p. 57; *Idea Book* (Springfield, Missouri: Home Missions Department, Assemblies of God, [1955]), p. 7.

[29] *Minutes,* 1945, pp. 31-36.

[30] Home Missions Department, *Missionary Manual* (Springfield, Missouri: National Home Missions Department, Assemblies of God, 1955), p. 10.

[31] *Ibid.,* p. 9.

[32] *Assemblies of God Home Missions* (Springfield, Missouri: National Home Missions Department, Assemblies of God, [1953]), pp. 3-4.

church extension. The following table indicates the number of new churches organized in recent years:

Period	New Churches
1945-47	237
1947-49	402
1951-53	508
1953-55	958 [83]

Jewish evangelism seems relatively insignificant compared to some of the other interest of the home missions department, though the appearance may be due in part to an inadequate means of evaluating results quantitatively. Departmental policy does not encourage the establishment of Jewish congregations. Rather, Jewish Christians are urged to associate themselves with local Assemblies of God churches. Specialists under home missions appointment labor in areas of concentrated Jewish population in close co-operation with local pastors. Statistics showing the annual number of Jewish converts are not available. [84]

A national prison representative works under the auspices of home missions primarily to promote prison evangelism. In addition to visiting and maintaining contact with state and federal prisons, he gives assistance to Assemblies of God ministers holding appointments as prison chaplains and acts as an enlistment officer recruiting other clergymen into this ministry. Free printed materials and counsel are furnished by the central office to persons engaged in prison evangelism. [85]

A ministry to the deaf is a relatively recent innovation of the department. The program of the central office has developed largely since 1948. Specialists for this unique work are trained in dactylology in four Assemblies of God Bible colleges and are then placed in the larger city churches to organize deaf groups within the framework of these

---

[83] *Idea Book*, p. 7; *Minutes*, 1955, p. 8.

[84] "History and Objectives, National Home Missions Department, Assemblies of God," (duplicated bulletin of the Home Missions Department, Assemblies of God, [1955]), p. 8.

[85] *Ibid.*, p. 9.

congregations. Bible classes and the regular worship services are transmitted to deaf constituents in sign language. To furnish additional opportunities for fellowship and association, religious camps and conventions are conducted periodically. A special magazine, *Silent Ambassador,* is also published for the deaf. A recent report shows thirty-one persons under appointment for this type ministry. They were working in seventy-two assemblies scattered throughout the Assemblies of God constituency.[36]

Supervision of the Assemblies of God work in Alaska is one of the oldest and most important functions of home missions. In 1947, just two years after home missions had been organized into a separate department, the biennial report to the General Council showed twelve churches or stations operating in Alaska under the department.[37] A more recent report indicates continuing vigorous development. Ninety workers staff a chain of churches and three children's homes. No Alaskan city with a population of 1,000 or more is without an Assemblies of God church.[38]

It would appear that organized work among the American Indians is a recent development, for in 1947 only one Indian church was reported.[39] Interest undoubtedly increased soon afterward, however, since the next biennial report showed missionaries laboring in eleven different states.[40] Ten years later the personnel in this field of endeavor numbered 118, and eighty-eight churches or stations were being maintained on some seventy reservations located in eighteen states.[41]

The home missions department has encouraged and assisted foreign-language groups within the United States to organize their Pentecostal believers into "branches" of

---

[36] "National Home Missions Department Report to District Home Missions Representatives" (duplicated report prepared by Home Missions Department, Assemblies of God, August, 1956), p. 2.

[37] *Reports and Financial Statements* (prepared and printed by the central offices of the Assemblies of God for the General Council of 1947), pp. 32-33. These printed reports were prepared for all the late General Councils and will hereafter be cited *Reports.*

[38] *Reports,* 1959, p. 96.

[39] *Reports,* 1947, p. 33.

[40] *Reports,* 1949, p. 35.

[41] *Reports,* 1959, p. 94.

the Assemblies of God. This has enabled such Pentecostal
Christians to develop distinctive types of worship in keeping with their backgrounds and at the same time eliminate
the handicap of a language barrier. Nine of these branches
are operated, several as well-organized bodies having their
own periodicals and literature.[42] The following table shows
the foreign-language groups of the Assemblies of God
with the number of churches connected with each:

Branch	Number of Churches
German	19
Greek	10
Hungarian	12
Italian	66
Latin American	362
Polish	19
Russian	12
Ukrainian	23
Yugoslavian	1 [43]

The report to the council of 1953 revealed that the department had become interested in the ministry of industrial chaplaincies. During the subsequent years, however, no organized program was reported for the training
or placing of industrial chaplains. In the report to the
council of 1955 it could only be stated that "an increase
of interest is being shown in this phase of our work and
a number of Assembly of God workers, although not officially appointed as industrial chaplains, are conducting
services in mills and factories." [44]

WOMEN'S MISSIONARY COUNCIL

The work of both the foreign and home missions departments has been complemented by a ladies' auxiliary
called the Women's Missionary Council (W. M. C.), an
agency that had an uncertain existence for a number of
years. It started on the local level in February, 1925, when
a group of women in Houston, Texas, "realizing the great
and ever-increasing need of the world for the gospel mes-

---

[42] *Assemblies of God Home Missions*, pp. 23-24.
[43] *Reports*, 1959, p. 96.
[44] *Reports*, 1955, p. 26.

sage," [45] organized themselves as a council to work in the interest of God's kingdom. Mrs. J. C. Calhoun was largely responsible for this phase of the organization, and her personal prestige and leadership contributed much to its early accomplishments. W. M. Morwood, Mrs. Calhoun's pastor, endorsed the project and used his influence to assist it. Within a few weeks three other women's groups were functioning in churches located at Goose Creek, Magnolia Park, and Beaumont—all in the Houston area.[46]

In August, 1925, the Texas and New Mexico District Council, while in session at Fort Worth, invited "the Women's Missionary Council to co-operate with them in labor for the advancement of the Master's Work, and extending the fellowship . . . of the District Council." [47] The invitation was accepted, and the women formed the first district W. M. C. group with Mrs. Calhoun as its president. In September of that same year the General Council in session at Eureka Springs, Ark., recognized the women's missionary council as the official ladies' missionary auxiliary.

The strange fact connected with this early period of development is that the auxiliary, though recognized and endorsed, was left to operate as an orphan with no central co-ordination. Its district organizations were seldom afforded much if any consideration in the district council programs. One defender writing of this sorry treatment stated in *Ruth Gleaners* in 1939 that "Women's Missionary Councils have been discouraged and disbanded for a lack of encouragement and too much criticism." [48] This lethargy and antipathy arose, no doubt, from a fear in the church that the W. M. C. might get out of control.

Surprisingly enough, interest in the organization increased in spite of the lack of official encouragement. Women in

[45] *Report of Organization and Development, Women's Missionary Council, Assemblies of God; District of Texas and New Mexico* (Houston, Texas: Women's Missionary Council, District of Texas and New Mexico, 1925), p. 2.

[46] *Ibid.*, pp. 9-10; "Texas Has First Missionary Council," *Ruth Gleaners*, I (June, 1937), pp. 1, 4. The *Ruth Gleaners* was a periodical published by the W. M. C. from 1937 to the early 1940's.

[47] *Report of Organization*, p. 9.

[48] Mrs. J. C. Wilder, "Not Merely a Money-Making Organization," *Ruth Gleaners*, III (October, 1939), p. 1.

other states emulated the action of the Texas women until
bodies were functioning in every district council. Finally,
in the council of 1951 the Women's Missionary Council
became an integral part of the General Council when provision was made for it to have a central administration.
The next council in 1953 gave the auxiliary departmental
status.[49]

These three agencies—foreign missions, home missions,
and the Women's Missionary Council—constitute the missionary arm of the Assemblies of God.

PUBLICATIONS

The development of a tremendous publishing plant by
the Assemblies of God is an indication of the emphasis
placed upon printed materials. The growth of this enterprise has been almost phenomenal.

DEVELOPMENT OF THE GOSPEL PUBLISHING HOUSE

At the organizing council in 1914 the limited printing
equipment of E. N. Bell and J. R. Flower, who edited
religious periodicals, and T. K. Leonard, who ran a small
printing press in connection with his church, was made
available for the use of the infant group. The equipment
was combined and installed in small quarters provided by
the church in Findley, Ohio, where T. K. Leonard was
pastor. Here all publications of the group were produced
for some six months.[50]

The second council made the first provision to expand
the enterprise by voting to expend $5,000 (the money had
still to be raised) for necessary equipment.[51] When the
Executive Presbytery met at the close of this council session, it decided to move the shop to St. Louis, Missouri,
for the sake of better quarters and a more central location. The move was made in January, 1915, to a rented
building at 2838 Easton Avenue, and there the printing

---

[49] "Women's Missionary Council" (Report prepared and duplicated by the
National Women's Missionary Council Department, Assemblies of God, Springfield,
Mo., [1956]), p. 1.

[50] Flower, "History of the Assemblies of God," p. 24. The periodicals were
farmed out for printing until after the move to St. Louis, when adequate
equipment was secured and installed.

[51] *Minutes,* November 15-29, 1914, p. 10.

plant became known as the Gospel Publishing House.

By 1918 the rented property in St. Louis had also become inadequate and a building was purchased in Springfield, Missouri, on West Pacific Street. There both the permanent headquarters of the Assemblies of God and its printing operation were established. The building was a two-story brick structure measuring forty-five by fifty feet. The upper story very conveniently housed the administrative and editorial offices while the lower level served as the printing plant.[52]

The growth of the publishing business made it necessary to enlarge the original building on Pacific Street four times between the years of 1918 and 1939. After the last addition the structure occupied an area 128 by 245 feet and provided over 50,000 square feet of floor space.[53] When this capacity was outgrown, the General Council in 1945 approved the construction of a new plant, and the White City Ball Park on Boonville Street in Springfield was purchased as a site.[54] After a delay occasioned by material shortages resulting from World War II, the new million-dollar concrete and masonry plant was begun with a ground-breaking ceremony on March 3, 1948.[55] By the closing days of December, 1949, the equipment was set, and the Gospel Publishing House began production in its spacious new quarters.[56]

The improvement of the printing plant kept pace with the housing development. None of the printing equipment belonging to T. K. Leonard, was moved to St. Louis when (in 1915) the headquarters offices were moved to that city. The periodicals were farmed out for printing during the first few months of residence, and until equipment could be secured. A secondhand linotype machine was purchased, and this equipment was supplemented with a

[52] *The New Gospel Publishing House* (Brochure published by the Gospel Publishing House, [1949]), p. 2.

[53] "The Romance of Your Publishing House," *Pentecostal Evangel*, No. 1322 (September 9, 1939), pp. 3-4.

[54] *Minutes*, 1945, pp. 27-29, 95-96.

[55] *Reports*, 1947, pp. 49-50; "We Start to Build Our New Plant," *Pentecostal Evangel*, No. 1766 (March 13, 1948), pp. 1, 11.

[56] "Moving Into the New Printing Plant," *Pentecostal Evangel*, No. 1857 (December 10, 1949), p. 13.

large, used flat-bed printing press, a cutting machine and
a new folding machine. These additions involved a considerable investment for the young business, and the $2,000
note connected with the transaction seemed a staggering
obligation.[57] The subsequent increase of production and
sales were sufficient, however, to meet all financial demands, and very soon annual reports reflected a favorable
financial position. The following table gives some indication of the increase of business through the years:

Period	Gross Sales
1917	$ 17,000
1918	23,000
1930-31	384,312
1954-55	4,125,659
1958-59	5,568,146[58]

PUBLISHING HOUSE MANAGEMENT

For many years the administration of the printing enterprise was relatively simple. The executive officers of the
church did the managing, hiring a few trained persons to
do the production work. By 1925 the operation had become so involved that a general manager was named to
head the Gospel Publishing House. Though the Executive
Presbytery remained the policy making body, the new executive was responsible for detailed direction of the business. After 1945, when the Executive Presbytery was enlarged and the functions of the General Council were somewhat reorganized, the general manager became subordinate
to a departmental director, who thus far has always been
an assistant general superintendent and has headed only
the production and merchandising divisions of the publishing house.[59]

---

[57] "Spreading the Pentecostal Message Across America and Around the World"
(duplicated paper prepared by the editorial office of the *Pentecostal Evangel*,
[1956]), pp. 1-2.

[58] *Minutes*, 1918, pp. 3-4; *Minutes*, 1931, p. 47; *Reports*, 1955, p. 37; *Reports*,
1959, p. 47.

[59] Statement by J. Z. Kamerer, Springfield, Mo., May 19, 1957, personal interview. Kamerer was general manager of the Gospel Publishing House for over
twenty-five years.

PERIODICALS OF THE ASSEMBLIES OF GOD

The Gospel Publishing House has been used largely to produce the official organs and Sunday school literature of the Assemblies of God. When the group organized in 1914, E. N. Bell and J. R. Flower not only offered their limited printing equipment to the new organization but also their established Pentecostal periodicals, *Word and Witness* and *Christian Evangel*. The two papers were accepted as the official organs of the body, and Bell and Flower, since both were elected general officers, were retained as the editors. Soon after the publishing house was moved to St. Louis, *Word and Witness*, a monthly, was discontinued, in order that all the resources and efforts of the central office might be concentrated on producing one strong Pentecostal weekly. The name of the other paper was changed about the same time from *Christian Evangel* to *Weekly Evangel* to avoid confusion with another organ, *Christian Evangelist*, that was published in St. Louis.[60] In 1918, when headquarters were moved to Springfield, the paper resumed the name *Christian Evangel* and was published bi-weekly rather than weekly. The following year the name was changed to its present form, *Pentecostal Evangel* and the periodical again became a weekly.[61]

Relatively few persons have filled the editor's chair of the official organ. In 1915, when only the *Weekly Evangel* was published, Bell and Flower were succeeded in the editorship by J. W. Welch. In 1919 Bell again filled the position for a short time, being succeeded by J. T. Boddy in 1920. The next year Stanley H. Frodsham, who had been assistant editor since 1916, became editor, a position he held until 1949, when Robert C. Cunningham, the present editor, was named in his place.[62]

The *Evangel* was for many years printed on flat-bed letter presses, a process that restricted the make-up of the paper because of the costs involved. Since the Gospel Publishing House moved into its new building in 1949, pro-

[60] Flower, "History of the Assemblies of God," p. 28.

[61] "Historical Highlights," *Pentecostal Evangel*, No. 2982 (April 4, 1954), pp. 16-17.

[62] "Spreading the Pentecostal Message," p. 2.

duction on offset presses has made possible a format greatly
improved by art work, more pictures, and two-color printing. The size of the organ varied from eight to sixteen
pages until 1956, when it was increased to thirty-two
pages.[63]

There has been little shift in the editorial policy of the
Pentecostal Evangel through the years, even with the change
of editors. The fact that the Executive Presbytery deter-
mines the broad practices of the paper undoubtedly accounts for this stability in policy. "The purpose of the
magazine is 'to set forth those things which are most surely
believed among us' (Luke 1:1) as well as to publish news
concerning the denomination, its churches, and its activities
in missionary and evangelistic work." [64] The content is intended for popular reading and general interest, being
slanted primarily to the laity of the church.

The advertising policy of the magazine is rather restricted.
The only display advertisements carried pertain to the various departments of the Assemblies of God. There is a
column of classified advertisements for the listing of goods
and services related to church work.[65]

The circulation of the *Pentecostal Evangel* has increased
through the years commensurate with the development of
the Gospel Publishing House and the growth of the Assemblies of God. By 1955 the regular weekly issues amounted
to 170,000 copies, while special editions were running as
high as 550,000.[66]

The second periodical with lasting influence published
by the Assemblies of God was one designed for youth.
This magazine was preceded by two abortive attempts. In
1926 the publishing house issued *Christ's Ambassadors,* a
Sunday school paper for young people. This was followed
in 1928 by *Christ's Ambassadors Monthly,* which continued
for two years. While the monthly was being published,
Carl E. Hatch, a youth worker in California, began editing

[63] *Ibid.,* p. 3.
[64] Robert C. Cunningham, Springfield, Mo., to Klaude Kendrick, June 16,
1958, L. S., p. 2. Cunningham is the present editor of *The Pentecostal Evangel.*
[65] *Ibid.*
[66] *Reports,* 1955, p. 80.

Christ's Ambassadors Herald, a paper which took on national scope and ultimately became the official organ of the youth department. In 1938 Hatch turned the magazine over to the General Council, and since that time it has been published by the Gospel Publishing House.[67]

The *Christ's Ambassadors Herald* has had three distinct editorial policies. During its early years the magazine was slanted almost entirely to older youth (the age span served by the youth department includes ages twelve through thirty-five). The reasons were, first, a strong feeling among the policy-makers favoring a format that provided as much spiritual reading material as possible on every page; and second, the costliness of a format that should have the visual features especially appealing to the teen-ager. When offset printing made this kind of format feasible, however, the content began to be directed almost completely to the other extreme. The present policy is shifting to a more central position, appealing to both teen-age and college-age youth.[68]

The content of the *Herald* falls "into five general categories: features, fiction, articles, anecdotes, and puzzles."[69] "Features" are defined as true stories of a biographical, "how we did it," or historical character. Only fiction that illustrates spiritual truths is used in the magazine. "Articles" is the term used to classify informative and instructional material, especially that of a doctrinal nature.

As time passed other departments of the Assemblies of God also began to issue periodicals. In June, 1939, the first number of *Our Sunday School Counselor* was printed. This sixteen-page magazine first appeared at irregular intervals and was distributed without charge as a service of the Sunday school department and the Gospel Publishing House. Since August, 1941, it has been a monthly subscription

---

[67] C. A. *Manual* (Springfield, Missouri: Gospel Publishing House, 1946), p. 7; "History of the Gospel Publishing House Publications" (manuscript prepared by officers of the Gospel Publishing House, [1951]), pp. 1-2.

[68] Dick Champion, Springfield, Mo., to Klaude Kendrick, June 16, 1958, L. S., p. 4. Champion is the present editor of the *Christ Ambassador Herald.*

[69] "Tips to Writers" (duplicated instructions for contributors to the *Christ's Ambassadors Herald,* prepared by the editor, 1958), p. 1.

114 *The Promise Fulfilled*

periodical.[70] The latest official voice of a department of the
Assemblies of God is *Team*, a thirty-two-page two-color
quarterly edited by the Men's Fellowship Department.
Team has been in regular circulation since September,
1954.[71]

SUNDAY SCHOOL LITERATURE

The printing of Sunday school literature now surpasses
quantitatively all other materials produced by the publishing house. During the first five years that the Assemblies
of God operated, no church school materials were prepared;
the only matter printed was the church organ and brief
religious tracts. But by 1919 considerable demand was expressed for the church to issue its own Sunday school literature. The growing Sunday schools found difficulty in
teaching the distinctive Pentecostal tenets from the unfavorable printed texts available from non-Pentecostal sources.[72]
The officers, therefore, decided to experiment with a limited
line of Sunday school literature, and brought J. Z. Kamerer,
an experienced printer from Findlay, Ohio, to Springfield
in 1919 to manage the Gospel Publishing House in this
enlargement of its operations. The first materials, lesson
leaflets and a quarterly for adults, were issued for the last
quarter of 1919, the initial printing amounting to only
5,000 copies of each item.[73] From this meager beginning the
Sunday school line has been expanded until every kind of
printed matter needed for the operation of a church school
program is now produced. The report for 1959 showed
that forty-seven different items were then being regularly
issued by the Sunday school literature department, and that
the total number of copies printed was 2,078,549.[74]

[70] Sunday School Department, *Survey of Services, Supplies and Literature
Available to Assemblies of God Sunday Schools*, 1955-56 (Springfield, Missouri:
Gospel Publishing House, [1956]), p. 8; hereafter cited as *Sunday School Survey*.

[71] Statement by Don Mallough, Springfield, Mo., May 21, 1957, personal interview. Mallough was Secretary of Men's Fellowship Department, 1954-60.

[72] Gayle F. Lewis, "A Brief Sketch and Outline of the Growth of the Gospel
Publishing House" (paper delivered to the General Council at Atlanta, Georgia,
in 1951), p. 1.

[73] J. Z. Kamerer, personal interview; J. Z. Kamerer, "History of Gospel Publishing
House Achievements, 1914-1949" (paper delivered to the Sunday School Convention
in Springfield, Missouri, in 1949), p. 3.

[74] *Reports*, 1959, pp. 112-113.

The general officers of the church did the writing and editing of all the literature during the first years of production. As the administration of the denomination required more of the officers' time, and the editorial responsibilities also increased, persons were added to the staff of the Gospel Publishing House to handle the writing role. By the time the new plant was completed in 1949, growth seemed to require reorganization. Accordingly, the writing function was assigned to a new editorial department operating independently of the management of the publishing house.[75]

In addition to periodicals and church literature, the presses of the Gospel Publishing House turned out books, hymnals, and other printed religious supplies. Thus the publication division came to make its contribution to the propagational function of the Assemblies of God by assuming the "great responsibility of spreading the Gospel through the printed page." [76]

---

[75] J. Z. Kamerer, personal interview.

[76] Lewis, "A Brief Sketch of the Gospel Publishing House," p. 3.

VII
Educational Departments of the Assemblies of God

THE Assemblies of God, like all the Pentecostal groups, was slow in developing educational agencies. Three factors probably contributed to this neglect. In the first place, the emphasis placed on certain Pentecostal doctrines tended to deprecate any type of formal training. A radical faction interpreted the words of Jesus, "Howbeit when he [the Holy Spirit], . . . is come, he will guide you into all truth," [1] to mean that the Holy Spirit would instruct all believers individually, thus making religious or secular training unnecessary. Second, another party put such stress upon premillennialism that time spent in preparation and study was considered wasteful, since Christ was expected to return to earth momentarily. Finally, a large number of the early Pentecostals, though not opposed to religious training, undoubtedly neglected it because of their extreme evangelical spirit and complete absorption in evangelism.

In regard to formal, institutional training, opposition possibly stemmed from incorrect evaluation. The early adherents came from social and economic strata that prevented many from advancing past the elementary or high school levels. Some of these persons had difficulty in according proper importance to higher education.

Fortunately, however, the leaders realized that training was essential if their evangelical program was to be most effective. Educational agencies developed gradually in spite of lethargy and opposition and became a contributing factor

---

[1] John 16:13.

in the growth and perpetuation of the Assemblies of God. This chapter will show the evolution of the three training arms of the church—the Sunday school, the denominational schools, and the youth organization.

THE SUNDAY SCHOOL DEPARTMENT

The religious education of the laity is primarily provided by the Sunday school. In the early years of the organization such work was completely unorganized and in some cases omitted altogether from the local church program. The writer had occasion to know a number of clergymen in the 1920's who did not participate in the Sunday school activity at all. In spite of these unfavorable tendencies, however, the church school soon gained proper appreciation and showed excellent growth and progress.

EARLY DEVELOPMENT OF ASSEMBLIES OF GOD SUNDAY SCHOOLS

The first leaders of the church did much to improve the attitude toward Sunday schools. An article by J. W. Welch, who was elected chairman of the Assemblies of God in 1915, in the first edition of *Our Sunday School Counselor* reflects the interest of the executives.

No pastor can afford to neglect this opportunity of promoting Sunday schools or be indifferent to the needs of the children and young people within the realm of his influence; so, in view of the importance of the Sunday school, I feel sure none of our pastors will fail to see this or hesitate to assume their responsibility.... Does some pastor object: "But think of the work connected with it all! I have enough to do without taking on the Sunday school! So I must let others carry that part of the load." I have said that myself, but when I took the matter to my Master, He showed me that some of my heavy burden was due to my interest and concern about matters of much less importance than the Sunday school, and I had better drop something, and take up more worthwhile things.[*]

J. Roswell Flower, the first secretary of the group, stated that his wife began writing comments on the International Sunday School lessons as early as 1914 with the object of stimulating greater interest in full gospel Sunday schools. The lessons thus revised with a Pentecostal slant were pub-

---

[*] J. W. Welch, "Our Counsellor's Message to Pastors," *Our Sunday School Counsellor*, June, 1939, pp. 2, 14.

lished for a number of years in *Christian Evangel,* the first weekly organ of the Assemblies of God.[3]

Sufficient concern for Sunday schools existed by 1919 to justify the introduction of an appropriate line of literature by the Gospel Publishing House.[4] By the 1930's the early apathy and antipathy were definitely waning. "Sunday school work was found to be one of the most fruitful ministries of the Church. Pastors and superintendents began demanding material for the purpose of improving this work in the individual assemblies."[5] To satisfy this need, the publishing house procured the services of R. M. Riggs, a successful pastor at the time, later general superintendent, to prepare a manual on Sunday school organization. The resultant volume, *A Successful Sunday School* published in 1933, continues to furnish the basic administrational pattern of Assemblies of God Sunday schools. This book was followed by a series of fourteen other texts that comprised a teacher's training course.[6]

The improved status of this area of religious training is further indicated by the appearance (in the minutes of the General Council) in 1935 of a written report of a Sunday school committee. A resolution was passed in the same session to use the *Pentecostal Evangel* and additional Sunday school literature to stimulate greater growth.[7]

ADMINISTRATIVE STRUCTURE OF DEPARTMENT

The policies controlling Sunday school work were laid down by the Executive Presbytery until 1935, but the actual administration was carried out by the manager of the Gospel Publishing House. In January of that year the Sunday school department was formerly organized; and M. L. Grable, a layman active in religious education, was named to head the new division. The department continued to operate (for a number of years) as a part of the Gospel Publishing House. As its services expanded, the personnel

---

[3] Statement by J. Roswell Flower, personal interview.
[4] "The Story of the Sunday School Department" (manuscript prepared by the Sunday School Department, Assemblies of God), pp. 3-4.
[5] *Ibid.,* p. 4.
[6] Information from J. Z. Kamerer, personal interview.
[7] *Minutes,* 1935, pp. 96-97.

increased proportionately. From one small office furnished with only a desk, a little steel table, and one typewriter, and staffed by Grable alone, the department grew to an aggregation of over thirty members with many well-equipped offices.[8]

In 1953 the General Council changed the administrative pattern of the department by separating its operation completely from the Gospel Publishing House. Like most other departments, it was now headed by an executive director selected from among the assistant general superintendents. Detailed administration was placed under a national Sunday school secretary.[9]

The Sunday school program is carried to the "grass roots" by district directors and sectional representatives. District councils started naming Sunday school officers in the 1930's. The Arkansas district had a director in 1926, and the Oklahoma district had such an officer at least by 1935.[10] In 1939 the General Council adopted a recommendation suggesting that all districts elect Sunday school officers to promote religious education in co-operation with the national department.[11] The forty-three districts gradually responded until all had directors, and many went on to select representatives under the director to serve the sections within the districts. The national department maintains close communication and co-ordination with the various district offices by means of a special publication, *Just Between Us.*[12]

WORKERS' TRAINING PROGRAM

Three activities of the department merit consideration because of their continued influence on religious education within the Assemblies of God. One, the workers' training course, has already been mentioned above. Its development commenced with the publication of *A Successful Sun-*

---

[8] Statement by M. L. Grable, Springfield, Mo., 1956, personal interview.

[9] *Minutes*, 1953, p. 17; see Chart 3.

[10] "Building Through VBS and Child Evangelism," *Our Sunday School Counsellor*, May, 1943, p. 8; "Sunday School Work in the Oklahoma District," *Our Sunday School Counsellor*, May, 1940, p. 2.

[11] *Minutes*, 1939, pp. 58-59.

[12] *Sunday School Survey*, 1956-1957, p. 20.

day School and the subsequent thirteen volumes issued in rapid succession. The original course included the following areas and texts:

Bible preview. Myer Pearlman, *Seeing the Story of the Bible*

Old Testament: Law and history. Myer Pearlman, *Through the Bible Book by Book*, Part I

Old Testament: Poetry and prophecy. Myer Pearlman, *Through the Bible Book by Book*, Part II

New Testament: Gospels and Acts. Myer Pearlman, *Through the Bible Book by Book*, Part III

New Testament: Epistles and Revelation. Myer Pearlman, *Through the Bible Book by Book*, Part IV

Principles and methods of teaching. Myer Pearlman, *Successful Sunday School Teaching*

The Life of Christ. Myer Pearlman, *The Life and Teachings of Christ*

Dispensations. Frank M. Boyd, *Ages and Dispensations*

Personal work. Helen Atkinson, *Personal Workers' Course*

Biblical introduction. Frank M. Boyd, *God's Wonderful Book*

Child study. Myer Pearlman, *Studying the Pupil*

Sunday school administration. Ralph M. Riggs, *A Successful Sunday School*

Doctrine. Myer Pearlman, *Knowing the Doctrines of the Bible*

Prophecy. Ralph M. Riggs, *Path of Prophecy* [13]

The course was designed to be offered to either individuals for home study or groups through church sponsored classes. A certificate was issued when each area of study was finished, and a diploma was given upon completion of the entire course.

The texts were written in popular style to appeal to those for whom the course was prepared. Though the work was elementary, it did much to better the quality of the staffs of Assemblies of God. In fact, the resultant improvement was so noticeable that the course was revised until it eventually included thirty-six books covering a wider area of study and making the program still more effective. [14]

The number of persons finishing studies is a good meas-

---

[13] *Sunday School Survey*, 1955-1956, p. 7.

[14] *Workers Training, Assemblies of God* (Springfield, Mo.: National Sunday School Department, Assemblies of God, [n. d.]), pp. 3, 7.

ure of the extent of participation in training courses. During the two-year period 1947-1948 only 21,053 certificates were issued, but for the period 1953-1954 the number increased to 102,636. In 1951 thirty-five per cent of the reporting churches of the Assemblies of God received credit for conducting workers' training studies, while in 1954 the number amounted to fifty-six per cent. Churches in congested areas have begun to sponsor union studies in recent years. This practice makes possible the teaching of several subjects simultaneously and the procuring of specialists as instructors.[15]

SUNDAY SCHOOL ORGAN

The second development of considerable importance in the work of the department was the publication of a Sunday school organ, *Our Sunday School Counselor*. A brief history of the periodical was included in the previous chapter. The magazine contains material for Sunday school officers and instructors of every age group. Its content is designed to be both inspirational and informative. The broad influence of the paper is revealed by its wide circulation, 31,000 copies. Since more than one member of a family often serve on a Sunday school staff, it is estimated that perhaps one half of the total teaching force of the church is touched by the organ.[16]

SUNDAY SCHOOL CONFERENCES

The last important activity of the Sunday school department has been the introduction of Sunday school conferences. Probably few involved in the planning of these early meetings realized the impact they would eventually have upon Christian education within the church. Ten conventions were held between 1940 and 1952, all at Springfield, Missouri. The first three sessions were conducted biennially and were not particularly imposing, although some thirty, or three-fourths, of the districts of the Assemblies of God were represented by their Sunday school officers at the second session and the third was considered sufficiently impor-

---

[15] *Reports*, 1955, p. 71; *Sunday School Survey*, 1955-1956, p .33.
[16] *Sunday School Survey*, 1955-1956, p. 8; *Reports*, 1955, pp. 71-72.

tant to be mentioned in the minutes of the General Council.[17]

Annual conferences were held starting in 1945 and continuing through 1952. All meetings prior to 1948 were held in the facilities of a local church, Central Assembly of God, but the attendance was so great from that year forward that the conventions had to be moved to Springfield's Shrine Mosque. The enrollments continued to climb until the conventions were reputed as being the largest Sunday school delegation ever to convene. The sixth in 1948 registered 2,500, the seventh in 1949, 3,000, the ninth in 1951, 6,521, the tenth in 1952, 9,218.[18]

Since Springfield had no building that could accommodate such a tremendous crowd, the convention program was altered the following year to provide for regional conferences rather than a single national one. This arrangement drew a record registration of 15,218. In 1954 a national convention was held at Kiel Auditorium in St. Louis. Since that time only regional meetings have been attempted.[19] In May, 1960, the first International Sunday School Convention was held in Minneapolis to provide stimulation and impetus for the church school program in bodies outside continental United States as well as in America.

Although the numerous departmental conferences, workshops, visual presentations, and inspiring addresses undoubtedly left a mark on the Assemblies of God, probably the greatest value of the conventions lay in the fact that their spirit and size brought a new awareness of the importance of the Sunday school.

DEVELOPMENT OF UNIFORM PROGRAM

Since the Sunday school endeavors in the beginning were completely unorganized, no uniform program was followed. The type of administration depended largely upon the concepts and objectives of the local leadership. Clearly defined goals were seldom found on this level, so that most of the

---

[17] Robert L. Hillegas, "Second Nation-wide Sunday School Convention Held in Springfield, Mo., January 20-23," *Our Sunday School Counsellor*, March, 1942, pp. 8-9, 14; *Minutes*, 1945, p. 89.
[18] *Reports*, 1949, p. 54; *Reports*, 1951, pp. 70-71; *Reports*, 1953, p. 55.
[19] *Sunday School Survey*, 1955-1956, pp. 14-16.

schools functioned in an aimless, haphazard fashion. By
1935 some leaders felt that a standard program was needed,
hence one of the first moves of Grable, after he was installed as head of the newly formed department, was to
inaugurate what he considered an "efficiency plan." This
was called the "First Class Sunday School" program. Its
principal feature was the establishment of twelve graded
objectives. Sunday schools earning eighty-one or more points
during a year were recognized as "First Class Sunday
Schools" and received a special award banner.[20] The twelve
graded objectives were:

1. Attendance—20 points. (A gain of at least 20% in average
   attendance each year)
2. Sunday school equal to church in size—10 points. (Having
   a Sunday school enrollment at least equal to church membership)
3. Attendance of pastor—5 points. (Pastor required to attend
   at least 95% of regular sessions as well as staff meetings)
4. Attendance of superintendent—5 points. (Superintendent required to attend at least 95% of regular sessions as well as
   staff meetings)
5. Attendance of teacher—20 points. (Teachers required to attend at least 90% of regular sessions as well as staff meetings)
6. Teacher training—5 points. (One subject completed each
   year; at least 12 classes of 45 minutes each)
7. Church attendance—9 points. (90% of pupils remain for
   morning worship service)
8. Evangelism—6 points. (3% of enrolled pupils make decisions
   for Christ)
9. Increase in regular offerings—5 points. (20% increase over
   previous year)
10. Increase in missionary offering—5 points. (20% of increase
    over previous year)
11. Cradle roll—5 points. (Cradle roll to equal 5% of Sunday
    school enrollment)
12. Home department—5 points. (Home department to equal 5%
    of Sunday school enrollment)[21]

In 1941 the "Sunday School Lighthouse Plan" replaced
the first program. In this change the basis for grading re-

[20] M. L. Grable, personal interview.
[21] *Sunday School Survey*, 1955-1956, pp. 16-17.

mained much the same, though point assessments were revised from time to time in order to realize better balance. The lighthouse proved an effective symbol for publicizing the program. After operating for seven years, the plan was followed by the one that has continued ever since—the "National Sunday School Standard." This new design was little more than a refinement of the first two, with additional adjustments being made in the grading to change the emphasis on some features, and innovations being introduced in the award system. Recognition was now given on the following basis: Below 70 points, Co-operative award; 70 to 79 points, Blue Crown award; 80 to 89 points, Silver Crown award; and 90 to 100 points, Gold Crown award.[22]

SUNDAY SCHOOL CURRICULUM

The development of a uniform Sunday school curriculum, like the establishment of a standard program, involved a number of changes. In January, 1937, the use of the International Uniform Sunday School Lessons, which the Assemblies of God had employed for many years, was discontinued because of a fear that "liberal" theology and "progressive" educational philosophy were being featured too prominently in them. That year the Gospel Publishing House introduced its Uniform Whole Bible Course, which was evangelical and "fundamental" in character. When the National Sunday School Association was formed in 1945 for the purpose of preparing a distinct course for evangelical groups, the Assemblies of God participated in the organization. The N. S. S. A. outlines, called the Uniform Bible Lesson Series, became the basis of the Word of Life Series, the latest curriculum offered by the Gospel Publishing House.[23]

The Sunday school department also struggled with the "uniform vs. graded lesson" controversy. A substantial segment of Pentecostal churchmen championed the uniform lesson for all ages because it enabled the family to study as a unit during the week. Others favored graded lessons,

---

[22] *Ibid.*, pp. 17-19.

[23] Statement by R. M. Riggs, Springfield, Mo., 1955, personal interview. Riggs was general superintendent of the Assemblies of God at the time of the interview.

feeling that texts appropriate for all ages were entirely too
restrictive in scope. The publishing house finally in 1936
issued experimental graded series for the primary and be-
ginner areas. When they were received favorably, others
were added until all areas through the intermediate (age
fourteen) had their distinctive graded literature.[24]

The accomplishments of the Sunday school department
have been most gratifying considering that its program did
not develop from idealistic goals or a long range design.
Statistics are lacking for the early years, but it is known
that at first only a minority of the churches were even
mildly interested in Sunday schools! From this unfavorable
beginning the Assemblies of God through the stimulation
of the Sunday school department, has become an enthusiastic proponent of the church training program. The 2,080
Sunday schools established during the two years prior to
the council of 1939 indicates the shift from opposition and
unconcern to zealous participation. A recent report shows
922,663 pupils enrolled in Assemblies of God Sunday
schools compared with a church membership of only 505,-
552.[25] A qualitative evaluation is more difficult to determine, since a means of measuring quality characteristics
is missing. It would seem, however, that the pupils receive
personal value from participating in the church training
program, for the Sunday schools have good holding records.
On the other hand, an observer cannot help noticing that
quantitative rather than spiritual and ethical goals receive
the greater emphasis, and that all sorts of material rewards
instead of the values of the educational experience itself,
are used to enhance attendance.

EDUCATION DEPARTMENT

The education department of the Assemblies of God is
limited in its scope of operation to the supervision of institutional education. This section will thus be concerned
only with the development of denominational schools.

---

[24] Statement by Ralph W. Harris, Springfield, Mo., 1956, personal interview.
At the time of the interview, Harris was head of the church school literature
department.
[25] *Minutes*, 1939, p. 89; *Reports*, 1959, pp. 9, 121.

EARLY ATTITUDE TOWARD FORMAL EDUCATION

The reasons that caused early Pentecostals to oppose or ignore the work of the Sunday school operated to produce similar attitudes toward formal institutional training. That this radical position was not held universally is indicated by the fact that no less than ten Pentecostal Bible schools were functioning prior to the founding of the Assemblies of God.[26] Most were small affairs generally carried on in connection with pastorates. Two schools were recognized and endorsed by the first council in 1914. One, located in Union, Mississippi, was under the direction of R. B. Chisolm; the other, the Gospel School in Findlay, Ohio, was headed by T. K. Leonard. This council further indicated that it placed some importance on formal training by recommending that

the students in other localities avail themselves of the courses offered in other Full Gospel or Pentecostal schools within their reach, and avail themselves of all opportunities for the study of the Word. We urge these students to constant prayer (Acts 6:4) and to the study of God's Word, as commended by Paul to Timothy (2 Tim. 2:15), and to the preaching of the Word everywhere (Acts 8:4) as opportunity affords in connection with their study.

As regards a school for the Southwest, we recommend the matter to be committed to the EXECUTIVE PRESBYTERY, with the authority to act upon the same.[27]

This was the initial provision for the establishment of an Assemblies of God Bible school, a directive that would receive no implementation for six years.

Some evidence of interest in education continued to exist during those early years even though the school was not established immediately. The council of 1917 encouraged young ministers to give "faithful and diligent" study to the Scriptures and to attend any accessible Bible training school. At the same time the body suggested that ten-day Bible conferences or "Itinerary Bible Schools," as they were called, be held in widely distributed areas to provide at least a little training for those who were unable to at-

---

[26] "Traces History of Bible Schools in Pentecostal Movement," *Pentecostal Evangel*, September 2, 1951, p. 6.
[27] *Minutes*, April 2-12, 1914, p. 7.

tend established schools.[28] During 1917 several additional
schools were recognized by the new church. One was directed by D. Wesley Myland, another the Mount Tabor
Bible Training School, by A. L. Fraser; both of these were
in Chicago. D. C. O. Opperman was prominently associated
with shorter term schools, most for only six weeks.[29]

FIRST BIBLE SCHOOL

When the first school was finally established by the
church itself in 1920, the curriculum provided only for
ministerial training. This, incidentally, was in keeping with
the practice of most newly organized church groups. The
training of a ministry customarily received first consideration. The school was organized after the Bible institute
pattern. Just prior to this time, because of the "modernistic"
tendencies of seminaries, A. B. Simpson in Nyack, N. Y.,
and Dwight L. Moody in Chicago had established a new
type theological school called the "Bible institute." The
objective of these schools was to provide a doctrinally sound
course of study for any person "called of God" regardless
of his educational background. This type school seemed
best suited to meet the needs of the Assemblies of God.[30]

The new institute, called Midwest Bible School, was located in Auburn, Nebraska, where a building had been
purchased with the help of district councils from several
surrounding states. In January, 1920, formal announcement
was made that operation would commence in the fall of
that year.[31] The old "faith" schools undoubtedly left their
mark on Midwest, for the council of 1920 reported that
the institute would compensate its faculty with offerings
rather than salaries, and that the other expenses as well
were to be cared for by unsolicited contributions.[32]

If this financial structure was not sufficient to condemn
the venture to failure, subsequent problems guaranteed
such an eventuality. The school first was plagued by an

[28] *Minutes*, 1914-1917, pp. 23-24.
[29] "Historical Highlights," *Pentecostal Evangel*, April 4, 1954, p. 16; Burnett,
"Forty Years Ago," March 28, 1954, p. 10.
[30] "Concerning Bible School," *Pentecostal Evangel*, August 5, 1950, p. 2.
[31] "New Bible School," *Pentecostal Evangel*, January 10, 1920, p. 8.
[32] *Minutes*, 1920, p. 43.

epidemic of influenza which delayed its opening. The small amount of support received during the first months of operation, when enthusiasm should have been the highest, probably reflected the formidable opposition and unconcern that haunted the enterprise. An early bulletin in the *Pentecostal Evangel,* mentioning the financial plight of the school, reported the teachers were receiving very little remuneration. In an effort to placate the fears of those who felt the undertaking might affect Pentecostal traditions the article went on to state that there was

not a denominational school on earth like this Bible school.... This school will stand for the Bible as the inspired Word of God, against all destructive criticism of the blessed old Book; for the atoning blood of the Lamb as the only way of salvation; for a never-changing and wonder-working God; for a Divine Saviour with all power in heaven and in earth; for a faith to look for the same wonders, signs and gifts of the Holy Ghost as promised in the New Testament.[33]

All measures taken, however, did little in improving the situation. Apparently both clergy and laity were still sufficiently wary of education that they ignored the fiscal needs of the school. The venture collapsed from lack of financial support after only one year of operation.[34]

CENTRAL BIBLE INSTITUTE

The same council that reported the failure of Midwest made provision for the establishment of another school. This endeavor was to be at headquarters in Springfield, Mo.[35] The new school was launched as Central Bible Institute in the fall of 1922, with D. W. Kerr, who had been connected with a school on the west coast, heading its administration. Though the school was opened in the basement of Central Assembly of God in Springfield, the response, nevertheless, was so favorable that larger quarters were needed very shortly. An appeal to the city of Springfield resulted in the gift of a beautiful wooded tract of land for a campus site. Encouraged and stimulated by this

---

[33] "Bible School Assured," *Pentecostal Evangel,* November 27, 1920, p. 1.
[34] *Minutes,* 1921, p. 64.
[35] *Educational Institutions of the Assemblies of God* (Springfield, Mo.: Educational Department, Assemblies of God [1951]), p. 6.

outside assistance, the General Council in 1923 made provision for the construction of a permanent brick building. Central Bible Institute moved into its new plant at the beginning of the fall semester of 1924. Starting there with one building and 106 students, the institute continued to develop until its facilities became adequate to accommodate an enrollment of over 500 pupils.[36]

Other schools made their appearance in the organization at about the same time that the Central Bible Institute began. In 1919 the Pacific Bible and Missionary Training School at San Francisco was endorsed by the General Council.[37] This school later became known as Glad Tidings Bible Institute, and then after its campus was moved to Santa Cruz, California, as Bethany Bible College. By 1921 four schools in addition to Pacific and the short-lived Midwest were receiving General Council recognition. They were Bethel Bible School, Newark, New Jersey; Beulah Heights Bible School, North Bergen, New Jersey; Elim School, Rochester, New York; and Southern California Bible School, Los Angeles.[38]

As time passed other Bible institutes came into existence, and changes occurred in the operations of some of those that were already established. Bethel, (1930) Beulah Heights, and Elim soon closed their doors. Southern California Bible School moved first to Pasadena and later to Costa Mesa, where it became known as Southern California College. Berean Bible Institute was established in San Diego in 1923 but operated less than two decades. Southwestern Bible Institute began at Enid, Oklahoma, in 1927. In 1941 it moved to Ft. Worth to amalgamate with Shield of Faith Bible School of Amarillo, Texas, and Southern Bible College of Houston, Texas. After remaining there for two years, it was finally located permanently on the former campus of Trinity University in Waxahachie, Texas. North Central Bible Institute was started at the Minneapolis Gospel Tabernacle in 1930 and expanded into

---

[36] "History of the Institute," *Central Bible Institute* Catalogue, XXVI (1948-49), p. 12; *Minutes*, 1923, p. 48; "The School that Began in a Basement," *Pentecostal Evangel*, May 28, 1927, p. 7.
[37] *Minutes*, 1919, p. 23.
[38] "Historical Highlights," *Pentecostal Evangel*, No. 2082 (April 4, 1954), p. 17.

a strong Minnesota school independent of the local church. In 1934 Northwest Bible Institute, later Northwest Bible College, was organized at Seattle, Washington, and later moved to Houghton, Washington, in 1959. Great Lakes Bible Institute of Zion, Illinois, which commenced operation in 1934, and Peniel Bible Institute of Stanton, Kentucky, which opened in 1935, eventually were united with Central Bible Institute. South-Eastern Bible Institute was launched in 1935 in Alabama; after moving to Atlanta, Georgia, in 1940, it was finally situated in Lakeland, Florida. Since 1938 Eastern Bible Institute has functioned in Green Lane, Pennsylvania. Three schools that started operations in the 1940's—South Central Bible College, Hot Springs, Arkansas, Metropolitan Bible Institute, Suffern, New York, and New England Bible Institute, Framingham, Massachusetts—all later merged with Central Bible Institute.[39]

TYPICAL BIBLE INSTITUTE PROGRAM

An account of the development of the program of Central Bible Institute, which is typical of all the Bible schools of the Assemblies of God, will serve to give an idea of the characteristics of those schools. Central has offered primarily two courses of study. The first, the customary three-year institute course, has been given since the very beginning of the school. It is terminal and vocational in nature, designed only to give training in areas of church service. The second, an undergraduate collegiate course in religion, was introduced in the 1948-1949 term. It combines a core of general education with religion and theology and thus broadens the training for the ministry. A diploma is issued to students finishing the three-year institute course, while

---

[39] *Educational Institutions*, pp. 3, 6; "A Vision Come to Life," *Pentecostal Evangel*, May 11, 1952, p. 13; "The Challenge of New England," *Pentecostal Evangel*, June 1, 1952, p. 6; "The Measure of a School Is Its Graduates," *Pentecostal Evangel*, June 8, 1952, p. 6; "Her March to Zion," *Pentecostal Evangel*, June 29, 1952, p. 7; "North Central—a Grandmother," *Pentecostal Evangel*, July 6, 1952, p. 11; "Training for Christian Service," *Pentecostal Evangel*, July 13, 1952, p. 11; "A School with a Vision," *Pentecostal Evangel*, July 27, 1952, p. 11; "Serving the Youth of Arkansas," *Pentecostal Evangel*, August 3, 1952, p. 7; "They Go into all the World," *Pentecostal Evangel*, August 17, 1952, pp. 7, 10.

the baccalaureate degree is conferred upon completion of the undergraduate program.[40]

In the early years of the Institute only one general curriculum was scheduled, and all students in a class took the same subjects. As the years passed, however, and other courses were added, only certain basic subjects were required for all students, the others being offered electives. At the beginning of the 1931-32 year the curriculum was organized into five departments—general Bible, Christian ministry, missions, Christian education, and music.[41] This departmental curricular pattern has remained substantially the same through the years, although the number and the titles of the departments have varied from time to time. The catalog for the 1941-1942 term, for example, listed nine departments, while that of the 1957-1958 recorded only eight.[42] Since a four-year undergraduate program began to be offered, the curriculum has usually been divided into departments of Bible, theology, religious education, missions, English and speech, languages, social science, and music.

Following the customary "institute" practice, Central's admission policy during the first years placed greater emphasis on religious devotion than upon educational background. According to an early bulletin,

Applicants should be at least nineteen (19) years of age. Exceptions to this rule may, for good reasons, be granted by the Committee on Management.

All applicants should have had a Common or Grammar school education or its equivalent. A High School or Academy course is most desirable, but those of more advanced years who have been denied this privilege, when they have approved [sic] themselves along other lines, will be permitted to take the regular Bible Course.

APPROVED CHRISTIAN CHARACTER, together with a willingness to do hard work and to submit cheerfully to the discipline of the school, will be required of all applicants.

A definite conviction of heart that God has called to His service,

---

[40] *Central Bible Institute Catalog,* 1922-1923, p. 17; *Ibid.,* 1948-1949, p. 26.
[41] *Ibid.,* 1931-1932, pp. 14-23.
[42] *Ibid.,* 1941-1942, pp. 29-41; *Ibid.,* 1957-1958, pp. 34-46.

is most desirable. But those who desire heartily a knowledge of the Word, that they may be fitted for service in case God should call, will also be accepted.[43]

In order to eliminate non-high school graduates who had not passed the customary secondary school age level, the policy in 1930 allowed no exceptions to the minimum age of nineteen years. A higher educational qualification was added at the same time, requiring all non-high school graduates to be admitted on examination. [44]

When the collegiate course was begun in 1948, the educational requirement was once more altered to permit admission only to those applicants who had "satisfactorily completed a course in a secondary school approved by a recognized accrediting agency, or the equivalent."[45]

The policies governing campus life at Central have always followed a rigid pattern. Style of dress, mixing of the sexes, absences from the campus, abstinence from tobacco and alcoholic beverages, and recreational activities are among the items that have been carefully supervised through the years.

DEVELOPMENT OF A CENTRAL ADMINISTRATIVE BODY

After several Assemblies of God schools had been formed, some type of central direction was needed in the interest of uniformity. Accordingly, a move was instituted that finally resulted in the establishment of an education department. As a first step the Executive Presbytery was in 1923 designated a Bible School Commission to supervise Central Bible Institute and to endorse other schools that operated acceptable programs.[46] No standards were established at that time, however, and recognition continued to be given on the basis of individual approval. Though the establishment of a Bible School Commission was a start in the right direction, it did not prevent wide variation in the programs of the different schools.

The next step, taken in the council of 1925, authorized the Bible School Commission to use the program of Cen-

[43] *Ibid.*, 1923-1924, p. 11.
[44] *Ibid.*, 1930-1931, p. 34.
[45] *Ibid.*, 1948-1949, p. 20.
[46] *Minutes*, 1923, pp. 58-59.

tral Bible Institute as a criterion for evaluating all affiliating schools.[47] This remained the educational policy
for ten years.

The committee on Bible schools that served the council
of 1931 asked for a more rigid policy in regulating the
endorsement of Bible schools. This set in motion an action
that culminated in the appointment in 1935 of a committee
on institutions charged with making a study of the complete structure of the Bible institutes of the Assemblies of
God and drafting a standard for institutional endorsement.[48] The report of this committee, which was accepted
at the next council, reflects a favorable shift in sentiment
toward education:

We believe that we have passed from the stage of mere individual vision to a united vision for the future perpetuation of the
great Pentecostal message. We must pass on this heritage to our
youth that they may go forth in the power of the Spirit, to proclaim
the message. A Spirit-baptized, heavenly-endued, divinely ordained,
and Biblically intelligent ministry is the cry and need of the church,
and must be had and maintained if the purpose of God is accomplished in us as a movement. The need is great. The call is
urgent. We can no longer delay. The time for action is here. Let
us put forth one united effort for the training of our future preachers,
especially with the schools sponsored by the General and District
Councils.[49]

The standards for approved Assemblies of God schools
recommended by the committee on institutions included
requirements concerning location, building and equipment,
management and ownership, faculty, admission of students,
curriculum, practical work, discipline, spiritual life, food
services, and extracurricular activities. Another recommendation of the committee called for the establishment of an
educational department headed by a national secretary of
education. The council of 1937 approved the committee's
work with only minor changes. A new department was

---

[47] *Minutes*, 1925, pp. 36-37.
[48] *Educational Institutions*, p. 6.
[49] "Report of the Committee on Institutions," *Pentecostal Evangel*, June 13,
1936, p. 10.

formed to direct the education and home missions affairs of the church.[50]

In 1945 education was separated from home missions and became an independent department. Its administrative pattern was similar to that of the other departments except that the Executive Presbytery was designated as the standing education committee of the General Council. That same year, upon the suggestion of the executive heads of all the affiliated schools, the standards for institutional endorsement were revised to include greater detail.[51]

The only other significant change in the educational structure occurred in 1955, when a new group, composed of the director of education, secretary of education, and eighteen other persons selected by the General Presbytery to represent the six geographical areas (northeast, north-central, northwest, southeast, southcentral, and southwest) of the Assemblies of God, replaced the Executive Presbytery as the standing education committee.[52]

ACCREDITING ASSOCIATION FOR BIBLE INSTITUTES AND COLLEGES

An agency other than the education department also contributed to the upgrading of Assemblies of God schools. This was the Accrediting Association for Bible Institutes and Colleges, formed in 1947 to provide a concerted voice for this type of educational institution. The purpose of this interdenominational accrediting association was to gain recognition for Bible institutes and colleges in American educational circles by assuring the maintenance of high scholastic standards among its member institutions. The Assemblies of God recommended that its schools apply for membership, and by 1951 all were accredited by the agency. Qualifying for this connection resulted in the improvement of a number of the programs of the schools.[53]

The Bible institutes and colleges have made a noteworthy contribution to the work of the Assemblies of God. A review of their accomplishment was included in the re-

[50] *Educational Institutions,* pp. 6, 11; *Minutes,* 1937, pp. 57, 103-111.
[51] *Educational Institutions,* p. 11; *Minutes,* 1945, pp. 22-26, 29-31.
[52] *Minutes,* 1955, pp. 36-44.
[53] *Educational Institutions,* p. 11.

port of the executive director of education to the General Council in 1953.

Through the years our schools have operated, they have produced 13,332 graduates. From 1914-1949, 36% of all ordained ministers and 74% of missionaries in the Assemblies of God were Bible school trained. In the last four years the percentage has increased to 60% for ordained ministers and 93% for missionaries. Our Bible schools are producing a large majority of our church workers and are thus doubtless having a great influence on our Movement.[54]

ACADEMIC EDUCATION

Interest in secular training has not developed in the Assemblies of God nearly so rapidly as in religious education. Only two senior high school programs are sponsored —Canyonville Bible Academy, Canyonville, Oregon, started in 1924, and Southwestern High School, Waxahachie, Texas, started in 1931 and operated as a division of Southwestern Bible Institute. In more recent years a number of parochial schools have been established under the sponsorship of local churches. These are supervised by state public school offices and operate largely outside the administration of the education department. Most of the constituents of the Assemblies of God have been satisfied to send their children to public schools for elementary and secondary education.

The first official appeal of the General Council for church-sponsored academic training came in the council of 1929 as a part of the report of the committee on Bible schools.

On account of the worldliness of many of our high schools and colleges and their antagonistic attitude for the most part to the Pentecostal message, there is a growing need of academic schools of our faith in different parts of our country to provide education without contamination of worldly and antichristian influences. We believe that our fellowship should look with favor upon the establishment of such schools, and should look forward to the time, if the Lord tarry, when we may have somewhere an institution of college grade, where the most complete and thorough education can be obtained under Pentecostal auspices.[55]

[54] *Reports,* 1953, p. 34.
[55] *Minutes,* 1929, p. 83.

The next action in this direction was not taken until 1945, when the General Council provided for an academic division in the education department to provide for and encourage academic education in the Assemblies of God. Caution was indicated, however, by the next resolution which stipulated that "no action be taken by the Educational Committee for the establishment of a Liberal Arts College unless such is authorized by the General Council in session."[56]

While the General Council moved slowly toward the field of liberal arts education, Southwestern Bible Institute acted without delay upon the apparent need and added a junior college course to its curriculum in the fall of 1945. The junior college met with immediate favor and became an important division of the school.

The education committee that served the council of 1947 recommended the founding of a liberal arts college

in which our young people who are not destined for the ministry can get a thorough training in a Pentecostal environment and under our leadership and instruction. It is to be understood that this committee does not recommend this college as a training ground for prospective ministers, but rather for the others of our young people who desire and require advanced education to fit them for their chosen life work.[57]

The General Council, however, rejected the recommendation of the committee, defeating by a substantial vote the motion to form a college.

Another district Bible school, Southern California Bible College, Costa Mesa, California, capitalized on this hesitation of the General Council by entering the academic field. A division of arts and sciences was incorporated into the California program in the fall of 1950.[58]

EVANGEL COLLEGE

In the meantime recommendations requesting the establishment of a central liberal arts college were submitted to each General Council session. The district councils of

---

[56] *Minutes*, 1945, pp. 22-23.
[57] *Minutes*, 1947, pp. 18-19.
[58] "Educational Program at Southern California Bible College to be Expanded," *Pentecostal Evangel*, May 6, 1950, p. 7.

Tennessee, Alabama, Oregon, West Central, and Michigan
also passed resolutions asking the General Council for the
same action. It was the council of 1953 that finally took
the necessary steps to found a liberal arts college by adopting the following resolution:

Be It Resolved, That this General Council in session authorize
the setting up of a Senior College Program, and be it
Further Resolved, That a committee of thirty-five (35) members,
consisting of the Executive Presbytery of the General Council, the
Administrative heads of our eleven endorsed schools, the chairman
of the Education Committee and eleven laymen be empowered to
set up this program as soon as possible.[59]

The senior college committee immediately attacked the
problem of founding a college. The first months following
the council of 1953 were devoted to individual study, directed and stimulated by the education department through
correspondence. The initial meeting of the committee convened in Springfield, Missouri, in December 1953. This
session outlined an approach to fulfilling its task, arranged
for a division of labor to effect the plan, and then adjourned to meet April 2, 1954, in St. Louis.

At the second sitting the committee prepared a formal
report of its work, making specific recommendations concerning the internal operation of the college. A board of
directors was then selected and charged with implementing
the suggestions in the report of the committee. Before adjourning *sine die,* the senior college committee also voted
to apply to the U. S. Government for the former O'Reilly
General Hospital in Springfield, Missouri, which had been
declared surplus property, for a college plant.[60]

The directorate had its first meeting on May 24-25,
1954, in Springfield, at which time a constitution and by-
laws were adopted, a college president was named, and the
tentative opening date of the college was set for the fall
of 1955. Subcommittees were given authority to act during
the interim between sessions. One very significant subcom-
mittee was to expedite the application for the O'Reilly

[59] *Minutes,* 1953, pp. 30-31.
[60] *Reports,* 1955, p. 57.

tract in compliance with the action of the senior college committee, while another was to determine the name for the college.[61]

Very shortly the appropriate group announced that the name of the projected college was Evangel College. Then on December 14, 1954, an agency of the federal government announced that the Assemblies of God had been awarded fifty-nine acres of the O'Reilly Hospital property for the establishment of its college. The value of the land and the seventy buildings on it was appraised at a little less than $1,000,000.[62] With the major problem of the college plant solved, the directorate held its second meeting on December 28-30, 1954. The session was devoted primarily to establishing definite objectives for the college, selecting an administrative staff, and exploring and determining means for financing the enterprise. The president was instructed to assemble a faculty, prepare a curriculum, activate the facilities, and have all in readiness to begin operation in September, 1955.[63]

After eight months of busy, detailed preparation, the college opened on schedule. Students were enrolled from twenty-six states, Alaska, and British Guiana, a response that seemed to indicate that the college would be widely received by the Assemblies of God. The launching of the new college was celebrated with an "open house" program on September 8.[64]

The establishment of the liberal arts college will probably mark a change in the educational pattern of the Assemblies of God. Where previously its youth largely attended Bible institutes and colleges, those having no intention of entering full-time religious work will now undoubtedly look with favor upon an academic program. This may, in turn, require the district schools to alter their programs to meet this trend. The big problem, of course,

---

[61] "Plans Laid for a Senior College," *Pentecostal Evangel*, June 27, 1954, p. 9.

[62] "O'Reilly Hospital Tract to 2 Groups," Springfield *Daily News*, December 14, 1954, pp. 1, 4; "Evangel College May Get Students from Bible Schools," Springfield *Daily Advertiser*, December 16, 1954, p. 1.

[63] "Minutes, Meeting of Board of Directors of Evangel College, December 28-30, 1954" (duplicated manuscript prepared by Evangel College), pp. 1-9.

[64] "Evangel College Opens," *Pentecostal Evangel*, October 30, 1955, p. 6.

will be the establishment of traditions and quality of work that will properly challenge and educate the youth of the church.

YOUTH DEPARTMENT

A consideration of the youth organization of the Assemblies of God fits appropriately into this chapter because that organization is primarily a training agency. Its program is designed to give young people experiences which will enable them to assume responsibilities in the church as they mature.

EARLY EFFORTS TO ORGANIZE YOUTH WORK

During the first decade of the development of the church, all youth work was left entirely to the local congregations. Though some had excellent programs, most pastors completely ignored the possibilities of planned youth activities. Organized young people's work on more than the local level first appeared in California. Both the northern and southern districts of that state are due credit for initiating early area organizations. In April, 1925, the youth leader of the Glad Tidings Assembly in Oakland, Vera Salmonsen, sent invitations to a number of youth groups in northern California to attend a rally at her home church on May 30. Thirteen bodies and some three hundred persons attended the sesson. Wesley R. Steelberg, then pastor of Bethel Full Gospel Church in Stockton, later general superintendent of the Assemblies of God, was moderator of this first meeting. During the course of the day's activities, the participants selected "Pentecostal Ambassadors for Christ" as the name for Assemblies of God young people in their region, and decided to hold similar gatherings semi-annually.[65]

Almost simultaneously another movement was developing in southern California through the promotion of A. G. Osterberg and Carl E. Hatch. In the spring of 1925 Osterberg, while pastor of the Fresno Full Gospel Tabernacle, organized his young people as "Christian Crusaders." This organization spread until it included groups throughout the

---

[65] C. A. Manual, pp. 8-9.

San Joaquin Valley. At the same time Hatch, who was in charge of the youth work at Bethel Temple in Los Angeles, formed a group under the name "Christ's Ambassadors." After hearing of the San Joaquin Valley activity, Hatch requested that the two areas unite their programs. Osterberg, who had in the meantime been elected superintendent of the Southern California-Arizona district, suggested that the program be enlarged to comprehend the entire district; and in 1928 the district council officially recognized the Christ's Ambassadors. Thus Southern California-Arizona gained the distinction of instituting the first district youth organization.[66]

Within a very short time the new movement became prominent. An article in the *Pentecostal Evangel* in 1926 suggested that youth groups everywhere embrace the name, Christ's Ambassadors. During the same year a paper for young people called *Christ's Ambassadors* was published by the Gospel Publishing House. Planned youth work received so much emphasis that during 1926 alone district C. A.[67] organizations were formed in Texas, Oklahoma, Colorado, and Indiana. Arkansas had preceded these by inaugurating a program in 1925.[68]

NATIONAL YOUTH ORGANIZATION

The council of 1927 gave the first official recognition by the General Council to the Christ's Ambassadors. An amendment to the bylaws of the Assemblies of God was passed in that session which defined the relationship of the C.A.'s to the local churches and district councils.[69] This gave such impetus to the youth movement that a brief reaction arose against its development. A fear existed, especially among some of the older clergymen, that the church might have difficulty controlling youth influence, if its emphasis continued unchecked. Because of this, the council

---

[66] "Dates and Data," p. 1; Carl Hatch, Sherman Oaks, California, to Robert Willis, Corpus Christi, Texas, February 28, 1952, L. S., p. 1.

[67] This abbreviated title came into popular use after 1926, when an emblem was designed using these letters.

[68] "Dates and Data," p. 1; Hatch to Willis, February 28, 1952.

[69] *Minutes*, 1927, pp. 73-75.

of 1931 disapproved the forming of a national youth organization.[70]

As the years passed and the youth movement demonstrated that it was no uncontrollable monster, opposition
to a national organization became less pronounced. Annual conferences of district youth leaders, begun by headquarters at Springfield in 1940, resulted in an appeal
being presented to the council of 1941 for the establishment
of a central Christ's Ambassadors department. This request
was favorably received, and the Executive Presbytery was
authorized to take appropriate steps to add such a division
to the national office. Accordingly, William E. Pickthorn,
pastor of the First Assembly of God in Memphis, Tennessee,
was appointed to head a study to determine the type of
administration that would best serve the interests of the
church. Ralph W. Harris, the Michigan District C. A.
president, was then called to Springfield to establish the
office. The forming of the national department was finalized
when the council of 1943 made the administrative structure suggested by the Pickthorn study a part of the bylaws
of the Assemblies of God.[71]

CENTRAL YOUTH ADMINISTRATION

The Christ's Ambassadors operate very similarly to the
Sunday school department. The central office is administered by a director, who is one of the five assistant general superintendents, a national secretary, and a corps of
subordinates who handle the detailed work. The program
is carried to the local churches through forty-three district offices, directed by district officers and sectional leaders.[72]

PROMOTION OF YOUTH PROGRAM

Excellent communication is maintained with the youth
constituency through a number of periodicals. The development of the *Christ's Ambassadors Herald,* the official organ
of the group, was sketched in the previous chapter. The

[70] *Minutes,* 1931, pp. 81-82.
[71] *Minutes,* 1943, pp. 58-62.
[72] "Christ's Ambassadors, Youth Organization of the Assemblies of God" (duplicated information prepared by the C. A. Department, Assemblies of God, [1951]),
p. 1.

national office keeps the district officers and sectional leaders informed of the central program through a publication entitled *CAPsule* (the capital letters stand for C. A. President). This confidential bulletin, prepared in a very informal style, is sent out with a questionnaire, which, when returned to Springfield, informs the central officers of district activities. Two papers are edited for special youth groups—*Campus Ambassador* for Assemblies of God students attending institutions of higher learning, and *Reveille,* for personnel of the armed services. A final periodical, the *C. A. Guide,* is a quarterly prepared to assist youth leaders and workers in implementing the C. A. program within the local bands.[73]

YOUTH PROGRAM

The activities of the C. A. program are designed to give training for adult church membership as well as opportunities for youth fellowship. Each member has experiences involving democratic religious processes, church music, stewardship, and leadership. Each year a special study is featured which is carefully outlined and carried to the individual groups through the *C. A. Guide.* For example, in 1951 the emphasis was upon evangelism. The first quarter was devoted to personal evangelism, the second to literature and evangelism, the third to group evangelism, and the last to missionary evangelism.[74]

The outstanding activity of the department has been the Speed-the-Light program.

Originally envisioned by Ralph W. Harris, who was the first National Secretary of the C. A.'s, this crusade among youth to raise money for the purchase of motor vehicles, airplanes, and boats for the use of Assemblies of God missionaries has literally speeded the gospel message in hundreds of mission fields. The program has been extended to purchase printing and radio equipment, and by them the gospel is spread to the uttermost parts of the earth.[75]

The Speed-the-Light project is financed by contributions from all Christ's Ambassadors of one or more dollars on

[73] *Ibid.*, pp. 3-4; C. A. *Manual*, p. 7.
[74] Statement by Dick Fulmer, Springfield, Mo., personal interview. At the time of the interview, Fulmer was National C. A. Secretary.
[75] *Workers Together* (Springfield, Mo., Gospel Publishing House, 1954), p. 32.

a designated Sunday of each year. During the first ten years of the campaign, which began in 1945, $1,147,565.34 was raised by the young people. By the end of 1958, $2,341,130.66 had been given to Speed-the-Light.[76]

An important division of the C. A. department is the servicemen's section. This office attempts to keep on file the names of all Assemblies of God men and women in the armed services and to maintain their interest in the church through regular correspondence and the distribution of appropriate literature. The division also regularly communicates with Assemblies of God military chaplains, Civil Air Patrol chaplains, and "contact pastors" (pastors situated near military installations who maintain contact with servicemen for the department). The servicemen's paper, *Reveille,* has been the most widely used and effective tool in this enterprise.[77]

The national office has been quite successful in reaching and organizing Assemblies of God young people. A late survey indicates 5,112 reporting groups with 96,000 members. Including bands that did not report, the central office estimates the total membership to be in excess of 100,000.[78]

Although much has been accomplished, it may be stated that the Christ's Ambassadors have merely come to the end of the beginning, and only now are ready to launch out in full-scale activity. The C. A. work is spreading around the globe. An outstanding proof of this is the surge of interest in Canada. . . .

The Christ's Ambassadors are being organized in Columbia, South America; in Nigeria and Liberia, West Africa; in China; in New Zealand; and in the Fiji Islands.[79]

The work of the three educational departments has served as an excellent complement to the efforts of the departments of propagation. The evangelical fervor and enthusiasm of propagational agencies have resulted in the addition of many new adherents to the Assemblies of God. The educational agencies have acted as a consolidating force, establishing the new communicants in the church.

---

[76] *Reports,* 1955, p. 29; *Reports,* 1959, p. 65.
[77] "Christ's Ambassadors, Youth Organization," pp. 2-3.
[78] *Reports,* 1959, p. 63.
[79] *C. A. Manual,* pp. 16-17.

VIII
Other Baptistic Pentecostal Groups

ALL PENTECOSTAL bodies can be classified by the position they hold on the doctrinal tenet of sanctification. Since most early Pentecostal believers had come from Holiness ranks, and were perfectionists, sanctification in the beginning was believed to be a "second definite work of grace." After 1910, however (as was noted in Chapter V), the Pentecostal movement was torn by a controversy over the doctrine; those who embraced the "finished work of Christ" or baptistic view held that sanctification was imputed in the experience of salvation, thus eliminating the "second experience" of the perfectionists. This chapter will consider the important baptistic bodies other than the Assemblies of God, while the next will deal with the perfectionist groups.

THE PENTECOSTAL CHURCH OF GOD OF AMERICA

Whereas most of the Pentecostal ministers who attended the first General Council of the Assemblies of God held in Hot Springs, Arkansas in April of 1914 joined up with the newly formed organization, there were others who held back, waiting to see the outcome of the effort. It seemed to be difficult for them to grasp the fact that independent, autonomous churches could be associated in a co-operative fellowship without losing their spiritual liberty. This feeling of uncertainty was intensified by the unfavorable preaching of radical, independent men who had opposed from the first any form of church organization. The emergence of a doctrinal issue during 1915 and 1916, which forced the adoption of a comparatively detailed statement of Fundamental Truths, with special emphasis given to the

Trinitarian position, occasioned still greater criticism, because it was construed by the apprehensive element as a trend toward conventional ecclesiasticism.

CHICAGO CONSTITUTIONAL CONVENTION, 1919

Following the holding of the General Council of the Assemblies of God in Chicago, in the fall of 1919, the dissident group finally took steps to effect an organization which would refrain from writing a doctrinal statement, but would be content with the simple statement that the Scriptures are the all-sufficient rule for faith and practice, thus simplifying the form of organization to that originally proposed for the Assemblies of God. Undoubtedly, a number of persons supported the move who were not themselves unhappy with the Assemblies of God. One such minister (a resident of Chicago) wrote that he went with the dissenters because he felt that greater unity would result from an affiliation based on a more general constitutional framework.[1]

At a called meeting in Chicago, on December 30, 1919, the group organized as the Pentecostal Assemblies of the U.S.A.[2] John C. Sinclair, of Chicago (who had attended the first General Council in 1914), and George Brinkman, a layman, also of Chicago, the editor of a new, free-distribution paper titled *The Pentecostal Herald,* were prominent in this move.

The constitution carefully set forth a liberal position on membership:

...We deem it advisable, in order to avoid creating unscriptural lines of fellowship and disfellowship, to affiliate on the basic principles of love, righteousness and truth, with due recognition of each other, allowing liberty of conscience in matters of personal conviction.[3]

The organization was "neither to legislate laws or government, nor to usurp authority over the various local Assem-

[1] T. A. Sandgren, Chicago, Illinois, to E. N. Bell, Springfield, Mo., November 19, 1921, A. L. S., 3 p.
[2] Pentecostal Church of God of America, *General Constitution and Bylaws,* 1947 (Kansas City, Mo.; Pentecostal Church of God, 1947), p. 3.
[3] Pentecostal Church of God, *Minutes of Meeting held February 15, 1922,* Chicago, Ill. (Chicago: Pentecostal Church of God, 1922), p. 3.

blies, or to deprive them of their scripturally recognized
local rights and privileges"; disapproving of fellowship on
the basis of a doctrinal statement, "we accept the Word of
God in its entirety, conducting ourselves in harmony with
its divine principles." [4] One cannot help noticing the sim-
ilarity between these founding declarations and those of
the Assemblies of God.

A meeting at Chicago in 1922 changed the name from
Pentecostal Assemblies of the U.S.A. to Pentecostal Church
of God. By that time the organization had grown to include
a combined ministerial membership of over two hundred. [5]

NATIONAL HEADQUARTERS

The central office of the group was located in Chicago
until 1927, when A. D. McClure was elected general superintendent and the headquarters were moved to the town
of his residence, Ottumwa, Iowa. The General Convention
of 1933 moved the office to Kansas City, Missouri. Then,
in order to avoid confusion with a local independent church
already operating as the Pentecostal Church of God, the
organization incorporated in the state of Missouri as the
Pentecostal Church of God of America. When, in 1950,
the church had grown sufficiently to justify the construction of its own headquarters' facilities, Joplin, Missouri was
selected as the site of the new central office building. [6]

POLITY OF THE CHURCH

Perhaps because of the previous association of various
leaders of the Pentecostal Church of God of America with
the Assemblies of God, the polity of the two groups is very
similar. In the early years, however, the body had certain
congregational characteristics which were more pronounced
than those of the Assemblies. In fact, the organization was
so loosely formed that it seemed its chief objective was the
issuing of ministerial credentials to those ministers who
wanted extreme independence but needed ministerial cre-

[4] *Ibid.*, p. 4.
[5] *Ibid.*, p. 1
[6] Clark, *Small Sects in America*, p. 109; Statement by J. W. May, Conroe,
Texas, April 27, 1955, personal interview. May was a former general superintendent
of the Pentecostal Church of God of America.

dentials for identification. One reason for this feeling was the simplicity of the procedure adopted for the ordination of ministers:

Two or more regularly ordained ministers in good standing shall have authority to ordain by imposition of hands and prayer such as have a call to the ministry and have proven their gifts and callings by actual success rather than the hopes of what they may be: This ordination shall be in conjunction with the pastor and local assembly.[7]

This practice was modified through the years until finally the church created a central credential committee to "decide all matters concerning credentials."[8]

The highest authority of the group is the General Convention. This biennial body is a representative assembly composed of the officers, ordained and licensed ministers, missionaries under appointment, and one lay delegate for each one hundred members or fraction thereof of each chartered congregation.

The next governing body in the scale of authority is the Executive Board, which includes all the general officers, district superintendents, and one district presbyter from each district. This body is considered the "Managing Directors and the Governing Body of the Organization, and its approval or disapproval of the acts of the Officers . . . fully bind the Corporation."[9]

Officers have been added to the administration as church activities have required additional supervision by the central office. A general superintendent has headed the organization from its very inception and is vested with the authority to act as chairman of all general meetings and have general supervision of all the operations of the group. By 1950 three assistant general superintendents had been added to the staff. They were probably needed because of the growth that was realized in the 1940's. May stated that during his tenure as general superintendent, 1942-1947, the number of districts doubled and the churches and ministers more than doubled.[10] The assistant superintendents are

---

[7] *Pentecostal Church of God Minutes*, 1922, p. 7.
[8] *Pentecostal Church of God Constitution*, 1953, p. 16.
[9] *Ibid.*, p. 11.
[10] J. W. May, personal interview.

elected by three geographical sections of the church—western, central, and eastern—that they are to serve and in which they must reside. These area selections are then confirmed by the General Convention. The specific duties of these officers are assigned by the Executive Board. A general secretary-treasurer and a director of world missions are the only other officers elected by the General Convention. All the additional ones—the executive secretary-treasurer of world missions, the editor of the general official publication, the director of Indian missions, and the director of religious education—are appointed by the Executive Board.[11]

The program of the General Convention is conveyed to the local congregations through district organizations. These are geographical areas that correspond roughly with state boundaries. Each district has its own representative government, which is a miniature of the national pattern. The district units are supervised by their officers, a superintendent, district presbyter, and secretary-treasurer. The districts in turn are divided into sections, over which sectional presbyters preside. The basic units of the church are, of course, the local congregations. These retain their sovereignty and participate in the sectional, district, and national programs on a voluntary, co-operative basis.[12]

DOCTRINAL POSITION

Though the Pentecostal Church of God had organized with a declaration that only a very general doctrinal statement would be the basis of the church's belief, it very soon felt, as had other religious bodies before it, the necessity of defining and limiting its theological scope. This was accomplished in a "Doctrinal Statement" adopted by the General Convention. The preface declared that the statement contained those things which were "most surely believed among us" and was intended to prevent "divisive

---

[11] R. Dennis Heard, Joplin, Missouri, to Klaude Kendrick, Springfield, Missouri, March 30, 1960, A.L.S., 1 p. At the time of the communication Heard had served for several terms as general superintendent of the Pentecostal Church of God.

[12] *Pentecostal Church of God Constitution*, 1953, pp. 19-23.

differences" of belief and "the disturbance of the peace and harmony of the churches." [13] The sixteen articles of the Doctrinal Statement did not present any basic doctrine not held by other baptistic Pentecostal bodies. A tenet on sanctification confirming the baptistic position was added to the original sixteen after 1947. The existence of other doctrinal difficulties may be presumed from the fact that the convention in 1949 authorized the publication of a book to define what the church believed "so that our churches will be in unity in doctrine." [14]

MISSIONARY PROGRAM

The missionary emphasis within the Pentecostal Church of God has not been as great as that in some of the other Pentecostal bodies. In its fortieth year the group had under appointment only thirty-six missionaries working in thirteen fields. [15] The Missions department was not considered sufficiently prominent to justify a full-time administrator or a distinct missionary board until the convention of 1949. Prior to that time the general secretary-treasurer served also as missionary secretary-treasurer, and the Executive Board acted as the missionary committee. [16] Work among the American Indians became such an important part of the program that a separate division under a director of Indian missions was established in 1949. [17]

PUBLISHING INTERESTS

The early publishing interests of the Pentecostal Church of God were concerned with the production of an official organ. The first paper recognized by the group was the privately published *Pentecostal Herald*. When the headquarters were moved from Chicago to Ottumwa, the general superintendent began to edit the *Pentecostal Messenger*, the permanent voice of the organization. [18] After moving to Kansas City the church established the *Mes-*

---

[13] Pentecostal Church of God Constitution, 1947, p. 5.
[14] Pentecostal Church of God Constitution, 1950, p. 36.
[15] Heard to Kendrick, March 30, 1960.
[16] Pentecostal Church of God Constitution, 1950, pp. 34-35.
[17] Ibid., p. 32.
[18] Pentecostal Church of God Minutes, 1922, p. 11; Pentecostal Church of God Constitution, 1947, p. 3.

senger Publishing House, which during its infant years produced only the *Pentecostal Messenger* and materials for the central office. Since 1938, however, a line of Sunday school literature has been developed.

TRAINING PROGRAMS

The Pentecostal Church of God has shown interest in ministerial training. Thus in the convention of 1946 Dr. John W. Waldron exclaimed:

In prophetic vision we see that very beautiful and outstanding General Headquarters, that fine Bible school, the consecrated staff of toilers, the growing groups of students, the anxious desire to make that necessary preparation for this modern day.[19]

As yet, however, very little progress has been achieved in establishing an institutional educational program. Two small Bible schools—Pentecostal Bible College, Gilroy, California, and Southern Bible College, Houston, Texas—are operated by the group. A high school in Gilroy, California, and a grammar school in Ontario, California, have been the only efforts thus far in developing a church-sponsored academic program.[20]

The Sunday school, in contrast to the institutional education program, has become a thriving activity in recent years. In 1953 the church established a central Sunday school department headed by a full-time director of religious education whose duty it is to assist Sunday schools and to improve and promote the Sunday school literature of the Pentecostal Church of God.[21]

YOUTH WORK

The youth organization of the church, the Pentecostal Young People's Association (P. Y. P. A.), began on the local level in 1932, when the first group was formally organized in Vallejo, California. Shortly afterward other bands were formed, and in 1933 the initial district P. Y. P. A. convention was held at West Los Angeles. All of the other districts soon followed the example of California and established district youth divisions. The national young

---

[19] *Ibid.*, p. 100.
[20] Heard to Kendrick, March 30, 1960.
[21] *Pentecostal Church of God Constitution*, 1953, pp. 34-35.

people's office was established in 1938, headed by a general president. The outstanding project of the P. Y. P. A. has been the financing of the Indian missions department, which now has fourteen missionaries on its staff who work with seventeen tribes.[22]

Slow growth characterized the early years of the Pentecostal Church of God. No mention is made of the group in the United States Census computation of Religious Bodies in 1926, and in 1936 only eighty-seven churches with a total membership of 5,713 are listed.[23] After this date development was more rapid. A late survey credits the denomination with 900 churches and 103,500 members.[24]

INTERNATIONAL CHURCH OF THE FOURSQUARE GOSPEL

A history of the Foursquare Church, as the International Church of the Foursquare Gospel is generally called, must of necessity begin with its founder, Aimee Semple McPherson. It is doubtful if a more controversial figure has been connected with the American church in the twentieth century.

To her followers she is simply the Lord's Anointed, sent to herald His second coming. To them, everything about her partakes of the miraculous and no further attempt is made to analyze the wonders of her works. At the opposite extreme are the scoffers who see nothing in her but a clever mountebank, devoid of genuine intelligence or sincerity.[25]

MRS. MCPHERSON'S EARLY LIFE

Aimee Kennedy was born and raised by a strong willed, religious mother who exerted a great influence on her daughter's life. Mrs. Kennedy came from an "old-fashioned Methodist" environment where "the mighty power of God" was manifested.[26] When the Salvation Army reached Amer-

[22] Pentecostal Church of God, *Pentecostal Young People's Association* (Kansas City, Mo.: Pentecostal Church of God, [n.d.]), pp. 9-17; Heard to Kendrick, March 30, 1960.
[23] U. S. Bureau of Census, *Religious Bodies: 1936*, II, 1343.
[24] Landis, *Yearbook of American Churches*, 1960, p. 88.
[25] Julia N. Budlong, "Aimee Semple McPherson," *Nation*, CXXVIII (June 19, 1929), p. 737.
[26] Aimee Semple McPherson, *This is That, Personal Experiences, Sermons and Writings of Aimee Semple McPherson* (Los Angeles: Echo Park Evangelistic Assoc., Inc., 1923), p. 14.

ica, she was attracted to its work and enlisted in its ministerial ranks. Later, when domestic responsibilities prevented her continuance in active service, she felt such deep regret that she vowed as a compensation for her failure to dedicate her child to the ministry.[27]

Aimee was born on a farm in Ontario, Canada, in 1890. Her childhood was no different from that of any other youngster raised in a rural area. She was introduced early to religion; and in spite of the inconvenience of distance, the family regularly attended services. During her high school days religion was somewhat replaced by other activities. She was especially interested in dramatics and became a locally popular performer.

She had a rare ability for personalizing every event, and a lively eloquence gave to everything she said embroidery and high coloring. These girlhood propensities were the blueprint for Sister's future technique, the recognized symptoms of her charm and human appeal.[28]

The Pentecostal message was brought to Aimee's community by Robert Semple during her senior year in high school. In recounting the first meeting, Aimee recalled that Semple "was straight and tall, well over six feet, broad shouldered ... He turned, and I saw an earnest, strong face, a pair of level, sincere, blue eyes. He spoke in a deep, ringing voice.... He was a man among men and spoke with the conviction of a strong character." [29] The preaching of the young evangelist stirred Aimee's religious sensibilities, which had been neglected during the past three years. "What he said sank into my heart like a swift flung arrow. It was a shaft of conviction from the bow of the Lord." [30] She renewed her Christian profession in the meeting and received the "Pentecostal experience."

[27] Carey McWilliams, "Aimee Semple McPherson: 'Sunlight in My Soul'," in Isabel Leighton, ed., *The Aspirin Age*, 1919-1941 (New York: Simon and Schuster, 1949), p. 52.

[28] Marcus Bach, *They Have Found a Faith* (Indianapolis: Bobbs-Merrill Co., 1946), p. 61.

[29] Aimee Semple McPherson, *In the Service of the King, Story of My Life*, (New York: Boni and Liveright, 1927), p. 76.

[30] *Ibid.*, p. 76.

Semple did more than arouse the religious flame in
Aimee. A few weeks after he ended his meeting, he returned
to Ingersoll, Aimee's hometown, and extended to his at-
tractive convert a proposal of marriage, which she readily
accepted. Immediately after their wedding, the couple
entered extensive evangelistic activities. The followers of
Mrs. McPherson mark this the beginning of her international ministry."[31]

MRS. MCPHERSON'S EARLY MINISTRY

The first phase of her career was devoted to holding
revival campaigns with her husband in both Canada and
the United States. They spent several months in Chicago
assisting W. H. Durham, father of the baptistic concept of
sanctification in modern Pentecostal circles.[32] This experience perhaps accounts for Mrs. McPherson's adherence to
this doctrine in her ministry both as an evangelist and as
a church organizer. The Semples also preached in Findlay,
Ohio, for T. K. Leonard, who was prominent in the founding of the Assemblies of God and may have influenced them
to become interested in that body. Mrs. McPherson's name
was carried on the rolls of the Assemblies for several years.[33]
After an extensive period of evangelism the couple volunteered for foreign missions work and embarked for China,
where Semple was stricken with malaria and died after a
short illness. Mrs. Semple and her infant daughter returned
to America a few weeks later.[34]

For some time following her return, Mrs. Semple was
not active in the ministry. Desiring the security of a home,
she finally entered into a marriage that brought her little
happiness. Harold McPherson was a kindly person and provided well for the family, but he had no inclination at
all toward religious work. Mrs. McPherson, on the other
hand, professing a growing feeling of guilt for abandoning

---

[31] *L. I. F. E. Bible College Student Handbook* (Los Angeles: L. I. F. E. Bible
College, 1949), p. 17.

[32] McPherson, *This is That*, p. 56.

[33] J. Roswell Flower, personal interview.

[34] "History of Foursquaredom" (unpublished mimeographed manuscript prepared
by L. I. F. E. Bible College), p. 1.

the ministry, re-entered evangelism in 1917 after her second child, Rolf, was born.[35]

One friendly writer maintains that Mrs. McPherson's loyalty to Semple's religion accounts for her success. As her attraction to his belief brought meaning to her life when she was drifting in high school, so now her return to this earlier loyalty started her toward prominence.[36] Whether this be the case or not, when she again entered evangelistic work, her success soon carried her from small churches, tents, and halls to the largest auditoriums in America.

MRS. MCPHERSON'S FOURSQUARE GOSPEL

Mrs. McPherson's message was similar to that of other Pentecostal preachers. She stressed the doctrines of salvation, baptism in the Holy Spirit, divine healing, and the second coming of Christ. In 1921, while conducting a meeting in Oakland, California, she based a sermon upon Ezekiel 1: 1-28, which gives a prophetic vision of four faces—those of a man, a lion, an ox, and an eagle. Perceiving these figures as types of her four basic doctrines, she was fascinated by the revelation.

A perfect Gospel! A complete Gospel for body, for soul, for spirit, and for eternity. A Gospel that faces squarely in every direction.

As the wonder—the power—the majesty of it cascaded o'er the battlements of heaven, filling, flooding, enveloping my very being, the fingers of the Spirit swept the aeolian harp strings of my heart and evoked a wondrous melody like the sound of a great Amen. The lost chord was found again!

In my soul was born a harmony that was struck and sustained upon four full, quivering strings, and from it were plucked words that leaped into being—THE FOURSQUARE GOSPEL.[37]

From this time the expression "Foursquare Gospel" was largely associated with the McPherson ministry and organization.

MRS. MCPHERSON'S ESTABLISHMENT IN LOS ANGELES

Mrs. McPherson held her first meeting in Los Angeles

[35] McPherson, *This is That*, pp. 69-96.
[36] Budlong, "Aimee Semple McPherson," *Nation*, CXXVIII (June 19, 1929) p. 738.
[37] Aimee Semple McPherson, *The Foursquare Gospel* (Los Angeles: Echo Park Evangelistic Assoc., 1946), pp. 22-23.

during the winter of 1918. She soon returned to conduct
several other campaigns, and after 1920 decided to build a
church and established her permanent residence there. As
she put it, "There it was that the Lord, most gently, but
unquestionably began to reveal to me His will, showing
me that there had been a method in the plan of His leading;
and that in this city of the Angels, we were to 'Build a House
unto the Lord.' " [38]

Though she had thought at first of building a modest
frame structure, as her planning progressed Mrs. McPherson
decided upon a much more elaborate sanctuary. An excellent
building site was obtained opposite Echo Park on Glendale
Boulevard, and construction commenced on a "pay as go"
basis.

Mrs. McPherson called the next three years sublime because of
the constant feeling of achievement they held for her. She was
"like a homing pigeon that brings twigs for the home nest one
by one and weaves them in, then speeds away to get another."
She told Foursquare friends in San Diego and Sydney, in Wichita
and Winnipeg, London and Los Angeles about "The staccato song
of the riveting hammers, welding steel to steel; the clatter of the
open-mouthed cement mixers whirling about to make the walls."
She told how the construction elevators were carrying their burdens
ever nearer the sky. She made them see the broad arches through
which the whole lost world might enter to find Jesus.

The result: money poured in from every country and city that
Sister had visited in her evangelistic barnstorming—one and a half
million dollars before the job was finished. [39]

The impressive sanctuary with its striking dome, stained
glass windows depicting the entire life of Chirst, great
proscenium arch, choir lofts, auditorium and balconies
seating 5,000, and red carpeted aisles was dedicated January 1, 1923, as Angelus Temple and became the heart of
Foursquaredom.

Mrs. McPherson had unusual organizing ability; though
thousands soon joined its ranks, Angelus Temple operated
smoothly under her direction. The following is Aimee's description of her administrative pattern:

---

[38] McPherson, *This Is That*, p. 507.
[39] Bach, *They Have Found a Faith*, pp. 66-67.

Angelus Temple is run upon the cabinet system, and operates like a wheel with twenty-four spokes. In the center there is a desk with two chairs—myself as pastor, caring for the spiritual end, and a certified accountant and bookkeeper, caring for the business details of this great organization, the books being open at any time to all members of the church.

At the end of each spoke is a desk about which are grouped seven chairs, composing department cabinets. The chairman of each cabinet has a seat at the council table and actively assists in the planning and executing of all details of the Temple work.[40]

This basic pattern has not changed through the years, though departments have been added or discontinued depending on needs and conditions. Departments were added until sixty, maintained by one hundred regular employees besides much donated help, served the church.[41]

DEVELOPMENT OF THE FOURSQUARE CHURCH

The transition of Foursquaredom from a local organization to one of national and international scope was a natural one. This statement is not meant to imply that Mrs. McPherson had any intention of starting another religious body when she was evangelizing or establishing Angelus Temple. In fact, the opposite was probably the case, for her meetings were conducted on an inter-denominational basis with churches and ministers of all communions co-operating with her. "Dedicated unto the cause of inter-denominational and world wide evangelism" were the words chiseled on the cornerstone of the temple.

Yet it was almost inevitable that another group should be formed. Large numbers of individuals had been attracted to Mrs. McPherson and her foursquare gospel program who would never be content to return to a church that functioned differently. An Evangelistic and Missionary Training Institute was started in 1923 as a department of Angelus Temple. Many of the students after receiving training in the school launched at once into mission and church work. Branch churches began springing up, especially in areas adjacent to Los Angeles.[42] According to Mrs.

---

[40] McPherson, *In the Service of the King*, p. 254.
[41] "History of Foursquaredom," p. 6.
[42] McPherson, *In the Service of the King*, p. 256.

McPherson, "they were not premeditated by us. We did not first draw the blueprints and then build a work to fit them but the work sprang up everywhere and we had to hasten to put the needful amount of scaffolding under it to hold it together." [43] Within two years after the opening of the Angelus Temple, thirty-two churches had been established in southern California alone, and some fifty other places were appealing to the mother church for services. With this number of groups on her hands, Mrs. McPherson was impelled toward formal organization.

The first steps in this direction may have been unconscious ones but were nevertheless significant. In 1921, when Angelus Temple was being built, Mrs. McPherson founded the Echo Park Evangelistic Association to further the gospel in accordance with her ideas and techniques. During her revival in Oakland, California, in 1922, the Foursquare Gospel Association was organized. Its purpose was to stimulate laymen and clergymen to promote the cause of evangelism. [44] These associations caused many persons to look to Mrs. McPherson for religious leadership.

The "kidnapping incident" may have been the factor that occasioned the formation of the Foursquare aggregation into a distinct religious body. In May, 1926, Mrs. McPherson mysteriously disappeared from a beach on the California coast. After being considered drowned, she reappeared in Douglas, Arizona, explaining that she had been kidnapped and held for ransom in northern Mexico. [45] When some doubted the veracity of the story, she was indicted on charges of conspiring to support a kidnapping hoax. [46] The charges were ultimately dropped, however, with the admission of the district attorney that they could not be substantiated.

During this unpleasant affair many clergymen who had previously supported Mrs. McPherson's evangelism became

---

[43] "The Church of the Foursquare Gospel," *Foursquare Magazine*, XXVII (May, 1954), p. 17.

[44] McPherson, *This Is That*, pp. 462-463.

[45] "Return," *Time*, VIII (July 5, 1926), p. 19.

[46] "Aimee McPherson Ordered Arrested," *New York Times*, September 17, 1926, pp. 1, 18; "Mother Collapses in McPherson Trial," *Ibid.*, September 30, 1926, pp. 1, 6; McWilliams, "Aimee Semple McPherson," *Aspirin Age*, pp. 64-72.

hostile toward her work. This unfavorable attitude may have speeded action toward church organization. At any rate, the International Church of the Foursquare Gospel was incorporated on December 28, 1927.[47]

POLITY OF THE CHURCH

The polity of the new organization had some episcopal characteristics. This undoubtedly arose in a measure from the influence of Mrs. McPherson's early church background, for the Methodist and Salvation Army communions in which her mother had been active were both episcopal. Even more significant was the position that Mrs. McPherson had held as the guiding genius of her movement, amenable to no one. It is not surprising that the new body was to be headed by a president with broad powers and that Mrs. McPherson was named to this position for life.

The president presides at all conventions, boards, cabinets, councils, and committees or designates someone to act for him. He holds the power of veto over the actions of the board of directors (the board can override the veto by a unanimous vote of all members other than the president). All officers, as well as all chairmen of cabinets, councils, and committees, are appointed by him. Subject to the recommendation and ratification of the board of directors, the president also hires all necessary personnel to carry out the objectives of the organization and sets all salaries of both officers and employed personnel. He likewise is required to sign all ministerial certificates of ordination and ratify with his signature the appointment of Foursquare pastors and missionaries.[48] The president is assisted in the detailed administration of the different functions of the church by six additional central officers—vice-president, secretary, treasurer, general superviser, director of foreign missions, and international director of youth and Christian education.

The highest administrative body is the Board of Directors, composed of five persons. Not only is the president a mem-

<hr>

[47] *Articles of Incorporation and By-Laws of the International Church of the Foursquare Gospel*, edition (Los Angeles: International Church of the Foursquare Gospel, 1952), p. 7; hereafter cited as *Foursquare By-Laws*.

[48] *Foursquare By-Laws*, 1952, pp. 28-29; Howard P. Courtney, Los Angeles, California, to Klaude Kendrick, Springfield, Missouri, April 7, 1960, L. S., 2 p.

ber by virtue of his office, but he also appoints the other members, subject to the approval of the annual convention. The Board of Directors has the responsibility of supervising and managing the affairs of the church. It is assisted by the Executive Council, a committee made up of the officers, members of the Board of Directors, and district supervisors. This body is responsible to study constantly the needs of the church and holds the prerogative of submitting recommendations dealing with the welfare of the group to the president and the Board of Directors.

The central legislative authority is vested in the Annual Convention, which customarily meets in February of each year. The voting constituency of this assembly includes the officers and directors of the church, all ordained and licensed ministers, and one lay delegate for each 100 members or fraction thereof of every chartered Foursquare church.

In order to facilitate the administering of the central program, the territory covered by the Foursquare Church is divided into geographical areas. The smallest unit is the division, which is headed by a division superintendent appointed by the president. The division superintendent is amenable to a district supervisor, whose area of administration includes a number of divisions. Under the president and Board of Directors the general supervisor directs the work of all the district supervisors.[49]

DOCTRINAL POSITION

Mrs. McPherson was personally responsible for the formal statement of doctrine of the Foursquare Church. According to the Articles of Incorporation, the

objects and purposes for which this corporation is formed are, generally, the propagation and dissemination of the Foursquare Gospel as presented in the "Declaration of Faith" compiled by Aimee Semple McPherson, founder, a copy of which is attached hereto and made a part hereof.[50]

The Declaration of Faith contains twenty-two articles that comprehend the basic tenets of the several baptistic Pente-

[49] *Ibid.*, pp. 14-32.
[50] *Ibid.*, p. 8.

costal bodies'.[51] Mrs. McPherson felt that it was "highly essential that the children of the Lord be well grounded in the faith, and know the Bible teachings upon which they base their Christian experience." [52] In fact, she considered indoctrination so important that she prepared an entire volume, *The Foursquare Gospel,* to define in detail the twenty-two articles of her Declaration of Faith.

Mrs. McPherson emphasized the doctrine that related to the "Pentecostal experience" more than many of the others. That she devoted an entire volume to the subject of the Holy Spirit indicates the importance she attached to that facet of the Foursquare Gospel.

Any success which has followed my ministry is attributed to the motivating power of the Holy Spirit in my life.

The tremendous power and ever-increasing momentum which enabled the Foursquare Gospel in seven short years following its inception, to encircle the earth, is naught but the impelling force of the Blessed Holy Spirit Baptism.[53]

GROUP COMMUNICATIONS

The Foursquare Church has maintained excellent contact with its membership. Soon after starting her evangelistic efforts in 1917, Mrs. McPherson began publishing a monthly paper entitled the *Bridal Call.* A weekly newspaper, the *Crusader,* made its appearance not long after the completion of Angelus Temple. These two remained the official organs of the church until shortly after the founder's death, when they were combined into an improved monthly called the *Foursquare Magazine.*[54] Mrs. McPherson also pioneered religious broadcasting. During her revivals, while radio was relatively new, she preached over a number of stations and was so impressed with the potential of this medium that she took steps to establish a station in connection with Angelus Temple.[55] The station, KFSG, was the third to be

[51] Aimee Semple McPherson, *Declaration of Faith* (Los Angeles: International Church of the Foursquare Gospel), pp. 7-30.

[52] McPherson, *Foursquare Gospel,* p. 133.

[53] Aimee Semple McPherson, *The Holy Spirit* (Los Angeles: Challpin Publishing Co., 1931), p. 11.

[54] "The Church of the Foursquare Gospel," *Foursquare Magazine,* XXVII (May, 1954), p. 17.

[55] McPherson, *This is That,* pp. 403, 463, 568.

commissioned in Los Angeles and the first church-owned station in America; it broadcasts religious programs exclusively.

EDUCATIONAL AND MISSIONARY PROGRAMS

The training program for the local churches is under the supervision of the international director of youth and Christian education and subordinate area officers, district directors. This department directs both the Sunday school and youth programs.[56] Institutional training is centered in one school that gives only religious instruction. The Evangelistic and Missionary Training Institute established in connection with Angelus Temple in February, 1923, was first designed primarily for the laity, but after a few years of operation the Bible institute type program was inaugurated. The name was changed in 1926 to Lighthouse of International Foursquare Evangelism, generally shortened to L. I. F. E. Bible College.[57] The school has a unique way of maintaining the interest and support of its constituency. All graduates who enter the ministry are ordained, and all ordained ministers who are not graduates of the school are made honorary alumni. Thus the alumni association, which is headed by the president of the church, has an automatic dues paying membership that includes all the active clergy.[58]

The missionary program of the church is supervised by a director of foreign missions, who works under a missionary cabinet. It is financed by three monthly offerings from the local congregations. The youth bands contribute on the first Sunday of the month, the Sunday schools on the second, and the churches on the third.[59]

The crisis that comes inevitably to an organization built completely around one individual confronted the Foursquare Church on September 27, 1944, when Mrs. McPherson died. *Life* graphically featured her funeral as one of the most

---

[56] *Foursquare By-Laws*, 1952, pp. 33, 82-87.

[57] McPherson, *This is That*, pp. 567-568; "The Church of the Foursquare Gospel," *Foursquare Magazine*, XXVII, pp. 17, 33.

[58] *Foursquare By-Laws*, 1952, pp. 79-81.

[59] *Ibid.*, pp. 33-35, 66.

spectacular ever to be conducted in the Los Angeles area.[60] She had, it would seem, retained the loyalty of her group in spite of her much criticized behavior. Rolf K. McPherson, son of the founder, immediately took up the mantle of his mother. Having grown up with the church and been its vice-president for some time past, he was well acquainted with its affairs. According to the magazine of the church,

Dr. Rolf K. McPherson has proven to be a leader with foresight, and one who has exhibited particularly good judgment in executive matters. His wisdom in forming a cabinet of capable and consecrated men, and in appointing trained and loyal co-workers to positions of trust, is paying off in material and spiritual accomplishments.[61]

Statistical information indicates that the passing of the founder has not retarded advancement.

Some five hundred and fifty branch churches grace key cities and rural communities across America and Canada, and more than two hundred and sixty mission stations are scattered throughout foreign lands. Within five years after her death (statistics as of December 31, 1949), one hundred and forty new churches were established; two hundred and fourteen properties in new cities or locations were acquired; a net valuation, including equipment, of $8,458,806.80 was realized; and annual missionary offerings jumped from $155,-300.37 to $251,415.13.... It is well to note that, in the year 1949 alone, 26,842 persons confessed Christ as their Saviour at the altars of Angelus Temple, its branch churches and foreign mission stations. This was an increase of 1,816 over the previous year and an increase of 6,392 over the 1947 figure.[62]

A recent report, listing 697 churches and 79,012 members, indicates continued growth.[63]

One of the district superintendents said in memorial at the founder's funeral, "We have lighted our torches from yours and by the grace of God we will carry on faithfully." [64] That statement may have been prophetic, for it appears that the McPherson tradition will be perpetuated.

---

[60] *Life*, XVII (October 20, 1944), pp. 85-89.
[61] "The Church of the Foursquare Gospel," *Foursquare Magazine*, XXVII, p. 36.
[62] Aimee Semple McPherson, *The Story of My Life*, In Memoriam (Los Angeles: Echo Park Evangelistic Association, 1951), pp. 236-237.
[63] Landis, *Yearbook of American Churches*, 1960, p. 56.
[64] Bach, *They Have Found a Faith*, p. 87.

THE OPEN BIBLE STANDARD CHURCH

The Open Bible Standard Church can be said to have evolved from two local congregations, one located in Des Moines, Iowa, the other, in Eugene, Oregon. Neither of these churches had any thought of establishing a new religious body when it was founded.

DEVELOPMENT OF DES MOINES PENTECOSTAL WORK

In 1926 a few persons who had embraced Pentecostal theology began meeting for worship and fellowship in an old abandoned fire station in Des Moines, Iowa.[65] This was the beginning of the first established Pentecostal church in that city.

The cause of Pentecost in Des Moines was greatly helped in January, 1927, by a meeting conducted by Aimee Semple McPherson. One account of the revival reported that she "preached to 3,000 souls yesterday, turned away a thousand, and made thirty-eight converts.... Hoyt Sherman Place proved entirely inadequate to shelter the thousands who crowded to see Mrs. McPherson." [66]

Having benefited by the meeting, the local group rented a more commodious building at 507 E. Grand and there on February 27, 1927, formally organized as the Des Moines Gospel Tabernacle. In a very few months the services of the new church were so well attended that a move was made to still larger quarters. Near the end of 1927 the group decided to affiliate with the newly chartered International Church of the Foursquare Gospel. At the same time the name of the local church was changed to Foursquare Gospel Lighthouse.[67]

Mrs. McPherson returned to Des Moines in March, 1928, for a second revival. This time services were held in the Coliseum, and reports indicated that the campaign was a great success. The Foursquare Gospel Lighthouse soon

[65] Gotfred S. Bruland, "The Origin and Development of the Open Bible Church in Iowa" (unpublished M. A. thesis, Drake University, Des Moines, Iowa, 1945), p. 1.

[66] "Aimee Speaks to 3,000 and Converts 38," *Des Moines Register*, January 29, 1927, p. 1.

[67] Bruland, "Origin of Open Bible Church in Iowa," pp. 4-5.

moved its quarters to the former Grace Methodist Church. A few weeks later a second church, seating 1,500, was being constructed on Locust street. A segment of the Foursquare Gospel Lighthouse congregation, having returned to the old Fifth and Grand street location to form a third church, had engaged the Rev. J. R. Richey to come from California to be their pastor.[68]

Richey distinguished himself as an able organizer and preacher. Within a few years he had developed his Des Moines congregation into a thriving church and, was able with the help of several other ministers, to reach out and establish Pentecostal churches in a number of surrounding cities. He was also responsible for starting a Bible institute in 1930. The young ministers who attended the school assisted Richey, both during their training and after their graduation, in founding Foursquare churches throughout the region.[69]

OPEN BIBLE EVANGELISTIC ASSOCIATION

At a meeting in 1932 the Iowa and Minnesota Division of the Foursquare Church, formed largely by the efforts of Richey, voted to withdraw from the International Church of the Foursquare Gospel. This action was taken because of unhappiness resulting from certain practices within the Foursquare fellowship.[70]

The same meeting which separated from the Foursquare communion voted to reorganize and incorporate under the laws of Iowa as the Open Bible Evangelistic Association.[71] The new organization had held its first convention in October, 1932. All the affiliating clergymen were ordained into the ministry of the Open Bible Evangelistic Association. Forty-six were included in the ceremony, two in absentia.[72]

---

[68] "Aimee's Church Plans Two New Missions," Des Moines *Register*, April 3, 1928, p. 5. "Aimee's Group Plans Church on East Side," Des Moines *Register*, April 25, 1928, p. 1.

[69] Open Bible Institute, *Fourteenth Annual Catalog* (Des Moines: Open Bible Institute, [1944]), p. 3.

[70] "Action Result of Publicity, Richey says," Des Moines *Tribune*, August 31, 1932, p. 1; Bruland, "Origin of Open Bible Church in Iowa," pp. 8-9.

[71] "Action the Result of Publicity," Des Moines *Tribune*, August 31, 1932, p. 1.

[72] "Convention Resume," *Open Bible Messenger*, I (November, 1932), p. 7.

In May, 1934, a map printed in the *Open Bible Messenger*, official organ of the Association, showed thirty churches scattered throughout Iowa, six of them in the city of Des Moines.

BIBLE STANDARD CHURCH, EUGENE, OREGON

In 1935 the Bible Standard Church with headquarters in Eugene, Oregon, amalgamated with the Open Bible. The history of this West Coast group went back to 1914, when Fred Hornshuh and Pat Hegan had held a tent revival in Eugene. At the conclusion of the meeting the converts had united to form a Pentecostal church that eventually became known as the Lighthouse Temple.[73] The church at first was affiliated with the Apostolic Faith Mission, Portland, Oregon. This relationship was finally strained, however, because Hornshuh and Hegan objected to a requirement that remarried divorcees separate before being admitted to church membership, and to the belief that the Apostolic Faith Mission was the only true church, a concept that prevented association or co-operation with other Pentecostal bodies. When the Apostolic Faith would not give any consideration to the appeals of Hornshuh and Hegan for a more moderate view of these matters; the Lighthouse Temple withdrew in 1919 and organized the Bible Standard Church.[74]

Hornshuh, who was elected moderator of the new group, began publishing the *Bible Standard Magazine* soon after assuming his executive post. This four-page periodical, printed in newspaper format, was accepted as the official organ of the church. In 1925 Hornshuh also founded the Bible Standard Training School in connection with the program of Lighthouse Temple. This was the only school ever sponsored by the Bible Standard Church.[75]

The group undoubtedly grew a good deal between the

[73] "Bible Standard Origin Told at Temple Birthday Celebration," *Open Bible Standard Messenger*, XVII (March, 1936), p. 6; "Lighthouse Temple," Eugene *Register Guard*, March 7, 1936.

[74] Statement by Fred Hornshuh, Portland, Oregon, August 25, 1956, personal interview. The Open Bible Standard Church's *Minister's Manual* (Des Moines: Open Bible Standard Churches, 1949), p. 2, states that the group organized in 1917.

[75] Hornshuh, personal interview.

time of its founding and the merging with the Open Bible. One newspaper account stated that "from this central church has sprung a large number of affiliated churches both in the United States and in foreign countries. Several missionaries are supported by the conference." [76]

OPEN BIBLE STANDARD CHURCH FORMED

It is difficult to determine when negotiations to unite the Open Bible and Bible Standard churches first started. They must have been well advanced by the time of the third annual convention of the Open Bible, held May 26 to June 2, 1935, for a delegation from the Bible Standard attended this convention, and a report of the meeting stated that "inasmuch as plans were already under way for union between the Bible Standard Conference and our own Association, it was deemed expedient to table further plans until the outcome might be known." [77] The convention voted unanimously to unite with the west-coast group and to send a deputation headed by Richey to the July conference in Eugene, Oregon, to complete the merger. [78]

The union was consummated in Eugene on May 25, 1935. Harry R. R. Neat wired the Des Moines office that the "Bible Standard Conference unanimously voted to unite with the Open Bible Evangelistic Association, Inc. Great enthusiasm for determined effort in spreading the gospel over land and sea, standing shoulder to shoulder together in extending the borders of the kingdom." [79] The following is the formal resolution that merged the two groups:

BE IT RESOLVED THAT:

Whereas the Bible Standard, Incorporated, and the Open Bible Evangelistic Association, Incorporated, have agreed to work together in a common bond of fellowship and be known from henceforth on, as one and the same organization;

1. That the name of the organization be OPEN BIBLE

[76] "Lighthouse Temple," Eugene *Register Guard*, March 7, 1936.

[77] "Convention Echoes," *Open Bible Messenger*, III (July, 1935), p. 9.

[78] "Bible Standard—Open Bible Unite," *Open Bible Messenger*, III (August, 1935), p. 3.

[79] Cited in "Bible Standard—Open Bible Unite," *Open Bible Messenger*, III (August, 1935), p. 3.

STANDARD EVANGELISTIC ASSOCIATION, INCORPOR-
ATED:

2. Since the Articles of Faith and the Constitution and By-Laws
of the Open Bible Evangelistic Association, Incorporated, are acceptable to both organizations, that they shall operate under the
same, with provision for amendment;

3. That the principal place of business of the Open Bible Standard
Evangelistic Association, Incorporated, shall be at Des Moines,
Iowa;

4. That the new corporate name be recorded at the Polk County
Recorder's office in Des Moines, Iowa;

5. That the Association be governed by a representative group
from both organizations, known hereafter as the Board of Directors
of the Open Bible Standard Evangelistic Association, Incorporated.[80]

The new body quickly developed a constitutional framework that would provide adequate services and administration for its constituency. An alteration of the charter
was made in 1946, when the name of the group was changed
to Open Bible Standard Churches, Inc.[81]

POLITY OF THE CHURCH

A modified congregational policy is the organizational
basis of the new group. The local churches being considered
sovereign units operate on the congregational principle,
while the national organization is formed on a basis that
places greater empahsis on central government. For purposes
of administration the group is divided into three area units
—district, division, and general conference.

The smallest unit is the district which is composed of
all the local churches within a prescribed geographical area
and supervised by a district superintendent. The districts in
turn are organized into divisions. Only two were formed at
the time of the merger in 1935, but three others have been
added in the intervening years. The divisional program is
under the direction of a divisional council consisting of
the divisional officers—divisional superintendent, district
superintendent, Bible school president or dean, young
people's representative, divisional Sunday school representa-

---

[80] "Official Minutes" (Manuscript minute book of the Open Bible Evangelistic
Association, Des Moines, Iowa), p. 17.

[81] Open Bible Standard Churches, *Minister's Manual* (Des Moines: Open Bible
Standard Churches, 1949), p. 3.

tive. The officers are responsible for directing and promoting their phases of divisional work in co-operation with the appropriate general officers.[82]

The central administrative unit is the General Conference. The voting constituency of this body includes all the ordained and licensed ministers of the church and one lay delegate from each district. The general board of directors, composed of the general and executive officers, the divisional and district superintendents, and a representative of each recognized Bible school, manages the business of the central church office. An executive committee made up of the general officers and two other directors supervise the routine detail of the body under the direction of this general directorate. The executive committee also serves as trustees for the group. Both the general officers—general chairman, vice chairman, secretary, treasurer, missionary secretary, and general field superintendent—and the executive officers—the national president of the youth organization and the national Sunday school superintendent—are elected by the board of directors.[83]

DOCTRINAL POSITION

Doctrinally, the Open Bible Standard Church can be classified as being arminian, trinitarian, and "fundamental." The basis of its position is the "Articles of Faith of the Open Bible Standard Churches," a statement containing nineteen articles and embodying essentially the same theology as that of the other baptistic Pentecostal groups.[84]

MISSIONARY PROGRAM

As might be expected, great importance is placed on missionary enterprise. The missionary secretary recently wrote that "Missions have always been the strongest cohesive single element of our group.[85] A detailed missionary policy that advocates the indigenous principle is carefully

---

[82] *Minister's Manual*, 1957, pp. 5, 11-13.
[83] *Ibid.*, pp. 4-5, 7-11.
[84] *Ibid.*, pp. 31-36.
[85] O. Ralph Isbill, Des Moines, Iowa, to Klaude Kendrick, Springfield, Missouri, July 2, 1957, L. S., 2 p.

outlined in the *Minister's Manual.*[86] Open Bible missionaries
are working in Africa, Alaska, Cuba, India, Japan, Jamaica,
Philippine Islands and South America. A recent report indicated that the missions force had grown from twenty-
two in 1947 to fifty in 1957.[87]

EDUCATION PROGRAM

The organization also has a growing Christian education
department. As was noted above, Richey established a Bible
school in 1930 in connection with his work in Des Moines.
Until the separation of the group from the Foursquare
church, this school was operated as a subsidiary of L.I.F.E.
in Los Angeles; afterwards it functioned as the Open
Bible Institute. In its early years the school offered only
night classes and served primarily lay members of the Des
Moines churches. By 1934 sufficient demand was evident
to justify day courses that featured ministerial training.
Since that time a typical Bible institute program has been
developed. Though the school began in a local church, it
was provided new quarters by a building program completed in the late 1930's.[88] The following Bible Institutes
have developed since the beginning of Open Bible Institute and pattern after its program: Bible Standard Institute,
Eugene, Oregon; California Open Bible Institute, Pasadena,
California; Dayton Bible Institute, Dayton, Ohio; and St.
Petersburg Bible Institute, St. Petersburg, Florida.[89]

PUBLICATIONS

The first convention of the Open Bible in October, 1932,
authorized the publishing of an official organ, and the first
number of the *Open Bible Messenger,* a monthly publication, appeared the next month.[90] When the Bible Standard
and Open Bible united, the periodical was called *Open
Bible Standard Messenger.* In July, 1944, the name became

[86] *Minister's Manual,* 1957, pp. 36-43.
[87] "General Chairman's Report, Open Bible Standard General Conference, July
17-21, 1957" (a duplicated report prepared by the general chairman of the
Open Bible), p. 2.
[88] Bruland, "Origin of Open Bible Church of Iowa," pp. 107-120.
[89] *Minister's Manual,* 1957, p. 52.
[90] "Dedications," *Open Bible Messenger,* I (November, 1932), p. 3.

Message of the Open Bible.[91] Besides this monthly organ, a bi-monthly missionary magazine, *World Vision*, a quarterly youth periodical, and a line of Sunday school literature, are published at the Inspiration Press, a well equipped auxiliary established by the church in the late 1930's.[92]

YOUTH WORK

The youth organization of the Open Bible Standard is called "United Overcomers." The program for young people, administered by the national Overcomers president, is promoted by a monthly letter, *Highlights*, sent to all local Overcomer presidents, and by monthly district youth rallies and summer youth camps.[93]

Though one of the youngest Pentecostal bodies, the Open Bible Standard has shown remarkable growth in the quarter of a century it has existed. A late report credits the group with 265 churches and 25,000 adult members.[94]

UNITED PENTECOSTAL CHURCH

The United Pentecostal Church differs from most other Pentecostal bodies in that it rejects the doctrine of the Trinity. This theological concept was introduced into Pentecostal ranks by Frank J. Ewart, who began preaching the doctrine in Los Angeles in 1914.[95] Ewart felt that this new truth, revealed to him some time previously, was a basic Biblical tenet. After an inward struggle he brought himself to part from the Trinitarian group and commence his "oneness" or "new light" ministry, as it was later called.

"ONENESS" DOCTRINE

The doctrinal tenet that developed as a consequence of this revelation to Ewart maintained that the Jehovah of the

---

[91] Bruland, "Origin of Open Bible Church in Iowa," pp. 20-36, 107-120.

[92] *Minister's Manual*, 1957, p. 52; Mrs. Dolores Rainey, Des Moines, Iowa, to Klaude Kendrick, Austin, Texas, July 2, 1957, L. S., 1 p. Mrs. Rainey was editor of the *Message* at the time of this communication.

[93] W. Rollie Clark, Eugene, Oregon, to Klaude Kendrick, Springfield, Missouri, July 22, 1957, L. S., 2 p. Clark was national youth president at the time of this communication.

[94] Landis, *Yearbook of American Churches*, 1960, pp. 86-87.

[95] Frank J. Ewart, *The Phenomenon of Pentecost, A History of the Latter Rain* (St. Louis: Pentecostal Publishing House, 1947), p. 51.

Old Testament, Jesus Christ, and the Holy Spirit were all manifestations of the one true God.

The Godhead is plainly taught in the creation of man who was made in the image and likeness of God. Man is a threefold being—body, soul, and spirit—but only one person; therefore, it is understood and clearly seen that God is a threefold being—Father, Son, and Holy Spirit—but only ONE person, and that one is the Holy One, Jesus Christ our Lord. He is not the second person, but is the First and Last, the Alpha and Omega, the Beginning and the End, and there is none beside Him.[96]

The emphasis placed on Christ in this concept results in the attachment of unusual importance to the name of Jesus. This is especially noticeable in the baptismal formula. Believers are baptized in the "name of Jesus" rather than of the "Father, Son, and Holy Ghost." [97] The prominence given to this type of water baptism is indicated by the fact that Ewart upon starting his "oneness" ministry immediately began rebaptizing by the new formula all persons who accepted his teachings.[98]

During the years immediately following 1914, the new message caused considerable confusion in Pentecostal ranks. A wave of conversions to the "name of Jesus" was made among Full Gospel believers. In fact, several leaders of the Pentecostal movement were rebaptized, though most very shortly returned to a belief in the Trinity.[99] The matter caused so much confusion and misunderstanding that the Assemblies of God in 1916 drafted for the first time a doctrinal statement clearly enunciating the Trinitarian position.

EARLY "ONENESS" ORANIZATIONS

When it became apparent that the Assemblies of God would not accept the "new light" many of the "oneness" proponents in the Pentecostal movement united to form the Pentecostal Assemblies of the World with headquarters in Indianapolis, Indiana.[100] This body at first was an inter-

---

[96] Oscar Vouga, *Our Gospel Message* (St. Louis: Pentecostal Publishing House, [n.d.]), p. 29.
[97] Ibid., pp. 15-16.
[98] Ewart, Phenomenon of Pentecost, p. 51.
[99] Ibid., pp. 54-55.
[100] Clark, Small Sects in America, p. 117.

racial group, but in 1924 the white clergymen withdrew and formed the Pentecostal Ministerial Association, an organization exercising authority only over its ministerial members and not over churches. This body soon developed into the Pentecostal Church, Inc., a white "oneness" church group.[101]

MERGERS FORM UNITED PENTECOSTAL CHURCH

In 1931 a number of small groups not associated with either the Assemblies of God or the Pentecostal Church, Inc., united to form the Pentecostal Assemblies of Jesus Christ. In its annual conference in 1944 the Pentecostal Assemblies of Jesus Christ passed a resolution to approach the Pentecostal Church concerning a merger. The Pentecostal Church in its conference the same year took favorable action on the suggested union. Negotiations began at once and shortly an acceptable plan of amalgamation was approved. The merger was effected at a general conference of the two bodies called in 1945 at St. Louis. In 1946 a Canadian group of "Oneness" bodies (organized at New Brunswick in 1933) entered the new affiliation.[102] Though the new church was organized in accord with congregational polity with full recognition of local sovereignty, a strong central administration developed. The highest legislative authority was vested in an annual general conference, a representative body composed of all certified ministers and one delegate from each local congregation. The general officers—general superintendent, two assistant general superintendents, general secretary-treasurer, foreign missionary secretary, home missionary secretary, and editor—and one presbyter from each district were designated as the General Board that functioned as the executive committee of the organization. The administration of the activities of the church were placed under the direction of general boards—foreign missionary board, board of Christian education, and board of

---

[101] Statement by Arthur T. Morgan and Stanley W. Chambers, St. Louis, Mo., 1955, personal interview. At the time of the interview Morgan was general superintendent and Chamber's general secretary-treasurer of the United Pentecostal Church.

[102] Morgan and Chambers, personal interview; Wynn T. Stairs, St. Louis, Mo., to Klaude Kendrick, L. S., July 18, 1957, 2 p. Stairs was the foreign missions secretary of the United Pentecostal Church.

publication—and were to be administered by the foreign missionary, home missionary, editorial, young people's and Sunday school departments.[103]

PUBLICATION, YOUTH, AND TRAINING ACTIVITIES

A Pentecostal Publishing House was established in connection with central headquarters in St. Louis. The principal publication is the monthly official voice of the group, the *Pentecostal Herald.*[104]

A national organization, the Pentecostal Conquerors, directs youth activities. The general young people's committee, comprised of the two youth officers and all district youth presidents, is the main policy body. The youth program is channeled to the local groups through district organizations.[105]

The United Pentecostal Church has been slow in developing educational facilities. It presently endorses four small Bible schools, namely, the Apostolic Bible Institute, St. Paul, Minnesota; Pentecostal Bible Institute, Tupelo, Mississippi; Western Apostolic Bible College, Stockton, California; and Conquerors Bible College, Portland, Oregon. Total enrollment in all the schools is approximately 300 students.[106]

CHURCH DOCTRINE AND PRACTICES

Aside from the unitarian concept, the doctrinal position of the United Pentecostal Church differs little from that of the other Baptistic Pentecostal bodies, though its views on some social practices are comparatively extreme. For example, the Articles of Faith state that the church disapproves of indulgence by any of its people

in any activities which are not conducive to good Christianity and Godly living, such as theatres, dances, mixed bathing, women cutting their hair, make-up, any apparel that immodestly exposes the body, all worldly sports and amusements, and unwholesome radio programs

---

[103] United Pentecostal Church, *Manual of the United Pentecostal Church,* 1955, (St. Louis: Pentecostal Publishing House, 1955), pp. 25-34, 43-70.

[104] Morgan and Chambers, personal interview.

[105] *Manual,* 1955, pp. 62-66.

[106] Morgan and Chambers, personal interview; S. W. Chambers, St. Louis, Mo., to Klaude Kendrick, Springfield, Mo., April 1, 1960, L. S., 2 p.

and music. Furthermore, because of the display of all of these evils on television, we disapprove of any of our people having television sets in their homes.[107]

The matter of cutting hair is considered so important that the central office distributed a special booklet on the subject giving fifteen reasons why women should have long hair.[108]

Despite its youth, the United Pentecostal Church has grown to be the largest "oneness" Pentecostal group. A recent survey reported 1,595 churches with 160,000 members.[109]

---

[107] *Manual*, 1955, p. 21.

[108] Murray E. Burr, *The Hair Question* (St. Louis: Home Missionary Department, United Pentecostal Church, [n.d.]), pp. 1-16.

[109] Landis, *Yearbook of American Churches*, 1960, p. 88.

IX

Pentecostal Wesleyan Perfectionist Groups

WHILE THE larger portion of the Pentecostal movement is organized into Baptistic groups, another segment is distinctive for holding the doctrine of Wesleyan perfectionism. This minority comes from the Holiness sects, of which "no less than twenty-five ... [arose] in various parts of the United States from 1893 to 1907." [1] After 1900 a number of holiness bodies accepted the Pentecostal experience and continued their development as Pentecostal organizations. This chapter will survey the principal Pentecostal perfectionist groups.

PENTECOSTAL HOLINESS CHURCH

The Pentecostal Holiness Church, as it is today, resulted from a merger in 1911 of the Fire-Baptized Holiness Church and the Pentecostal Holiness Church.

FIRE-BAPTIZED HOLINESS CHURCH

The Fire-Baptized Holiness Church had been formed as a consequence of the influence of the National Association for the Promotion of Holiness organized primarily through the efforts of John S. Inskip in the 1880's. The Iowa Holiness Association, one of the larger area entities of the National Association, played the leading role in the establishment of the new group. Through contact with it Benjamin Hardin Irwin, a moderately successful lawyer, became an active Holiness minister, and it was Irwin who founded the Fire-Baptized sect. He learned from the writings of John Fletcher of a religious experience beyond

---

[1] Gaddis, "Perfectionism in America," p. 458.

salvation and sanctification known as the "baptism of fire,"
an experience supposed to have been quite common among
early Methodists. Being deeply impressed by his discovery,
Irwin eventually sought and claimed to have received such
a "baptism of fire." He immediately began preaching his
new doctrine and found a receptive hearing among the
devoutly religious people of the Holiness associations. A
"baptism of fire" movement soon swept over Iowa,
Nebraska, Kansas, Oklahoma, Texas, North and South
Carolina, Georgia, and Florida.[2]

Irwin probably had no intention of starting a new group,
yet it was inevitable that one would result from his teaching.
Association leaders who supported traditional holiness
theology refused to embrace the new experience, branded
it as the "Third Blessing Heresy," and vigorously opposed
it as a "doctrine of demons." This made the followers of
Irwin so uncomfortable that steps were taken to provide
other facilities for their worship. Accordingly, the first local
bodies of what would become the Fire-Baptized Holiness
Churches were formed in 1895. During the next three years
groups were established in most of the states where the
new teaching had spread. By 1898 state associations were
functioning in nine states, and steps were being taken to
organize four other states and two Canadian provinces. At a
conference called by Irwin at Anderson, South Carolina,
July 28-August 8, 1898, representatives of all the state associations agreed to a central organization, the Fire-Baptized
Holiness Association.

The new church formulated a discipline that was episcopal in character, democratic processes being noticeably
absent. Irwin was accepted as general overseer rather because of his prestige than by formal election. He continued
to be the leading spirit of the body only until 1900, when
he fell into disrepute and dropped out, turning his paper,
Live Coals of Fire, over to his assistant, the Rev. Joseph
H. King. At a specially called convention in Olmitz, Iowa,
July 1, 1900, King was elected to succeed Irwin as general

[2] Campbell, *Pentecostal Holiness Church*, pp. 193-196.

overseer, a position he retained until the body was merged with the Pentecostal Holiness Church.[3]

Irwin's defection virtually paralyzed the Fire-Baptized Church and during the next several years it underwent a crisis. "A short time after the new general overseer had come into office every state organization in the West had disappeared and there remained only Georgia and North Carolina left intact on the Eastern seaboard. The work in Canada also disappeared." [4] According to King's memoirs many of his former friends then became his "bitter enemies," and "throughout the church there was great discouragement, and many backslid as a result of it." [5]

In spite of the temporary setback, the organization was probably benefited by the new arrangement. King voluntarily inaugurated changes which tended to democratize the church and to limit the authority of the general overseer. He also corrected some religious extravagances and erroneous teachings that had disturbed the group during Irwin's administration. This action laid a sound foundation for subsequent growth.[6] Another significant alteration voted by the convention in 1902 was the changing of the name of the organization to Fire-Baptized Holiness Church.[7]

It was shortly after the Azusa Street revival in 1906 that the Fire-Baptized Holiness Church became Pentecostal. King first heard of the Los Angeles meeting through A. H. Argue [8] while attending a camp meeting in Canada. He found upon studying the scant literature of the new movement that the tenets of the Pentecostals were very similar to those of his own group. Both taught that the baptism in the Holy Spirit occurred after the experience of sanctification, the only difference being in what they regarded as evidence of the experience—the Pentecostals believed that it was "tongues", the Fire-Baptized folk, physical demon-

---

[3] King & King, *Yet Speaketh*, pp. 85-104.
[4] Campbell, *Pentecostal Holiness Church*, p. 205.
[5] King & King, *Yet Speaketh*, p. 104.
[6] Campbell, *Pentecostal Holiness Church*, pp. 202-204.
[7] Pentecostal Holiness Church, *Discipline of the Pentecostal Holiness Church*, 1949 (Franklin Springs, Georgia: Pentecostal Holiness Church, 1949), p. 6.
[8] See p. 69.

stration. During the last week of 1906 G. B. Cashwell, a
Holiness Church minister from Dunn, North Carolina, returned to the South after receiving the Pentecostal experience in the Azusa revival. In his revivals many Holiness
Fire-Baptized people, including King, accepted the Pentecostal message and "tongues" experience. The general
convention that met in 1907 at Anderson, South Carolina,
revised the doctrines of the church to include the newly
accepted tenet.[9]

EARLY DEVELOPMENT OF THE PENTECOSTAL HOLINESS CHURCH

Like the Fire-Baptized Holiness Church, the Pentecostal
Holiness Church began in the Holiness movement. The
exact time of formal organization seems uncertain. The
Discipline states that the church came into being at Goldsboro, North Carolina, in 1898.[10] Campbell, on the other
hand, gives good evidence to indicate that it was established
in 1900 at Fayetteville, North Carolina, through the influence of A. B. Crumpler, who had organized a state
Holiness association at Magnolia, North Carolina, in 1897.
Goldsboro, North Carolina, where Crumpler was pastor of
the largest local church of the group, became headquarters
for the organization.[11]

The second convention, held in Magnolia, North Carolina,
in 1901, voted to change the name from Pentecostal Holiness to Holiness Church. The *Discipline* states that "the
word 'Pentecostal' was eliminated from the name due to
the fact that none of them spoke in tongues as the Spirit
gave utterance as the disciples on the day of Pentecost." [12]
This would seem to indicate that the group did not wish
to be mistaken for a "tongues" body in the early days of
the modern Pentecostal revival. As was true of the Fire-
Baptized people, it was Cashwell's revival in Dunn, North
Carolina, starting on December 31, 1906, that began the
conversion of Crumpler's group to the Pentecostal position.
During Cashwell's meeting "scores of the preachers of the

---

[9] King & King, *Yet Speaketh*, pp. 112-124.
[10] *Discipline*, 1949, p. 6.
[11] Campbell, *Pentecostal Holiness Church*, pp. 221-224.
[12] *Discipline*, 1949, p. 6.

Holiness Church went down to the altar ... and it was not long until they were rejoicing in the new found [Pentecostal] experience." [18] From this revival ministers took the Pentecostal message throughout the group.

GROUP ACCEPTS PENTECOSTAL EXPERIENCE

The "new" experience was the main topic at the next annual convention, but the meeting adjourned without taking any official action on the matter. Crumpler, president of the body, became very outspoken against the innovation during the year that followed. When the Pentecostal faction continued to grow, he with several other members withdrew from the group in 1908. After this defection the annual convention proceeded to revise the *Discipline* to harmonize with the Pentecostal position.[14] The next annual convention of 1909 voted to resume the original name, the Pentecostal Holiness Church.[15]

MERGERS FORM PRESENT DAY GROUP

Various leaders of the Holiness movement began in the early 1900's to favor consolidation among the several Holiness organizations to eliminate the confusion and unwholesome competition inevitably resulting from their multiplicity. No kind of amalgamation between the Fire-Baptized Holiness Church and Pentecostal Holiness Churches was possible prior to 1906, however, because the Pentecostal Holiness group branded the "baptism of fire" of the other body as the "third blessing heresy." When both groups accepted the Pentecostal "baptism of the Holy Spirit" as a religious experience to be received subsequent to sanctification, the third experience difficulty was removed, and steps toward uniting commenced in 1908. In a special called combined convention at Falcon, North Carolina, in January, 1911, the merger was approved.[16]

Both of the bodies were quite small at the time of the consolidation. At the combined convention in 1911 the

---

[18] Campbell, *Pentecostal Holiness Church*, p. 241.
[14] *Ibid.*, pp. 224-247.
[15] *Ibid.*, p. 251. *Discipline*, 1949, p. 6, states this action took place on the year before at Dunn, North Carolina.
[16] *Discipline*, 1949, p. 7.

Fire-Baptized Holiness Church was represented by only
thirty-two delegates, and the Pentecostal Holiness Church
had fewer still. In fact, only six annual state conventions
were functioning in 1911.[17] From this time, however, the
new organization developed much more rapidly.

In 1915 the Tabernacle Presbyterian Church merged with
the group. This small body had come into being when,
after Holiness became an issue in the Carolina-Georgia area,
certain ministers who accepted the experience of sanctification withdrew from the Presbyterian communion, which
rejected Wesleyan perfectionism, and organized a Holiness
group called the Tabernacle Presbyterian Church. Their
later acceptance of the Pentecostal experience prepared the
way for a merger with the Pentecostal Holiness Church.[18]

POLITY OF GROUP

The Pentecostal Holiness Church more than any other
Pentecostal body patterns its polity after the episcopal type.
This is readily understood when one remembers that substantial roots go back to the Methodist Church. In keeping
with the episcopal organization, the group is divided into
conferences—general, annual, missionary, and district—to
facilitate administration.

The General Conference is a representative body of the
entire organization. This conference met biennially until
1915, when the convention provided for quadrennial sessions.[19] The activities of the General Conference are directed
by the General Board of Administration, an executive committee created in 1917 to meet annually. This board was
enlarged as its responsibilities increased until its constituency included the officers of the General Conference, the
superintendent of each annual conference and four members
at large (two to be laymen) elected by the General Conference. The General Board elects from its membership
five sub-boards—Foreign Missions, Home Missions, Edua-
tion, Publication, and Orphanage—composed of five mem-

---

[17] Campbell, *Pentecostal Holiness Church*, pp. 257-259.

[18] *Discipline*, 1949, p. 7.

[19] Campbell, *Pentecostal Holiness Church*, p. 259.

bers each to supervise these various functions of the church.[20]

The General Conference is a representative body composed of the General Board of Administration, the superintendents of the annual conferences, at least one clerical delegate from each annual conference (but not more than one for every twenty-five ministers) and at least one lay delegate from each annual conference (but never more than the clerical representation). All of the delegates are elected by their respective annual conferences.[21]

A general superintendent with the honorary title of Bishop, four assistant general superintendents, a general secretary, and a general treasurer serve the General Conference as officers.[22]

The annual conference is also a representative body composed of a superintendent, the ordained and licensed ministers within the area, and at least one lay delegate (but not more than one for every fifty members) from each local church within the area. This conference has two important functions. Both the ministers and churches are subject to its prerogative of assigning pastorates, though local congregations can express their desires for certain pastors. It also examines and approves all candidates for the ministry. The annual conference is administered by three officers—a superintendent, assistant superintendent, and secretary-treasurer. These officials with two additional elected members serve as the official board of the conference.[23]

Similar in character to the annual conference is the missionary conference. The principal distinction is that the former administers geographical areas within the United States, while mission fields outside continental United States constitute the areas of the latter.

The district or quarterly conference was a Methodist in-

---

[20] King & King, *Yet Speaketh*, p. 303; Pentecostal Holiness Church, *Discipline of the Pentecostal Holiness Church*, 1953 (Franklin Springs, Georgia: Board of Publication, Pentecostal Holiness Church, 1953), pp. 40-41; J. A. Synan, Hopewell, Va., to Klaude Kendrick, Springfield, Mo., May 11, 1960, L. S., 2 p.

[21] *Ibid.*, pp. 34-35.

[22] J. A. Synan to Klaude Kendrick, May 11, 1960.

[23] *Discipline*, 1949, pp. 31-33, 38, 39.

stitution introduced into the Pentecostal Holiness Church
by G. O. Gaines. While superintendent of the Georgia
Conference, he organized quarterly meetings in his area.
The results were so gratifying the General Conference
adopted the innovation in 1917.[24] The district conference
is a geographical entity of the annual conference and has
meetings every three months. Its constituency is comprised
of the superintendent of the annual conference, pastors and
their assistants, evangelists, mission workers, and delegates
(chosen on the same basis as that of the annual conference)
of churches within the district. The district conference supervises the work of the ministers and churches within its
area.[25]

DOCTRINAL POSITION OF THE CHURCH

The doctrinal position of the Pentecostal Holiness Church
is stated in the three opening sections of the *Discipline*.
The first contains the church's creed and covenant. The
second, entitled "Articles of Faith," and dealing with the
twelve basic doctrines of the church, states no tenet, other
than the perfectionist view of sanctification, that is not held
by other Pentecostal bodies. The third, termed "Doctrinal
Exegesis," gives short expositions on all the main beliefs of
the group.[26] The following brief and comprehensive doctrinal statement was published in a recent issue of the
church's official organ:

The Pentecostal Holiness Church believes in Justification by faith
(The New Birth) as taught by Martin Luther. We believe in
Sanctification as preached by John Wesley. It might be pointed out
that we do not teach "absolute perfection" but that sanctification
is a progressive work of grace as well as an instantaneous second
work of grace. We believe in the baptism of the Holy Spirit as the
early Apostolic Church received and taught; and in divine healing
for the body as the privilege of Christians of all generations, but
also acknowledging and appreciating the great work of medical science
in behalf of suffering humanity.... The church definitely believes
in the Holy Trinity, in the apostles' creed, in the Communion of the
Saints, in the Great Commission, in eternal bliss for the finally
righteous and in eternal punishment in hell as the portion of the

---

[24] King & King, *Yet Speaketh*, pp. 303, 308.
[25] *Discipline*, 1953, pp. 33-34.
[26] *Ibid.*, pp. 9-27.

ultimate rejectors of the saving grace of our Lord Jesus Christ. And finally, we believe in the personal, pre-millennial second coming of our Lord.[27]

The Pentecostal Holiness Church holds a distinctive position concerning the ordinance of water baptism. Candidates for baptism have the right of choice between the various modes as practiced by the several evangelical denominations.[28] (All other Pentecostal bodies with this exception practice immersion.) Parents are allowed the option of requesting either dedication or baptism for children.

MISSIONS PROGRAM

Missionary activity, which has been prominent since the very inception of the group, is administered by the Board of Foreign Missions that directs the disbursement of all missionary funds, examines and approves all missionary candidates, and supervises all the missionary conferences. The early efforts, however, were made on an individual basis rather than as a formally supervised program of the church. A number of missionaries were evident in foreign fields as early as 1910 for Mr. & Mrs. A. G. Garr, a missionary couple, influenced Bishop King at that time to make a world tour and visit Pentecostal mission centers. During his two-year trip King encountered many Pentecostal missionaries.[29] By the beginning of its fifth decade of operation, the church had a corps of thirty-five missionaries and 403 national workers in Africa, Alaska, Argentina, China, Costa Rica, India, Jamaica, and Mexico.[30] This extensive operation is financed by allotting fifty per cent of all general church funds to missions.[31]

In contrast to the early organized foreign missionary program, home missions was left for many years primarily to the unsupervised evangelistic efforts of individuals and established local churches. The General Conference in 1941 established a home missions board which became a part of

[27] *Pentecostal Holiness Advocate*, XXXVI (January 29, 1953), p. 4.
[28] *Discipline*, 1953, p. 43.
[29] King & King, *Yet Speaketh*, p. 142.
[30] *Pentecostal Holiness Advocate*, XXXVII (June 18-25, 1953), p. 12.
[31] M. E. Parrish, Franklin Springs, Georgia, to Klaude Kendrick, July 19, 1957, L. S., 2 p.

the General Board of Administration in 1945. Since that time expansion in America has followed a planned program. The delay in providing a home missions policy may account in part for the slow growth of this early Pentecostal organization.[32]

BENEVOLENT ENTERPRISES

Though the Pentecostal Holiness Church has been associated with the establishment of several benevolent institutions, only two remain—the Falcon Orphanage, Falcon, North Carolina, and a home for the aged at Carmen, Oklahoma. The orphanage was long operated as a private corporation largely dependent upon the gifts of Pentecostal Holiness people for support. King relates that it was founded while he was Overseer of the Fire-Baptized Holiness Church as the result of a spontaneous and unpremeditated impulse that developed during the Falcon Camp Meeting in 1909. The Culbreth family became the leading spirits of the enterprise during the early years. In 1943 the home was turned over to the church, and since 1945 it has been administered by an orphanage board selected from the General Board of Administration. The home for the aged is a recent establishment of the Western section of the church.[33]

EDUCATIONAL PROGRAM

Several schools have served the organization through the years. The oldest was established by N. J. Holmes in the 1890's. Its early history is somewhat indefinite because Holmes was engaged in informal Bible training before actually founding a formal educational institution. The school underwent several changes of name, becoming the Holmes Bible College in 1946. It now offers undergraduate work in theology.[34]

In 1918, when property in Franklin Springs, Georgia, was

[32] Campbell, *Pentecostal Holiness Church*, p. 325.

[33] *Ibid.*, pp. 360-373; King & King, *Yet Speaketh*, pp. 138-141; Synan to Kendrick, May 11, 1960.

[34] *Pentecostal Holmes Advocate*, XXXVI (April 30, 1950), p. 7; N. J. Holmes and Wife, *Life Sketches & Sermons*, (Royston, Georgia: Press of the Pentecostal Holiness Church, 1920), p. 117; Campbell, *Pentecostal Holiness Church*, pp. 423-476.

purchased for a headquarters for the group, G. F. Taylor was designated to establish a school and publishing house on the site. Franklin Springs Institute, later named Emmanuel College, was opened in 1919 but developed slowly partly because the establishment of several other schools, all short-lived, channeled much needed support from Emmanuel. Fires on the campus added to the financial distress of the school. After 1933, however, support noticeably improved, and the college gradually developed into a very creditable institution of learning. After Taylor's administration, emphasis was placed on academic training. High school work was first offered, to be followed in 1937 by the introduction of a junior college department. The school intends eventually to expand this area to include a complete undergraduate program.[35]

In 1946 the Western Board of Education purchased property in Oklahoma City and established Southwestern Bible College, which offers both junior college work and undergraduate theology.[36]

A board of education formed in 1933 supervises the educational interests of the church, co-ordinating the efforts of all agencies concerned with training activities of the church.[37]

YOUTH WORK

A youth group, the Pentecostal Young People's Society (called since 1941 the Pentecostal Holiness Youth Society), was created by the General Conference in 1925.[38] The General Conference of 1945 provided for this organization to be directed by a general youth board. The program of the society is transmitted to the local church groups through the youth offices of the conferences, thus conforming to the general administrative pattern of the church.[39]

---

[35] Campbell, *Pentecostal Holiness Church*, pp. 477-501.

[36] *Pentecostal Holiness Advocate*, XXXVII (May 14, 1953), p. 36; J. A. Synan, Franklin Springs, Georgia, to Klaude Kendrick, August 6, 1957, L. S., 5 p.

[37] J. A. Synan to Klaude Kendrick, August 6, 1957.

[38] King & King, *Yet Speaketh*, p. 320.

[39] Campbell, *Pentecostal Holiness Church*, pp. 377-384.

SUNDAY SCHOOL PROGRAM

Although a Sunday school department was not formally organized until 1945, the Sunday schools have held a prominent place in the Pentecostal Holiness Church through the years. The services offered the local church schools have been greatly expanded since the program has come under the direction of a departmental agency of the General Board of Administration.[40]

PUBLICATIONS

A number of papers were published during the premerger period. Mention has already been made of *Live Coals of Fire*, which was edited by Irwin for the Fire-Baptized Holiness Church. King was given control of this periodical after Irwin's defection; the paper known after 1907 as the *Apostolic Evangel*, continued to be published intermittently until 1927. Crumpler edited for the early Pentecostal Holiness body the *Holiness Advocate*, but it was discontinued when he withdrew from the organization in 1908. In 1917 the General Conference authorized the publication of the *Pentecostal Holiness Advocate* as the official organ of the church.

A publishing house opened in 1919 in connection with the new headquarters at Franklin Springs came to produce all the group's Sunday school literature and periodicals, as well as a line of religious books. Construction of a new $350,000 plant and headquarters was begun in 1958.[41]

The growth of the Pentecostal Holiness Church has not been outstanding but has improved steadily through the years. A recent survey reported 1,203 churches, 1,077 ordained ministers, and a membership of 49,594 for the organization.[42]

THE CHURCH OF GOD

The Church of God of Cleveland, Tennessee, had an origin similar to that of the other Holiness bodies. The early constituents became dissatisfied with their convention-

[40] *Ibid.*, pp. 384-387.
[41] *Pentecostal Holiness Advocate*, XXXVII (July 2, 1953); *Pentecostal Evangel*, No. 2331 (January 11, 1959), p. 9.
[42] Landis, *Yearbook of American Churches*, 1960, p. 88.

al church connections and withdrew to establish a new group, one that later accepted the Pentecostal experience.

CHRISTIAN UNION FORMED

In 1884 Richard G. Spurling and his son Richard, Jr., became concerned over what they deemed laxity in their Baptist church and began to promote a reformation movement. Convinced after two years of crusading that reform was impossible, they decided to organize a new group on strictly Bible principles, hoping "to restore primitive Christianity and bring about a union of all denominations."[43] Accordingly, a conference of all "Christians ... that are desirous to be free from all men-made [sic] creeds and traditions"[44] was called at Barney Creek Meeting House, Monroe County, Tennessee, on August 19, 1886. When Spurling challenged the conference to take the New Testament as the only rule of faith and practice and to "sit together as the Church of God to transact business, eight persons responded to his appeal and organized as the Christian Union."[45] This was the humble beginning of the Church of God.

When the senior Spurling died soon afterwards, his son succeeded to the leadership of the group. Continuing to preach at Barney Creek Church the younger Spurling also accepted appointments to speak throughout the area, but his early efforts seem to have attracted little attention.[46] In the 1890's, however, the endeavors of the Christian Union were more rewarding. Three of Spurling's colleagues conducted in 1896 a meeting at Camp Creek, North Carolina, that resulted in many professions of salvation and sanctification. In the absence of a constituted authority, much of this gain was never consolidated, and many converts were led by other ministers into what Spurling and his associates regarded as error or fanaticism. This pointed up the need for some sort of church government. As a

[43] Clark, *Small Sects in America*, p. 100.
[44] Church of God, *Book of Minutes* (Cleveland, Tennessee: Church of God Publishing House, 1922), p. 8; hereafter cited *Book of Minutes*.
[45] *Ibid.*, pp. 8-9.
[46] E. L. Simmons, *History of the Church of God* (Cleveland, Tennessee: Church of God Publishing House, 1938), p. 11.

consequence of an appeal by Spurling for action, the group in May 15, 1902 organized as the "Holiness Church at Camp Creek." [47]

During 1903 and 1904 three new churches and a number of members were added to the organization. Two later leaders, A. J. Tomlinson and M. S. Lemons, entered the church at this time.[48]

The first general assembly of the group "was held January 26 and 27, 1906, at the home of J. C. Murphy, Cherokee County, North Carolina, about one-half mile from the school house where a great revival had broken out ten years before.[49] The minutes of this meeting indicate that the assembly was primarily interested in fellowship, worship, and religious instruction. "We do not," said the first recorded action, "consider ourselves a legislative or executive body." [50] Tomlinson, the host pastor, was selected as moderator, and a decision was made to hold similar meetings each year in the month of January.

NAME CHANGED TO CHURCH OF GOD

At the second annual assembly, held January 9-15, 1907, in Union Grove, Tennessee, the "Church of God" was chosen as the permanent name for the group. The growing influence of Tomlinson was indicated by his being selected again as moderator.[51] The following year the assembly was held in a new church in the Tennessee town of Cleveland, which was to become the headquarters for the organization.

GROUP ACCEPTS PENTECOSTAL DOCTRINE

The most significant event at this time was the introduction of the modern Pentecostal revival to the group. Though "tongues" had been noted on several occasions since 1896 in Church of God meetings, the phenomenon was still considered a manifestation similar to other expressions of religious enthusiasm such as shouting or weeping. In 1907

---

[47] *Ibid.*, pp. 11-12.
[48] A. J. Tomlinson, *Answering the Call of God* (Cleveland, Tennessee: White Wing Publishing House, [n.d.]), p. 17.
[49] A. J. Tomlinson, *The Church of God Marches On* (Cleveland, Tennessee: White Wing Publishing House, [1939]), p. 6.
[50] *Book of Minutes*, p. 15.
[51] *Ibid.*, pp. 20-25.

the congregation in Cleveland, Tennessee, enjoyed a great revival in which a number of persons spoke in "tongues," a thing many of the members had never witnessed before. Not a few considered the new demonstrations fanaticism. In this state of religious confusion the third annual assembly convened in Cleveland during January, 1908. At this convention, G. B. Cashwell, who had attended the Los Angeles revival in 1906 and then returned to the South to evangelize, was invited to preach. It was while he was ministering in Cleveland that Tomlinson received his Pentecostal baptism along with many others.[52] The "tongues" experience is mentioned from this point in the records of the church[53] which would seem to indicate that the Church of God, as a body, embraced Pentecostal doctrine at this time.

EARLY ORGANIZATIONAL DIFFICULTIES

The annual assembly of 1909 instituted a trend toward more formal and conventional organization by passing the following resolution:

WHEREAS, the following office is considered in harmony with New Testament order and on account of the present needs for general welfare of the churches and the promotion of the interest of the same, we hereby institute the name General Moderator, whose term of office shall commence at the closing of each yearly assembly and expire the following year at the same time or until his successor is selected.[54]

Previously the moderator was selected to serve only during the time of the assembly. Now he was to function during the entire year and was to issue credentials to ministers, keep records of the activities, look after the general interest of all churches, fill vacancies, and act as moderator and clerk of the annual assemblies. At the next assembly the title of the office was changed to "general overseer."[55]

Tomlinson was elected annually to the office of overseer until the Tenth Annual Assembly in 1914. In that session the necessity of annual elections was questioned. Though

---

[52] Tomlinson, *Diary of A. J. Tomlinson*, I, 25-29; Simmons, *History of the Church of God*, p. 21.
[53] *Book of Minutes*, pp. 31-32.
[54] *Ibid.*, p. 35.
[55] *Ibid.*, p. 38.

the minutes do not record any definite action on the matter, undoubtedly many considered that the overseer was elected with indefinite tenure by this assembly. Tomlinson recounted that his selection "was marked by such demonstrations of the Spirit of God that it was made final." [56] The election of an overseer was not brought before the assembly again until 1923.

Other administrative personnel were added as the group developed. The assembly in 1911 made provision for state overseers to direct the work of the church on the local level,[57] while the twelfth assembly in 1916 established a council of twelve elders (the Council of Elders became the Supreme Council in 1929) to assist the general overseer in the administration of the church.[58]

An action of the assembly in 1920 was to precipitate great difficulty. For several years prior to this time the assemblies had struggled to formulate a satisfactory financial plan for the church. This session instituted a system that Tomlinson recommended. He asked that all churches send their tithes to headquarters for equitable apportionment among all the clergy. Seven men were to "regulate and make, or order, the distribution among the ministers according to their needs and the efficiency of their works and the responsibility of their position in which they serve." [59] Though a majority of the clergy did not object to the plan, a number became quite dissatisfied with the management of the fund, which Tomlinson in practice distributed without consulting the board of seven. In the face of growing unhappiness the overseer satisfactorily defended his financial administration to the assembly of 1921, and no action was taken against the plan. The session did provide for a more definite delineation of responsibility, however, by adopting a formal constitution.[60] Until this time the organization had dealt with each problem as it arose, being guided by tradition rather than constituted authority.

[56] Tomlinson, *Church of God Marches On*, p. 9.
[57] *Book of Minutes*, pp. 51-52.
[58] *Ibid.*, pp. 242, 244.
[59] Simmons, *History of the Church of God*, p. 37.
[60] Charles W. Conn, *Like a Mighty Army Moves the Church of God, 1886-1955* (Cleveland, Tennessee: Church of God Publishing House, 1955), p. 167.

Tomlinson had supported the drafting of the constitution, but in the assembly of 1922 he attacked the instrument and asked that it be abrogated. He also criticized the method of selecting the Council of Elders and asked for authority to appoint the Council himself.[61] So much dissatisfaction existed by this time that there appeared to be little inclination to comply with these requests. Rather, the body further restricted the overseer's authority by establishing two new offices—an editor-publisher and a superintendent of education—to carry out functions previously controlled by the overseer. The two officers were also to serve with Tomlinson as an executive council to manage all general funds, appoint all state overseers, and arrange for assemblies. [62]

Such restraint of his former almost unlimited authority was a severe blow to Tomlinson. He tendered his resignation but upon the insistence of friends reconsidered and retained his post as overseer.[63] Before adjournment, the assembly appointed a committee of three persons to investigate thoroughly Tomlinson's financial administration.

The committee upon having the books completely audited and finding them unsatisfactory, submitted an unfavorable report to the Council of Elders in June, 1923. Impeachment proceedings were then filed against Tomlinson, and on July 26, 1923, he was relieved of his office for mishandling church funds.[64] Tomlinson left the Church of God and started an organization that became known as the Church of God of Prophecy (a subsequent defection from which gave rise to the Church of God, World Headquarters).

POLITY OF THE GROUP

After the Tomlinson administration the Church of God quickly developed into a conventional religious group. This was accomplished without a constitutional organization, for the instrument that had been adopted in 1921 was repealed in 1926, and from that time the group operated as a theocracy, using the Bible as the basis for government and

---

[61] Simmons, *History of the Church of God*, p. 38.
[62] Conn, *Like a Mighty Army*, p. 173.
[63] Tomlinson, *Answering the Call of God*, p. 21.
[64] *Ibid.*, pp. 21-22; Simmons, *History of the Church of God*, p. 40.

discipline.[65] The organizational pattern of the church gradually assumed episcopal characteristics. This change was unusually pronounced since the early form was strictly congregational. With the alteration of polity three areas of administration eventually evolved—the General Assembly, meeting annually until 1946 and afterwards biennially; state annual conferences; and district quarterly conferences.[66]

The officers of the General Assembly are the general overseer, two assistant overseers, and general secretary and treasurer. Since 1930 all of these officers have been nominated by the General Council, a body composed of all the ordained ministers, and elected by the General Assembly. The term of office for all general officers was limited to four years by the assembly in 1944 in order to avoid the abuse of authority. The officers form an executive committee, which with twelve elders constitute the Supreme Council. This council meets semi-annually and assists the officers with matters of policy.[67] The activities of the church are supervised by general boards selected by the Supreme Council, which also appoints officers on the state and district level.

PUBLICATIONS

A publishing auxiliary, established in 1917, encountered financial difficulties during the early years, but eventually developed into a profitable business. As demand required increased production, three expansions of the facilities were necessary.[68] The official organ of the organization, *The Church of God Evangel*, began publication in 1910,[69] first as a biweekly periodical, since 1914 as a weekly. In addition to printing the periodicals of the church, the publishing house produces a complete line of Sunday school literature.

[65] Conn, *Like a Mighty Army*, p. 199.

[66] Church of God, *Supplement to Church of God Minutes*, 1951 (Cleveland, Tennessee: Church of God, 1951), pp. 3, 10; hereafter cited as *Supplement*, 1951.

[67] *Ibid.*, pp. 26-29; Conn, *Like a Mighty Army*, pp. 263, 324; James A. Cross, Cleveland, Tenn. to Klaude Kendrick, Springfield, Mo., April 12, 1960, L. S., 3 p.

[68] Conn, *Like a Mighty Army*, p. 147.

[69] *Book of Minutes*, p. 39.

MISSIONS PROGRAM

The missionary department, headed by the executive secretary of foreign missions, is directed by the Missions Board. This committee was established in 1926 to make extensive distribution of missionary literature, examine missionary candidates, provide support for all appointed missionaries, and administer all mission funds. The missionary program is financed by contributions from the churches of an amount equal to at least five per cent of the tithe. One-half of this fund is dispersed to finance the foreign program while the other half is used to forward home missions in the state in which the contribution was made.[70]

EDUCATIONAL FACILITIES

Educational facilities were discussed by the organization as early as 1911, at which time the overseer's report emphasized the need for a training school.[71] A committee was accordingly selected to explore the possibility of launching an educational program, but the Bible Training School was not established in Cleveland, Tennessee, until 1917.[72] Enrollment had grown to such proportions by 1938 that the plant of the Murphy Collegiate Institute, which would accommodate 300 students, was purchased to house the school. A few years later the Church of God purchased the old campus of Bob Jones University in Cleveland, Tennessee, and moved the school back to the headquarters city, where it was renamed Lee College. Both a junior college and a Bible college curriculum are offered by the institution.[73] Two other schools, Northwest Bible and Music Academy of Minot, North Dakota, and West Coast Bible School of Pasadena, California, are operated by the group.

SUNDAY SCHOOL AND YOUTH PROGRAMS

Regular Sunday schools were established with the early churches. The first assembly

highly favored [Sunday schools] as a means to teach the children to reverence God's Word, the house appointed for worship, and to

---

[70] *Supplement*, 1951, pp. 25-26, 31; Paul H. Walker, Cleveland, Tennessee, to Klaude Kendrick, July 8, 1957, L. S., 2 p. Walker at the time of the letter was Foreign Missions Executive Secretary.

[71] *Book of Minutes*, p. 44.

[72] *Ibid.*, p. 300.

[73] Conn, *Like a Mighty Army*, p. 267.

elevate the morals of a community. The Assembly, therefore recommends, advises and urges every local church to have a Sunday school every Sunday.[74]

A number of local churches and a few districts established youth programs prior to 1929, but the Young People's Endeavor, the national organization, was not formed until that year.[75] The youth work became so involved by 1946 that a national youth director was selected to administer the department. As further assistance was needed, state directors were added. The youth and Sunday school activities function nationally under one board now called the National Sunday School and Youth Board.

Two excellent informational and inspirational youth periodicals are published by the national office. The *Lighted Pathway*, a monthly first issued in 1929, is the official organ of the Young People's Endeavor. In 1952 a quarterly, the *Pilot*, appeared to assist local youth leaders in developing more effective programs.[76]

DOCTRINAL POSITION OF THE GROUP

The Church of God had no formal outline of its teachings until 1910, when the *Church of God Evangel* published a list, prepared by a special committee, of the prominent teachings of the church. This catalog, which included twenty-eight items (a twenty-ninth was added by the forty-fifth assembly in 1945), was endorsed by the General Assembly in 1911.[77] Forty-two years after the first assembly the church accepted a Declaration of Faith containing fourteen articles.[78]

The doctrines comprehended in the two statements do not differ from those held by other Pentecostal perfectionest groups except on two counts. The first is that the washing of the saints' feet is an ordinance equal in importance to the Lord's Supper. The second is the somewhat extreme interpretation of personal holiness exemplified in

---

[74] *Book of Minutes*, p. 17.

[75] Simmons, *History of the Church of God*, p. 70.

[76] Conn, *Like a Mighty Army*, pp. 212-213, 298; O. W. Polen to Klaude Kendrick, July 8, 1957, L. S., 2pp. Polen was National Youth Director at the time of the letter.

[77] *Book of Minutes*, pp. 45-47.

[78] Conn, *Like a Mighty Army*, pp. 280-281.

the twenty-sixth teaching which states that the Church of God is "against members wearing jewelry for ornament or decoration, such as finger rings (this does not apply to wedding bands) , bracelets, earrings, lockets, etc." [79]

The Church of God has shown remarkable growth in recent years, from only 1,081 churches with 44,818 members in 1936 to 3,082 churches and 155,541 members twenty-four years later.[80]

THE CHURCH OF GOD IN CHRIST

The early history of the Church of God in Christ, the largest Negro Pentecostal body, like that of the Apostolic Faith, the Church of God, and the Foursquare Church, revolves around the personal ministry of a founder and first leader.

C. H. MASON, FOUNDER

The founder in this case was C. H. Mason, a Negro born and raised in Tennessee by former slave parents who were members of the Missionary Baptist Church. His mother, a deeply religious woman, exerted a great influence on his early life. While he was quite young, he felt that "God endowed him with supernatural characteristics, which were manifested in dreams and visions, that followed him through life up to the age of forty-one years." [81]

Mason was licensed to the ministry in 1893, though he had only an informal Bible training. Thinking that a formal education would help his ministry, he entered Arkansas Baptist College later that year, but remained only three months, claiming that the Lord had shown him "that there was no salvation in schools and colleges." [82] From this time forward neither Mason nor his followers attached much importance to formal Bible or secular training.

The same year that he left school Mason, in close fellowship with C. P. Jones, became associated with the Holiness movement. These two and others held in Mississippi in

---

[79] *Minutes of the Forty-seventh General Assembly*, 1958, p. 159.

[80] Bureau of the Census, *Religious Bodies: 1936*, II, 400-407; Landis, *Yearbook of American Churches*, 1960, p. 33.

[81] Mary Mason, *The History and Life Work of Bishop C. H. Mason, Chief Apostle, and His Co-Laborers*. (Memphis, Tenn.: 1934), p. 12.

[82] *Ibid.*, p. 17.

1895 a revival that resulted in the organization of a Negro Holiness body, the Church of God. In order to distinguish it from the several other Churches of God, the name was changed in 1897 to Church of God in Christ, a title based on 1 Thess. 2:14.[83]

CHURCH OF GOD IN CHRIST ACCEPTS PENTECOST

In 1906 Mason received news of the Azusa street meeting in Los Angeles. With two colleagues, J. O. Jeter and D. J. Young, he traveled to the west coast and attended the services. During his five-weeks' visit he not only became convinced of the genuineness of the Pentecostal baptism in the Holy Spirit but also claimed the "tongues" experience. Mason returned to Memphis to find a Pentecostal revival already started within his group as a result of the ministry of Glen A. Cook of Los Angeles. Very shortly he was heading a strong full gospel faction within the Church of God in Christ.[84]

The Pentecostal defection was the principal issue of the General Assembly that met at Jackson, Mississippi, in 1907. The controversy could not be healed, consequently the non-Pentecostal faction, headed by C. P. Jones, withdrew from the Church of God in Christ. Mason shortly afterward called an assembly in Memphis, where the Church of God in Christ was reorganized as a Pentecostal body.[85] From this beginning the church developed into a flourishing group.

POLITY OF THE GROUP

The body has operated with a relatively simple organization, especially in the early years. In the beginning all administration was effected through the office of the chief apostle or bishop, a position held continuously since 1907 by Mason. In 1933 four assistant bishops were added to help meet new demands within the group.[86] As the church became complex, the United States and mission fields were organized into smaller geographical entities conforming

---

[83] *Religious Bodies*, 1936, II, 448.
[84] Mason, *Life of Bishop C. H. Mason*, pp. 18-22.
[85] *Religious Bodies*: 1936, II, 448.
[86] Church of God in Christ, *Manual of the Church of God in Christ* (fourth ed., Memphis: O. T. Jones and J. E. Bryant, 1947), p. 6.

to state areas. These were under the supervision of state and foreign bishops. Eventually there was further division into districts presided over by superintendents and district missionaries.[87] Annual convocations are held at the state level to care for local business, and an annual general convocation handles any matters referred to it by state bishops or state convocations. Consistent with this episcopal type polity, pastors are assigned to local churches by the officers of the body.[88]

DOCTRINAL POSITION

The tenets emphasized by this group differ little from those of other perfectionist Pentecostal churches. The doctrine is Trinitarian and stresses repentance, regeneration, justification, sanctification, speaking in tongues as the evidence of the baptism in the Holy Spirit, the gift of healing, and the pre-millennial return of Christ. Ordinances include foot washing in addition to the Lord's Supper and baptism by immersion.[89]

The institutional development of the Church of God in Christ has been much slower than that of the other Pentecostal bodies. This is probably due to the fact that the economy of colored constituents did not improve at the same rate as that of white Pentecostals.

CHURCH PROGRAMS

Though the national and state organizations have superintendents of Sunday schools, this training agency has never developed into a thriving activity. The Church of God in Christ is one of the few Pentecostal groups that has a Sunday school enrollment that is smaller than its church membership. The fact that several of the local assemblies in the larger cities have well administered programs may indicate a trend toward improvement.[90]

Several other auxiliaries function within the local

---

[87] Statement by J. O. Patterson, Memphis, Tennessee, 1956, personal interview; one of the Assistant Bishops of the Church of God in Chirst; Frank S. Mead, *Handbook of Denominations in the United States* (Nashville: Abington Press, 1956), p. 65.

[88] *Religious Bodies: 1936*, II, 448.

[89] Mead, *Handbook of Denominations*, p. 65; *Manual*, 1947, pp. 6-28.

[90] Patterson, personal interview; *Manual*, 1947, p. 47.

churches. A women's organization, headed by a general
supervisor, has existed on a national basis since 1911. Its
officers are designated by the title of "mother." All churches
are encouraged to have a Sunshine Band, a lay group to
foster the proper training of children, and active sewing
circles to promote the general welfare of the congregations.
An organization called the Young People's Willing Workers
is, according to the *Manual*, intended (1) to unite Holiness
young people, (2) to increase spiritual strength, (3) to
stimulate more life in service, (4) to educate in scriptural
knowledge, (5) to keep the unity of the spirit, and (6)
to promote holy living.[91] The Willing Workers are headed
by a national president who is also a bishop of the church.

A missionary band was formally organized during the
meeting of the Council of Elders in 1926. The work of the
missions was placed under an executive secretary appointed
by the senior bishop and a home and foreign missions
board. Greater emphasis has been placed upon work in the
United States, but a foreign missionary corps of some thirty
persons is maintained by the church.[92]

PUBLICATIONS

Though the Church of God in Christ has never owned
a printing establishment, it has published a number of
items. It offers the local bodies a complete line of Sunday
school literature that is printed by outside firms. An official
organ, *Whole Truth*, is published monthly primarily for
the purpose of keeping its readers informed of church activities. A source book, *Bible Band Topics*, is issued to aid
the work of the women's department, while *Evangelists
Speak* is directed to a clergy as a source of inspirational
sermon material.[93]

TRAINING FACILITIES

The only denominational school, a junior college, is
located at Lexington, Mississippi. Though no theological
school is presently operated, interest has now been aroused
in formal ministerial training, and the establishment of

[91] *Manual*, 1947, pp. 54-59.
[92] *Ibid.*, pp. 61-65; Patterson, personal interview.
[93] Patterson, personal interview.

an institution to give such training is being studied by appropriate committees of the church.[94]

In spite of its limited institutional development, the Church of God in Christ has grown remarkably in the last two decades. In 1936 there were only 772 churches with a membership of 31,564.[95] A recent survey indicates that the churches have increased to 3,800 and the membership to 380,428.[96]

[94] *Ibid.*

[95] *Religious Bodies: 1936, II,* 441.

[96] Landis, *Yearbook of American Churches,* 1960, p. 36.

X

Pentecostal Co-operative Action

THE Pentecostal churches tend to be somewhat aloof from the rest of Christendom. Having risen in great measure from the Holiness movement, they retain an honest fear that any type of ecumenical action may lead to what they conceive to be the spiritless ecclesiasticism from which they originally revolted. At the same time their theological peculiarities and ecstatic demonstrations have kept them from enjoying cordial relations with the older denominations.

EARLY EXCLUSIVENESS OF PENTECOSTALS

Donald Gee, editor of *Pentecost*, (a periodical published by request of the Pentecostal World Conferences), has very cogently stated the Pentecostal position. After observing that Pentecostals share the "universal desire ... for more interfellowship," he goes on to explain that

> many sincere believers within the Pentecostal Revival regard participation in any ecumenical movement as a sharing in a subtle drift toward a final apostasy foretold in the Apocalypse. Others fear that fellowship with non-Pentecostal bodies must inevitably weaken our distinctive testimony and injure our spiritual power. Some sections would boycott a World Council of Churches purely on the ground of objection to all organization beyond local assemblies. . . .
> This is not to say that Christian Councils, even on a worldwide scale, are uncalled for or useless. . . . There are inestimable benefits from brethren speaking face to face who otherwise might become estranged. . . . We have no praise for those misguided isolationists, within or without the Petecostal movement, who deliberately hold aloof from Councils.[1]

Pentecostals have avoided participation both in the World Council of Churches and in the National Council of Church-

---

[1] *Pentecost*, No. 6 (December, 1948), p. 17.

es. Partly this is because the older denominations seem to regard the Pentecostal sects as "not yet qualified for recognition" in the family of churches, but mainly it is because Pentecostals themselves entertain serious objections to the Councils as presently constituted. The nature and extent of these objections have been spelled out by *United Evangelical Action* in a critique of the World Council of Churches.

1. Setting itself up as an "ecumenical" ecclesiasticism the council has refused to adopt as a basis of fellowship the absolute minimum of fundamental evangelical Christian doctrine necessary to such a body....

2. It has admitted into its membership a host of "liberals" who are committed to a theology and philosophy which are definitely anti-Christian in the Biblical sense....

3. It has created an organization which to all intents and purposes is under the control of an "oligarchy." Real control lies in the hands of a few men who are definitely "liberal" in their viewpoint....

4. The ramifications are such that it is already beginning to function as a "super church," bringing pressures or exerting controls over both member and non-member churches....

5. Its concept of the nature of the church, the character of Christ and of essential doctrine is inadequate. It has at no time unequivocally stated its belief in the Bible as the inspired, the only infallible authoritative Word of God; in the deity of our Lord Jesus Christ, in His virgin birth, in His sinless life, in His miracles, in His vicarious and atoning death through His shed blood, in His bodily resurrection, in His ascension to the right hand of the Father, and His personal return in power and glory; in regeneration by the Holy Spirit as essential to the salvation of lost and sinful man; in the present ministry of the Holy Spirit by whose indwelling the Christian is enabled to live a Godly life; in the resurrection of both the saved and the lost—they that are saved unto the resurrection of life and they that are lost unto the resurrection of damnation.

6. It has adopted an approach to the problem of Christian unity which is un-Protestant and un-Biblical and, therefore essentially un-Christian.

7. It has seriously threatened the development of a distinctly evangelical foreign missionary program and formed alliances which will further secularize the whole Missionary Movement.

8. It has encouraged social revolution through liaison relation-

ships with the Commission of Churches for International Affairs and other such bodies. . . .

9. Its relations with the Greek Orthodox Churches and its general attitude toward the Roman Catholic Church threaten to weaken if not eventually destroy the distinctive testimony of Protestantism.

10. It has deliberately omitted or shamefully neglected to include provisions for the preservation and perpetuation of all the values and liberties inherent in historic Protestantism.[2]

PARTICIPATION IN N. A. E.

While there has been no association with the National Council or the World Council, Pentecostals have joined ranks with organizations whose positions are more in accordance with their own. Outstanding among these is the National Association of Evangelicals, organized in 1942 after it was discovered that over 320 denominations with millions of members in the United States could not, for reasons of conscience, affiliate with any existing organization, and that among them there was "a growing conviction of a need for correlation of many Christian activities on a soundly evangelical basis and without interference with the internal affairs of constituent bodies."[3] The Statement of Faith of the National Association of Evangelicals is such that all fundamental, evangelical Christians can enter it without reservations.

1. We believe the Bible to be the inspired, the only infallible, authoritative word of God.

2. We believe that there is one God, eternally existent in three persons: Father, Son and Holy Ghost.

3. We believe in the deity of our Lord Jesus Christ, in His Virgin birth, in His sinless life, in His miracles, in His vicarious and atoning death through His shed blood, in His bodily resurrection, in His ascension to the right hand of the Father, and in His personal return in power and glory.

4. We believe that for the salvation of the lost and sinful man regeneration by the Holy Spirit is absolutely essential.

5. We believe in the present ministry of the Holy Spirit by whose indwelling the Christian is enabled to live a Godly life.

---

[2] *United Evangelical Action*, XIII (January 15, 1955), p. 10.
[3] National Association of Evangelicals, *Progress*, (Chicago: N. A. E., 1945), p. 1.
[4] *Ibid.*

6. We believe in the resurrection of both the saved and the lost; ...

7. We believe in the spiritual unity of believers in our Lord Jesus Christ.[4]

From the very beginning a number of Pentecostal groups have been associated with the N. A. E., and several were represented on the original board of administration.[5] The action of the Assemblies of God may be taken as an example of the Pentecostal attitude. The first General Council after the N. A. E. was organized voted to participate in it. Six years later, 1949, a motion was presented at the General Council to determine feeling concerning the Association:

WHEREAS, There has been a desire on the part of a number of our ministers to discuss the affiliation of the Assemblies of God with the National Association of Evangelicals, be it hereby

RESOLVED, That this General Council re-affirm its action to affiliate with the aforesaid Association as taken in the session of 1943.[6]

After thorough discussion the motion passed by an over-whelming majority.

The specific objectives of the N. A. E. are:

One—To provide a vehicle through which all believers in the Lord Jesus Christ may become united and articulate in relation to matters of common interest and concern.

Two—To foster brotherliness, good will and fellowship among ... in every denomination, assembly, or association.

Three—To establish a common front for the promotion of evangelical truth. . . .

Four—To guard the religious freedom guaranteed as under our national constitution. . . .

Five—To provide services to our constituents which will enable them to accomplish more quickly and efficiently the mission of the church. . . .[7]

These objectives the Pentecostal groups can endorse and support.

Participation in the N. A. E. has resulted in much good

---

[5] "Basic Unity of Evangelical Christianity," *Pentecostal Evangel*, No. 1519 (June 19, 1943), p. 8.

[6] Assemblies of God, *Minutes and Constitution with By-Laws* (Springfield, Mo.: Gospel Publishing House, 1949), p. 28.

[7] National Association of Evangelicals, *United in the Faith* (Chicago: N. A. E., 1948), p. 1.

to the Pentecostal groups, especially to their educational activities. An Accrediting Association of Bible Colleges, formed by evangelical schools, has made much progress in standardizing the work offered in Pentecostal schools, and has provided a sound basis, which was previously lacking, for transferring of credits between schools.

WORLD PENTECOSTAL FELLOWSHIP

The Pentecostals' greatest co-operative activities of recent years have been within their own ranks. The roots of inter-Pentecostal association reach back to an International European Pentecostal Convention held in Amsterdam in 1921.[8] Called through the mutual agreement of several national groups, and for fellowship purposes only, this convention was not based on any kind of formal organization. Similar conventions met intermittently through the years, the last in Stockholm in 1939.[9] Though attended primarily by European groups, these meetings contributed to the development of Pentecostal co-operative action by demonstrating the value of fellowship between kindred believers.

By the late 1930's interest in a world Pentecostal conference was apparent. In the General Council of the Assemblies of God in 1937 the presence of representatives of several American Pentecostal groups and of churches in South Africa, Canada, and Britain gave an international as well as an inter-denominational flavor. At this gathering a decision was reached to call a world conference in London in 1940,[10] but the war made it impossible.

In 1946 a Pentecostal prayer convention was held in Basle, Switzerland. When the desperate and critical condition of many war victims among the European groups was brought vividly to their attention, the convention decided to call a world-wide conference of representatives from all Pentecostal churches to lay the need before them. Pentecostal leaders all over the world were accordingly asked to attend a conference at Zurich, Switzerland, in May, 1947. The main purposes of the conference would be

---

[8] *Pentecost*, No. 6 (December, 1948), p. 17.
[9] *Pentecost*, No. 1 (September, 1947), p. 1.
[10] H. W. Greenway, *World Pentecostal Conference, 1952* (London: British Pentecostal Fellowship, [n. d.]), p. 3.

to offer an opportunity for united prayer and waiting upon God to all ministering brethren, that they may receive from the Lord a clear revelation of His will for the Pentecostal Movement in this hour of crisis ... and to discuss the possibilities of co-ordinate effort in rehabilitation of the work in Europe, and in spreading the full Gospel testimony in every country.[11]

Donald Gee reported that the delegates to this first World Pentecostal Conference could be classified in three categories. One came for the practical purpose of helping Pentecostal believers suffering in the aftermath of the war, by establishing machinery for co-ordinated world relief. Another gathered mainly for spiritual discussions, feeling that "the best methods for organizing relief, and for maintaining evangelical agencies must fail and wither if the dynamic of Pentecostal power at their heart ceases to inspire."[12] The third attended merely for the thrill and blessing of a large convention.

Out of these conflicting elements emerged a unity that became increasingly impressive as the conference proceeded. The foundation for a great world fellowship was laid and several important resolutions were passed. One authorized the opening of an international office in Basle, Switzerland. Another made provision for publishing an international Pentecostal organ. The paper was placed in the hands of one man, rather than a group, the editor being made personally responsible for all that was published. This was done to keep the periodical from being associated with any one of the many Pentecostal denominations. Donald Gee was selected as editor, and in September, 1947, the first edition of *Pentecost* was issued.[13] Another resolution of importance recommended that different geographical sections of the world organize into area conferences.[14] This was entered into at once with much enthusiasm, and as a result several such conferences very shortly were functioning.

Unfortunately the conference in Zurich stopped short of providing a constitutional basis for co-operation between international groups. To care for this lack the second World

[11] *Ibid*.
[12] *Pentecost*, No. 1 (September, 1947), p. 1.
[13] *Ibid.*, p. 18.
[14] *Pentecost*, No. 5 (September, 1948), p. 5.

Conference of Pentecostal Churches was called to convene in Paris during May, 1949,[15] to consider mainly the momentous matter of a formally organized world council.

Many leaders felt the time had arrived for the acceptance of a regular constitution by which the World Fellowship might be better served.[16] It was found, however, that to propose was one thing, to adopt, altogether another.

One group desires a World Fellowship and feels it must be organized before it can be recognized by all. The other group is equally anxious to have a World Fellowship but they hold that it already exists; they insist we just need to believe this without organizing it and it will be universally recognized.

The two factions seem like two little boats in a tempestuous sea. One moment they get so close that it seems they are getting knitted together. Then comes another wave caused by the speech of an extremist on one side or the other and there they drift farther apart than ever. Misunderstanding seems to be the root of all the trouble.[17]

After two days of discussion much of the misunderstanding and suspicion fortunately abated. The conference then assigned a committee of fifteen the task of working out a plan for organizing the fellowship. Next morning the committee's report was quickly and unanimously passed. This constitutional document recognized the sovereignty of all participating bodies and gave assurance that rights of churches would not be violated. World Pentecostal Conferences were to be held every three years, each conference being directed by its elected presidium. A secretary assisted by an elected advisory committee of five persons was provided to serve the interests of the Fellowship during and between conferences. The declaration further stipulated that all necessary expenses would be covered by voluntary contributions, and the paper *Pentecost* was to continue as the official voice of the organization. The following purposes and objectives for the Fellowship were also listed:

(a) To encourage fellowship and facilitate co-ordination of effort among Pentecostal believers throughout the world.
(b) To demonstrate to the world the essential unity of Spirit-

[15] *Ibid.*
[16] Greenway, *World Pentecostal Conference*, 1952, pp. 4-5.
[17] *Pentecostal Evangel*, No. 1833 (June 25, 1949), p. 9.

baptised believers, fulfilling the prayer of the Lord Jesus
Christ: "that they all may be one" (John XVII. 21).

(c) To co-operate in an endeavour to respond to the unchanging
commission of the Lord Jesus, to carry His message to all
men of all nations.

(d) To promote courtesy and mutual understanding, "endeavour-
ing to keep the unity of the Spirit in the bond of peace,
until we all come in the unity of the faith" (Eph. IV. 3, 13).

(e) To afford prayerful and practical assistance to any Pentecostal
body in need of such.

(f) To promote and maintain the scriptural purity of the Fellowship of Bible study and prayer.

(g) To uphold and maintain those pentecostal truths, "most
surely believed among us?" (Luke I. 1).[18]

The World Pentecostal Fellowship thus formally organized received support in its formative period from several of
the prominent United States Pentecostal groups. Representatives of the Assemblies of God, Open Bible Standard, and
Foursquare churches served on the program of the first
conference, and others participated in the planning for the
meetings that followed.[19] The Fellowship has rendered many
services to the Pentecostal movement. And the tone of
subsequent conferences has indicated that the organization
has received general acceptance and that many of the early
fears have disappeared.

NORTH AMERICAN PENTECOSTAL FELLOWSHIP

As was noted above, an important resolution passed at
the first World Conference in Zurich recommended the or-
ganizing of area fellowships. Representatives of eight North
American Pentecostal groups accordingly met in Chicago in
May, 1948, to explore the possibility of forming a North
American conference. Five of the larger United States or-
ganizations (namely, the Pentecostal Holiness Church, the
Church of God, the International Church of the Four-
square Gospel, the Open Bible Standard Churches, and the
Assemblies of God), were among the bodies represented.[20]
Representatives of the Pentecostal Assemblies of Canada also

---

[18] Greenway, *World Pentecostal Conference*, 1952, p. 6.

[19] *Pentecostal Evangel*, No. 1725 (June 7, 1947), p. 6; *Pentecostal Evangel*,
No. 1833 (June 25, 1949), pp. 8-9.

[20] *Pentecost*, No. 5 (September, 1948), p. 5.

participated. Though little action was attempted, the fellowship and understanding realized contributed much to later organization. The meeting agreed that another conference would be held in the fall to effect a formal organization.

The convention met at Des Moines, Iowa, on October 26-28, 1948. Its chief task

was the formation and adoption of a constitution and by-laws and this was accomplished easily and quickly due to the warm spirit of brotherhood and mutual confidence that was manifested. Decisions were reached by unanimous vote; not a single time was a vote of dissension heard.[21]

Evidently the Pentecostals in North America did not hold the extreme fears of co-operative organizations expressed by some of the Europeans at the World Conference in Zurich and later in Paris. To allay what apprehension there was, the constitution clearly stated that the purpose of the North American Fellowship was

to give expression to the inherent principles of spiritual unity and fellowship of Pentecostal believers, leaving inviolate the existing forms of church government adopted by its members; and recognizing that every freedom and privilege enjoyed by a church or group of churches, shall remain their undisturbed possession.[22]

The direction of the affairs of the Fellowship was placed under a board of administration of thirteen members. The officers—chairman, two vice-chairmen, secretary, and treasurer—were to serve ex officio on the board and also to constitute an executive committee. Each member group was allowed voting representation of one delegate for each 5,000 members up to 25,000, and one delegate for each 15,000 members thereafter.[23]

The constitution included a brief "Statement of Faith," designed to be acceptable to any Pentecostal group. Membership was offered to all

Pentecostal Evangelical institutions, churches, and groups of churches which shall subscribe to the Statement of Faith of the Association,

---

[21] *Pentecostal Evangel*, No. 1802 (November 20, 1948), p. 13.

[22] *Pentecost*, No. 7 (March, 1949), p. 7.

[23] *Pentecostal Evangel*, No. 1853 (November 12, 1949), p. 7.

212   *The Promise Fulfilled*

and which agree to be governed by the principles, purposes, and objectives of the fellowship as set forth in the Constitution and by-laws.[24]

The second annual conference of the Fellowship, embracing fourteen groups and representing a constituent membership of over 1,000,000, met in Oklahoma City in October, 1949. Sessions were well attended, those at night numbering as many as 4,000 persons.[25] Subsequent annual conferences have confirmed the value of the Fellowship.

Six years of association in the Pentecostal Fellowship have drawn the leaders ... together in a way that is benefiting the entire Pentecostal Movement. It is helping all members to recognize the essential unity of Spirit-baptized believers and is enabling them to demonstrate that unity to the world.[26]

Five committees—missions, youth, radio, education, and publication—function from session to session and effect an interchange of ideas and material that helps substantially the activities of all the groups. These committees have also sponsored foreign missions forums and youth seminars.[27]

LOCAL INTER-GROUP ACTIVITIES

A major result of high-level co-operation in the North American Fellowship has been greater local association and co-operation. In fact, only since the formation of the world and area fellowships has there been within the modern Pentecostal movement any noticeable fellowship at the community level. David J. DuPlessis, former secretary of the World Fellowship, thus describes the change:

United rallies under the auspices of local fellowships became regular features of the revival. Evangelists found auditoriums and canvas cathedrals crowded with thousands instead of the erstwhile hundreds. Missionaries found that co-operation, instead of competition, brought landslides of souls from among the great multitudes that attend special services.[28]

A few examples will indicate the large scale of the new inter-group activities. On March 29, 1948, a youth rally

---

[24] Pentecostal Evangel, No. 1802 (November 20, 1948), p. 13.
[25] Pentecost, No. 10 (December, 1949), p. 2.
[26] Pentecostal Evangel, No. 2063 (November 22, 1953), p. 15.
[27] Ibid.
[28] Greenway, World Pentecostal Conference, 1952, p. 4.

was announced for the young people of Assemblies of God,
Foursquare, Pentecostal Church of God and Independent
Full Gospel Churches in the Los Angeles area. The meeting took place in the Shrine Auditorium which seats 7,800.
Not only was the auditorium filled but police estimated
that 6,000 more were turned away. A report of the rally
stated that "many revivals are resulting from this one
meeting, and God is confirming in every way His approval
in the uniting of full gospel hearts in a combined effort
to propagate our tenets of faith and reach youth with the
Saviour." [29]

Six local Pentecostal groups, namely, Assemblies of God,
Foursquare, Pentecostal Holiness, Pentecostal Church of
God, Church of God and Independent Full Gospel, co-
operated in another youth rally on September 27, 1948, in
the Hollywood Bowl. A crowd of 21,000 persons jammed
the amphitheater.[30] "Never before in history has there been
so great a Full Gospel youth rally in all the world," [31] was
the opinion of Howard Rusthoi, a leader of the Foursquare
Church. It was estimated that the youth of 800 Pentecostal
churches in the area participated in this mass service. In
1951 a Golden Gate Pentecostal Fellowship comprising
thirty-eight churches was formed in the San Francisco area.[32]

The spirit of local co-operation appeared not only in
services of the rally and convention type, but also in evangelistic efforts. Indeed, some co-operative revivals have been
backed by such mass support that adequate facilities could
not be found to accommodate the crowds. According to
secretary DuPlessis, few cities have auditoriums

large enough to hold the crowds that flock to the "city-wide"
campaigns of our Pentecostal evangelists. Several of them have now
equipped themselves with tents seating from 4,000 to 8,000. Even
these are usually too small.... It is no longer an unusual thing
for 15,000 to 20,000 people to turn out to the tent campaigns....
Very seldom does one find a Pentecostal Assembly in any city
that does not fully co-operate with all the others in these city-
wide campaigns.[33]

[29] *Pentecost*, No. 4 (June), p. 4.
[30] *Pentecostal Evangel*, No. 1798 (October 23, 1948), p. 13.
[31] *Pentecost*, No. 6 (December 1948), p. 6.
[32] *Pentecost*, No. 16 (June, 1951), p. 10.
[33] *Pentecost*, No. 14 (December, 1950), p. 5.

An example of this kind of co-operation is seen in the work of Oral Roberts. Though he is a minister of the Pentecostal Holiness Church, all Pentecostal churches often take part in his revivals. In his Jacksonville, Florida, meeting early in 1952 twenty-five churches participated. It was reported that 152,000 persons attended the sixteen day revival and that 3,863 walked the "sawdust trail." A little later in Los Angeles nearly 200,000 attended, and 4,100 conversions were reported.[34]

Thus it would seem that fifty years of institutional development has brought the Pentecostal movement to seek and encourage co-operative action. This undoubtedly will result not only in better understanding between Pentecostals and other evangelicals but also in happier relations among kindred Pentecostal groups and the elimination of much useless duplication and unhealthful competition.

---

[34] *Pentecost*, No. 20 (June, 1952), p. 16.

XI

Modern Pentecost: an Appraisal

BY THOSE persons who refer to sectarianism as the "Modern Babel" or the "Scandal of Christianity," [1] the Pentecostal sects are held to deserve little more than derision as just another link in the chain of religious disunity. It would seem wiser and fairer, however, to accept the Pentecostal movement as one in a long series of schismatic reactions precipitated by the American environment and concept of religious liberty. Sects are, as one writer has stated, "sometimes a nuisance, but they are the legitimate fruit of the tree of liberty. To curb their freedom is to place the freedom of all of us in jeopardy." [2]

It has been estimated that some seventeen million Americans have joined new religious organizations since the turn of the century. [3] Whatever the exact number, it is obviously tremendous, and a phenomenon of such magnitude cannot be taken lightly. The success of the new religious groups indicates a deep religious impulse not altogether satisfied by the older orthodox bodies. This condition arises to a great extent from the shift of population, underway since the last century, from rural areas to cities. The influx from the country has caused social and economic changes that produced demands for which the older city churches had little experience or aptitude to handle.

---

[1] Charles W. Ferguson, *The Confusion of Tongues* (New York: Doubleday, 1929), ch. 1; Peter Ainslie, *The Scandal of Christianity* (Chicago: Willet, Clark, and Colby, [n. d.]).

[2] A. G. Smith, "Fringe Religions," *American Mercury*, LXX (April, 1950), p. 442.

[3] John T. Nichol, "The Role of the Pentecostal Movement in American Church History," *The Gordon Review*, II (December, 1956), p. 133.

The big churches, with all their intelligence and decency, and with all the tremendous advantage of large and well-equipped physical structures, have failed conspicuously and lamentably to reach and really serve the rural-to-urban migrant.[4]

In contrast, most of the Pentecostal groups achieved rapid growth by directing their program to such new city residents. In serving them and other victims of social and economic change, the modern Pentecostal movement has contributed immeasurably to American religious life.

The Pentecostals have developed an unusually *esprit de corps* within their ranks. They care for their religion—care enough both to give to and live for it. Active devotion, deep sincerity, and vital enthusiasm have characterized their unusual success.

The movement can, on the other hand, be justly criticized for taking little interest in the improvement of the social order. This apathy can, according to John T. Nichol,

be explained in part as the legacy of dissent; that is, sectarian ethics are designed to meet the exigencies of a small and close-knit brotherhood drawn for the most part from the propertyless and disinherited classes. Its moral rubrics are determined by this fact and it is understandable, therefore, why the Charismatic Sects stress meekness, simplicity, thrift, opposition to many forms of luxury.[5]

A further explanation is to be found in the Pentecostal's absolute confidence in the revivalistic concept. As individual lives are changed for good through the influence of the Gospel, society will be improved. It is a question, nevertheless, whether this position is adequate to meet completely the ethical demands of modern society.

Critics are also justified in denouncing the "primitivism" of the Pentecostal movement. As Nichol observes, "many adherents are inimical to modern scholarship, which they call 'modernism.' Some have almost made a positive virtue of ignorance, and devote much of their polemic to assaults on education."[6] Hedley has said in a more plainly disapproving tone that "such self-conscious antipathy to learn-

[4] George Hedley, *The Christian Heritage in America* (New York: Macmillan, 1946), p. 143.
[5] Nichol, "The Role of the Pentecostal Movement," p. 133.
[6] *Ibid.*

ing augurs badly for the religious tutelage of many millions of Americans." [7] Chiding of this sort has moved many Pentecostal groups into action. Their concepts of religion and higher education are presently being re-evaluated with a trend toward improvement.

Though the Pentecostals have placed a renewed emphasis upon doctrines of personal religious experiences, and have grown to be the largest "tongues" group since the Apostolic church, they have introduced no new tenet to Christendom. It is true, however, that in their teaching some groups have become bizarre, overstressing one tenet and neglecting others. Too often they tend to be exclusive and to be very critical of all who do not agree with them, thus becoming difficult to live with and developing a "holier-than-thou" complex. It should be remembered, though, that Pentecostalism is relatively young. Generally the offensive characteristics of a new group are lost after a few generations. There are indications that in the Pentecostal movement this transformation has already begun.

With all their faults and weaknesses, the Pentecostals are with us, commanding a more and more prominent place on the contemporary American religious scene. It is time and past time for the modern church to reassess its evaluation of the new movement.

A practice very common among the "respectable churches" is to denounce these underprivileged groups; to call them all "Holy Rollers"; to sneer at them as troublemakers.... It is well to bear in mind that Baptists, Methodists, Disciples, and Quakers were once troublemakers for the respectable churches—the Congregationalists, the Presbyterians, and the Episcopalians. And only a little farther back in time, the Episcopalians, the Congregationalists, and the Presbyterians were in turn, troublemakers.[8]

If Pentecostals can come to be regarded not as heretics or schismatics but rather as sincere followers of Christ fast taking their place among the historical churches, then a desirable *rapprochement* will undoubtedly be achieved. It will result not only in a better understanding but also in a greater accomplishment of common goals.

---

[7] Hedley, *Christian Heritage in America*, p. 144.
[8] Sweet, *Religion in America*, p. 177.

Appendix

OFFICERS OF THE GENERAL COUNCIL OF THE ASSEMBLIES OF GOD

A RECORD OF PLACES AND DATES FOR THE HOLDING OF GENERAL COUNCILS TOGETHER WITH LIST OF OFFICERS CHOSEN TO SERVE THE FELLOWSHIP.

Hot Springs, Arkansas—April 2-12, 1914
Constitutional Meeting

EUDORUS N. BELL, Chairman   J. ROSWELL FLOWER, Secretary

Chicago, Illinois—November 15-29, 1914

A. P. COLLINS, Chairman   J. ROSWELL FLOWER, Secretary
DANIEL C. O. OPPERMAN, Asst. Chairman   BENNETT F. LAWRENCE, Asst. Secretary

St. Louis, Missouri—October 1-10, 1915

JOHN W. WELCH, Chairman   J. ROSWELL FLOWER, Secretary

Third and Fourth Councils, St. Louis, Missouri
October 1-7, 1916 and September 9-14, 1917

JOHN W. WELCH, Chairman   STANLEY H. FRODSHAM, Secretary

Springfield, Missouri—September 4-11, 1918

JOHN W. WELCH, Chairman   STANLEY H. FRODSHAM, Secretary

Chicago, Illinois—September 25-30, 1919

JOHN W. WELCH, Chairman   EUDORUS N. BELL, Secretary & Editor
                                             J. ROSWELL FLOWER, Foreign Mission Secy.

Springfield, Missouri—September 21-27, 1920

EUDORUS N. BELL, Chairman   JOHN W. WELCH, Secretary
                                             J. T. BODDY, Editor
                                             J. ROSWELL FLOWER, Foreign Mission Secy.

St. Louis, Missouri—September 21-28, 1921

EUDORUS N. BELL, Chairman   JOHN W. WELCH, Secretary
                                             J. ROSWELL FLOWER, Foreign Mission Secy.
                                             STANLEY H. FRODSHAM, Editor

(E. N. BELL died in Springfield, Mo. June 15, 1923. No one was chosen to succeed him in office until the next General Council. After 1921, General Councils were convened biennially.)

St. Louis, Missouri—September 13-18, 1923

JOHN W. WELCH, Chairman   J. R. EVANS, Secretary
DAVID H. McDOWELL, Asst. Chairman   WILLIAM FAUX, For. Missions Secy.
                                             J. R. FLOWER, Foreign Missions Treas.

Eureka Springs, Arkansas—September 17-24, 1925

W. T. GASTON, Chairman   J. R. EVANS, Secretary
DAVID H. McDOWELL, Asst. Chairman   WILLIAM FAUX, For. Missions Secy.-Treas.

(Resolutions affecting constitutional order had been considered sufficient
until the General Council of 1925 at which time essential resolutions were
assembled to create a formal constitution. The proposed constitution, prepared by the administration, was rejected. A constitution and bylaws was
finally adopted in the 1927 General Council.)

Springfield, Missouri—September 16-22, 1927

W. T. GASTON, General Superintendent   J. R. EVANS, General Secretary
D. H. McDOWELL, Asst. Gen. Supt.   NOEL PERKIN, Foreign Missions Secy.
STANLEY H. FRODSHAM continued to serve as Editor until 1949

Wichita, Kansas—September 20-26, 1929

ERNEST S. WILLIAMS, Gen. Superintendent J. R. EVANS, General Secretary
Office of Assistant left vacant   NOEL PERKIN, For. Missions Secy.
                                         continued to serve until 1959

San Francisco, California—September 8-13, 1931

ERNEST S. WILLIAMS, Gen. Supt.   J. R. EVANS, General Secretary
Continued to serve until 1949.   Continued to serve until 1935
J. ROSWELL FLOWER, Asst. Gen. Supt.
  (served without portfolio)

Philadelphia, Pa.—September 14-20, 1933

All officers re-elected. In the 1933 General Council the basis for representation
on the General Presbytery was changed so that each district, in the future
would be represented by three members—the District Superintendent and
two others to be nominated by the District Councils and elected by
the General Council.

Dallas, Texas—September 12-19, 1935

ERNEST S. WILLIAMS, Gen. Supt.   J. ROSWELL FLOWER, Asst. Gen. Supt.
                                         and General Secretary-Treasurer.

Memphis, Tenn.—September 2-9, 1937

Same officers with the exception of election of   J. R. FLOWER retaining office
FRED VOGLER, Asst. General Superintendent   of General Secretary-Treasurer

Springfield, Missouri—September 2-12, 1939

All officers re-elected

Minneapolis, Minn.—September 5-11, 1941

All officers re-elected

Springfield Missouri—September 1-9, 1943

All officers re-elected with exception of FRED VOGLER, who was replaced by
RALPH M. RIGGS, Asst. Gen. Superintendent.

Springfield, Missouri—September 13-18, 1945

In the 1945 meeting, four assistant General Superintendents were elected, and
given portfolios by the General Superintendent—in home missions, youth, education,
publications, etc.: RALPH M. RIGGS, GAYLE F. LEWIS, FRED VOGLER, WESLEY
R. STEELBERG.

Grand Rapids, Michigan—September 4-11, 1947

All officers re-elected and office of General Secretary and General Treasurer separated. WILFRED A. BROWN elected General Treasurer. J. R. FLOWER retained as General Secretary.

Seattle, Washington—September 8-14, 1949

ERNEST S. WILLIAMS retired from office, and WESLEY R. STEELBERG elected to serve as General Superintendent. BERT WEBB elected one of the four assistant general superintendents. All other officers re-elected.

Atlanta, Georgia—August 16-23, 1951

All officers re-elected. WESLEY R. STEELBERG died in Cardiff, Wales on July 8, 1952. GAYLE F. LEWIS was chosen by the General Presbytery to fill the unexpired term of Brother STEELBERG, on September 2, 1952, and JAMES O. SAVELL was chosen to succeed G. F. LEWIS as Assistant General Superintendent.

Milwaukee, Wisconsin—August 26-September 2, 1953

RALPH M. RIGGS, General Superintendent. The four Assistant General Superintendents were GAYLE F. LEWIS, BERT WEBB, JAMES O. SAVELL and THOMAS F. ZIMMERMAN. All were assigned to departmental portfolios.

.J ROSWELL FLOWER, General Secretary
WILFRED A. BROWN, General Treasurer
NOEL PERKIN, Foreign Missions Secy.

Oklahoma City, Okla.—September 1-6, 1955

All officers re-elected. WILFRED A. BROWN was not present at the 1955 General Council, due to serious illness. He died on September 19, 1955, and ATWOOD FOSTER was nominated Treasurer to fill the unexpired term. His appointment was approved by the General Presbytery.

Cleveland, Ohio—August 28-September 3, 1957

Only two changes made in the Executive Officers, CHARLES W. H. SCOTT elected to succeed JAMES O. SAVELL, and MARTIN B. NETZEL elected to succeed ATWOOD FOSTER.

San Antonio, Texas—August 26-September 1, 1959

THOMAS F. ZIMMERMAN elected General Superintendent to succeed RALPH M. RIGGS, who was within a few months of reaching retirement age. J. ROSWELL FLOWER and NOEL PERKIN retired. The slate of Executive Officers who were elected included:

THOMAS F. ZIMMERMAN, General Superintendent

GAYLE F. LEWIS, Asst. Gen. Supt. _____ Home Missions and WMC Dept.

CHARLES W. H. SCOTT, Asst. Gen. Supt. _____ Dept. of Education, Sunday School, and Benevolences

BERT WEBB, Asst. Gen. Supt. _____ Publications

HOWARD S. BUSH, Asst. Gen. Supt. _____ Youth, Men's Fellowship, Evangelism.

J. PHILIP HOGAN, Asst. Gen. Supt. _____ Foreign Missions

BARTLETT PETERSON, Gen. Secretary _____ Radio Department
MARTIN B. NETZEL, Gen. Treasurer

Bibliography

INTERVIEWS

Hugh M. Cadwalder, Kerrville, Texas 1954, by Klaude Kendrick.
J. Roswell Flower, Springield, Mo., 1955, by Klaude Kendrick.
Dick Fulmer, Springfield, Mo., 1956, by Klaude Kendrick.
M. L. Grable, Springfield, Mo., 1956, by Klaude Kendrick.
Ralph W. Harris, Springfield, Mo., 1956, by Klaude Kendrick.
Fred Hornshuh, Portland, Oregon, 1956, by R. Bryant Mitchell.
J. Z. Kamerer, Springfield, Mo., 1957, by Klaude Kendrick.
Don Mallough, Springfield, Mo., 1957, by Klaude Kendrick.
T. W. May, Conroe, Texas, 1955, by Klaude Kendrick.
Arthur P. Morgan and Stanley W. Chambers, St. Louis, Mo., 1955, by Paul Chamless.
W. B. McCafferty, Waxahachie, Texas, 1954, by Klaude Kendrick.
J. O. Patterson, Memphis, Tenn., 1956, by Warren Grant.
R. M. Riggs, Springfield, Mo., 1955, by Klaude Kendrick.

LETTERS

(Letters to E. N. Bell are in the Pentecostal File, Gospel Publishing House, Springfield, Mo.; to Klaude Kendrick and Robert Willis in Kendrick's possession; and to Brother Carothers, in Charles F. Parham's scrapbook.)

A. H. Argue, Winnipeg, Canada, to E. N. Bell, Springfield, Mo., November 17, 1921.

Mary A. Arthur, Galena, Kansas, to E. N. Bell, Springfield, Mo., December 7, 1921.

Mrs. Robert A. Brown, New York, N. Y., to E. N. Bell, Springfield, Mo., April 5, 1922.

S. W. Chambers, St. Louis, Mo., to Klaude Kendrick, Springfield, Mo., April 1, 1960.

Dick Champion, Springfield, Mo., to Klaude Kendrick, Austin, Texas, June 16, 1958.

W. Rollie Clark, Eugene Oregon, to Klaude Kendrick, Springfield, Mo., July 22, 1957.

Howard P. Courtney, Los Angeles, Calif., to Klaude Kendrick, Springfield, Mo., April 7, 1960.

James A. Cross, Cleveland, Tenn., to Klaude Kendrick, Springfield, Mo., April 12, 1960.

Robert C. Cunningham, Springfield, Mo., to Klaude Kendrick, Austin, Texas, June 16, 1958.

Mother Dobson, Houston, Texas, to E. N. Bell, Springfield, Mo., November 12, 1921.

Carl Hatch, Sherman Oaks, California, to Robert Willis, Corpus Christi, Texas, February 28, 1952.

R. Dennis Heard, Joplin, Mo., to Klaude Kendrick, Springfield, Mo., March 30, 1960.

O. Ralph Isbill, Des Moines, Iowa, to Klaude Kendrick, Springfield, Mo., July 2, 1957.

W. C. Moody, Butler, Pa., to E. N. Bell, Springfield, Mo., November 17, 1921.

Harold H. Moss, North Bergen, N. J., to E. N. Bell, Springfield, Mo., April 24, 1922.

M. E. Parrish, Franklin Springs, Ga., to Klaude Kendrick, Springfield, Mo., July 19, 1957.

O. W. Polen, Cleveland, Tenn., to Klaude Kendrick, Springfield, Mo., July 8, 1957.

Mrs. Dolores Rainey, Des Moines, Iowa, to Klaude Kendrick, Springfield, Mo., July 2, 1957.

T. A. Sandgren, Chicago, Ill., to E. N. Bell, Springfield, Mo., November 19, 1921.

W. J. Seymour, Los Angeles, Calif., to Brother Carothers, Houston, Texas, July 12, 1906.

John C. Sinclair, Portland, Oregon, to E. N. Bell, Springfield, Mo., January 3, 1922.

Wynn T. Stairs, St. Louis, Mo., to Klaude Kendrick, Springfield, Mo., July 18, 1957.

Howard D. Stanley, Topeka, Kansas, to E. N. Bell, Springfield, Mo., January 17, 1922.

J. A. Synan, Franklin Springs, Ga., to Klaude Kendrick, Springfield, Mo., August 6, 1957.

J. A. Synan, Hopewell, Va., to Klaude Kendrick, Springfield, Mo., May 11, 1960.

Paul H. Walker, Cleveland, Tenn., to Klaude Kendrick, Springfield, Mo., July 8, 1957.

OTHER UNPUBLISHED MATERIALS

Bruland, Gotfred F. "The Origin and Development of the Open Bible Church in Iowa." Unpublished M.A. thesis, Drake University, Des Moines, Iowa, June, 1945. Pp. 134.

"Christ's Ambassadors, Youth Organization of the Assemblies of God." Duplicated information prepared by the Christ's Ambassadors Department, Assemblies of God. [1951]. Pp. 4.

Flower, J. Roswell. "A History of the Assemblies of God." Unpublished mimeographed manuscript prepared for Central Bible Institute, Springfield, Mo. Pp. 31.

"Foreign Missions Department Report to General Presbyters, September 5-7, 1956." Duplicated report prepared by the Foreign Missions Department, Assemblies of God, 1956. Pp. 17.

Gaddis, Merrill Elmer. "Christian Perfectionism in America." Unpublished Ph.D. dissertation, University of Chicago, 1929. Pp. 602.

"General Chairman's Report, Open Bible Standard General Conference, July 17-21, 1957." Duplicated report prepared by the General Chairman of the Open Bible Standard Church.

"History and Objectives, National Home Missions Department, Assemblies of God." Duplicated bulletin of the National Home Missions Department, Assemblies of God, [1955]. Pp. 10.

"History of Foursquaredom." Unpublished mimeographed manuscript prepared for L. I. F. E. Bible College, 1951. Pp. 9.

"History of the Gospel Publishing House." Manuscript prepared by officers of the Gospel Publishing House, [1951]. Pp. 6.

Kamerer, J. Z. "History of the Gospel Publishing House Achievements, 1914-1949." Paper delivered to the Sunday School Convention, Springfield, Mo., 1949. Pp. 6.

Lewis, Gayle F. "A Brief Sketch and Outline of the Growth of the Gospel Publishing House." Paper delivered to the General Council of the Assemblies of God, Atlanta, Ga., 1951. Pp. 3.

Moore, Everett LeRoy. "Handbook of Pentecostal Denominations in the United States." Unpublished M. A. thesis, Pasadena College, 1954. Pp. 346.

"National Home Missions Department Report to District Home Missions Representatives." Duplicated report prepared by the National Home Missions Department, Assemblies of God, August, 1956.

"Official Minutes." Manuscript minute book of the Open Bible Evangelistic Association, Des Moines, Iowa.

Parham, Charles F., Scrapbook.

"Pointers for All Who Write for the Pentecostal Evangel." Duplicated paper prepared by the editor of the *Pentecostal Evangel*, April, 1958. Pp. 3.

"Spreading the Pentecostal Message Across America and Around the World." Duplicated paper prepared by the editorial office of the *Pentecostal Evangel*, [1956]. Pp. 3.

"The Story of the Sunday School Department." Manuscript prepared by the Sunday School Department, Assemblies of God.

"Tips to Writers." Duplicated instruction for contributors to the *Christ's Ambassadors Herald* prepared by the editor. Pp. 6.

"Women's Missionary Council." Report prepared and duplicated by the National Women's Missionary Council Department, Assemblies of God, [1956]. Pp. 7.

NEWSPAPERS

Des Moines *Register*, 1927-1928.
Des Moines *Tribune*, 1932.
Eugene (Oregon) *Register Guard*, 1936.
Galveston *Daily News*, 1905.
Galveston *Tribune*, 1905.
Houston *Chronicle*, 1905.
Houston *Suburbanite*, 1905.
Kansas City *Times*, 1901.

New York Times, 1926.
Springfield (Mo.) *Daily News*, 1954.
Springfield (Mo.) *Daily Advertiser*, 1954.
Topeka *State Journal*, 1900-1901.

PERIODICALS

"Aimee Semple McPherson, Thousands Mourn at Famed Evangelist's Funeral," *Life*, XVII (October 20, 1944), pp. 85-89.

Apostolic Faith (Baxter Springs, Kansas), 1926-1944.

Brown, Ira V., "Watchers for the Second Coming: the Millenarian Tradition in America," *Mississippi Valley Historical Review*, XXXIX (December, 1952), pp. 441-458.

Budlong, Julia N., "Aimee Semple McPherson," *Nation*, CXXVIII (June 19, 1929), pp. 737-739.

The Faithful Standard, 1922.

Foursquare Magazine (Los Angeles), 1954.

"Growth of U.S. Churches," *Time*, LVII (April 2, 1951), p. 81.

Hall, John F., "An Emperor Receives the New Testament," *Bible Society Record*, XCII (September, 1947), pp. 100-101.

Missionary Challenge (Springfield, Mo.), 1943-1951.

Nichols, John T., "The Role of the Pentecostal Movement in American Church History," *The Gordon Review*, II (December 1, 1956), pp. 127-135.

Open Bible Messenger (Des Moines, Iowa), 1932-1935.

Open Bible Standard Messenger (Des Moines, Iowa), 1936.

Osterberg, A. G., "The Azusa Revival," *Voice of Healing*, July, 1954, p. 5.

Our Sunday School Counsellor (Springfield, Mo.), 1939-1958.

Pentecost (London), 1947-1948.

Pentecostal Evangel (Springfield, Mo.), 1919-1958.

Pentecostal Holiness Advocate (Franklin Springs, Ga.), 1950-1953.

"Return," *Time*, VIII (July 5, 1926), p. 19.

Ruth Gleaners, 1937-1939.

Schlesinger, A. M. "A Critical Period in American Religion, 1875-1900," *Massachusetts Historical Proceedings*, LXIV (1932), pp. 523-547.

Smith, A. G., "Fringe Religions," *American Mercury*, LXX (April, 1950), pp. 429-442.

United Evangelical Action, XIII (January 15, 1955), p. 10.

Wright, Carroll D., "Are the Rich Growing Rich and the Poor Poorer?" *Atlantic Monthly*, LXXX (September, 1897), pp. 300-309.

Word and Witness (Malvern Arkansas; Findlay, Ohio; St. Louis, Mo.), 1913-1915.

World Challenge (Springfield, Mo.), 1955-1958.

CATALOGS, CONSTITUTIONS, DISCIPLINES, MANUALS, MINUTES, REPORTS, AND YEARBOOKS

Assemblies of God, *C. A. Manual*. Springfield, Mo.: Christ's Ambassadors Department, Assemblies of God, 1946. Pp. 90.

——. *Minutes and Constitution*, 1914 to 1959.

——. *Missionary Manual*. Revised to 1956. Springfield, Mo.: Foreign Missions Department, Assemblies of God, 1956. Pp. 77.

——. *Missionary Manual*. Springfield, Mo.: National Home Missions Department, Assemblies of God, 1955. Pp. 50.

——. *Reports and Financial Statements*, 1947 to 1959

Central Bible Institute. *Catalog*, 1922 to 1958.

Church of God. *Book of Minutes*. Cleveland, Tenn.: Church of God Publishing House, 1922. Pp. 303.

——. *Supplement to Church of God Minutes*, 1951. Cleveland, Tenn.: Church of God, 1951. Pp. 48.

Church of God in Christ. *Manual of the Church of God in Christ*. Fourth ed. Memphis: O. T. Jones & J. E. Bryant, 1947. Pp. 96.

Evangel College. "Minutes, Meeting of Board of Directors of Evangel College, December 28-30, 1954."

International Church of the Foursquare Gospel. *Articles of Incorporation and By-Laws*, 1949 and 1952 editions.

L. I. F. E. Bible College. *Student Handbook*. Los Angeles: L. I. F. E. Bible College, 1949. Pp. 71.

Open Bible Institute. *Fourteenth Annual Catalog*. Des Moines: Open Bible Institute.

Open Bible Standard Churches. *Minister's Manual*, 1949 and 1954 editions.

Pentecostal Church of God of America. *General Constitution and By-Laws*, 1947 and 1953 editions.

——. *Minutes of Meeting Held February 15, 1922, Chicago, Illinois*. Chicago: Pentecostal Church of God, [1922]. Pp. 19.

Pentecostal Holiness Church. *Discipline of the Pentecostal Holiness Church*, 1937 to 1953 editions.

United Pentecostal Church. *Manual of the United Pentecostal Church*, 1955. St. Louis: Pentecostal Publishing House, 1955. Pp. 234.

BOOKS

Abell, Aaron Ignatius. *The Urban Impact on American Protestantism*, 1865-1900. Cambridge: Harvard University Press, 1943. Pp. 275.

Ainslie, Peter. *The Scandal of Christianity*. Chicago: Willett, Clark, & Colby, n. d. Pp. 212.

Ante-Nicene Fathers. Edited by Alexander Roberts and James Donaldson. 10 vols. New York: Charles Scribner's Sons, 1885.

Bach, Marcus. *They Have Found a Faith.* Indianapolis: Bobbs-Merrill Co., 1946. Pp. 300.

Baird, Henry M. *The Huguenots and the Revocation of the Edict of Nantes.* 2 vols. New York: Charles Scribner's Sons, 1895.

Bartleman, Frank. *How Pentecost Came to Los Angeles, As it was in the Beginning.* 2d ed. Los Angeles: Frank Bartleman, 1925. Pp. 167.

Bushnell, Horace. *Christian Nurture.* New Haven: Yale University Press, 1947, p. 351.

Beardsley, Frank Grenville. *The History of Christianity in America.* New York: American Tract Society, 1938. Pp. 244.

Brumback, Carl. *What Meaneth This? A Pentecostal Answer to a Pentecostal Question.* Springfield, Mo.: Gospel Publishing House, 1947. Pp. 348.

Campbell, Joseph E. *The Pentecostal Holiness Church, 1898-1948, Its Background and History, Presenting Complete Background Material Which Adequately Explains the Existence of this Organization, Also the Existence of Other Kindred Pentecostal and Holiness Groups, As an Essential and Integral Part of the Total Church Set-up.* Franklin Springs, Ga.: Publishing House of the Pentecostal Holiness Church, 1951. Pp. 573.

Carter, Paul A. *The Decline and Revival of the Social Gospel: Social and Political Liberalism in American Protestant Churches, 1920-1940.* Ithaca, N. Y.: Cornell University Press, 1954. P. 265.

Catholic Encyclopedia, an International Work of Reference on the Constitution, Doctrine, Discipline, and History of the Catholic Church. Edited by Donald Attwater. 15 vols. New York: Robert Appleton Company, 1912.

Chafer, Lewis Sperry. *Systematic Theology.* 8 vols. Dallas: Dallas Seminary Press, 1947-48.

Clark, Elmer T. *The Small Sects in America.* Revised ed. Nashville: Abingdon-Cokesbury Press, 1949. Pp. 256.

Conn, Charles W. *Like a Mighty Army Moves the Church of God, 1886-1955.* Cleveland, Tenn.: Church of God Publishing House, 1955. Pp. 380.

Curran, Francis S. *Major Trends in American Church History.* New York: American Press, 1946. Pp. 198.

Cutten, George Barton. *Speaking with Tongues, Historically and Psychologically Considered.* New Haven: Yale University Press, 1927. Pp. 193.

Davenport, Frederick Morgan. *Primitive Traits in Religious Revivals, a Study in Mental and Social Evolution.* New York: Macmillan Company, 1917. Pp. 323.

Elliott, Jonathan. *The Debates in the Several State Conventions, on the Adoption of the Federal Constitution, as Recommended by the General Convention at Philadelphia, in 1787. Together with the Journal of the Federal Convention, Luther Martin's Letter, Yate's Minutes, Congressional Opinions, Virginia and Kentucky Resolutions* of 1798-1799, and other *Illustrations of the Constitution.* 2d ed. 5 vols. Philadelphia: J. B. Lippincott Co., 1888.

Encyclopedia of Religion and Ethics. Edited by James Hastings. 12 vols. New York: Charles Scribner's Sons, 1955.

Etter, Mrs. M. B. Woodworth. *Signs and Wonders God Wrought in the Ministry for Forty Years.* Indianapolis: Author, [1916]. Pp. 584.

Eusebius Pamphilus. *Ecclesiastical History.* Translated by C. F. Cruse. London: Bell and Daldy, 1870. Pp. 430.

Ewart, Frank J. *The Phenomenon of Pentecost, A History of the Latter Rain.* St. Louis: Pentecostal Publishing House, 1947. Pp. 109.

Ferguson, Charles W. *The Confusion of Tongues.* New York: Doubleday, 1929, p. 464.

Frodsham, Stanley, *With Signs Following, the Story of the Pentecostal Revival in the Twentieth Century.* Revised edition. Springfield, Mo.: Gospel Publishing House, 1941. Pp. 279.

Gee, Donald. *The Pentecostal Movement, Including the Story of the War Years, 1940-47.* London: Elim Publishing Company, Ltd., 1949. Pp. 236.

Goss, Ethel E. *The Winds of God, The Story of the Early Pentecostal Days (1901-1914) in the Life of Howard A. Goss.* New York: Comet Press, 1958. Pp. 178.

Grant, Heber J. *Gospel Standards, Selections from the Sermons and Writings of Heber J. Grant.* Compiled by G. Homer Durham. Salt Lake City: Deseret News Press, 1941. Pp. 384.

Greenway, H. W. *World Pentecostal Conference, 1952.* London: British Pentecostal Fellowship, n. d. Pp. 76.

Hedley, George. *The Christian Heritage in America.* New York: Macmillian Company, 1948. Pp. 177.

Hodges, Melvin L. *The Indigenous Church.* Springfield, Mo.: Gospel Publishing House, 1953. Pp. 157.

Hodges, Serena M. *Look on the Fields, a Missionary Survey.* Springfield, Mo.: Gospel Publishing House, 1956. Pp. 201.

Holmes, N. J. and Wife. *Life Sketches and Sermons.* Royston, Ga.: Press of the Pentecostal Holiness Church, 1920.

Hopkins, Charles Howard. *The Rise of the Social Gospel in American Protestantism,* 1865-1915. New Haven: Yale University Press, 1942. Pp. 352.

Johnson, Charles Albert. *The Frontier Camp Meeting: Religious Harvest Time.* Dallas: Southern Methodist University Press, [1955]. Pp. 325.

King, Joseph H. and Blanche L. *Yet Speaketh, Memoirs of the Late Bishop Joseph H. King.* Written by himself and supplemented by Mrs. Blanche L. King. Franklin Springs, Ga.: Publishing House of the Pentecostal Holiness Church, 1949. Pp. 388.

Knox, R. A. *Enthusiasm; a Chapter in the History of Religion with Special Reference to the Nineteenth and Eighteenth Centuries.* New York: Oxford University Press, 1950. Pp. 622.

LaBerge, Mrs. Agnes N. O. *What God Hath Wrought.* Chicago: Herald Publishing Company, n. d. Pp. 128.

Landis, Benson Y. *Yearbook of American Churches, Information on All Faiths in the U.S.A., 1957.* New York: National Council of Churches of Christ in the U.S.A., 1956. Pp. 314.

——. *Yearbook of American Churches, 1960.* New York: National Council of Churches of Christ in the U.S.A., 1959. Pp. 314.

Lawrence, B. F. *The Apostolic Faith Restored.* St. Louis: Gospel Publishing House, 1916. Pp. 119.

Lee, Umphrey. *The Historical Background of Early Methodist Enthusiasm.* New York: Columbia University Press, 1931. Pp. 176.

Mackie, Alexander, *The Gift of Tongues.* New York: George H. Doran Company, 1921. Pp. 275.

Mason, Mary. *The History and Life Work of Bishop C. H. Mason, Chief Apostle, and His Co-Laborers.* Memphis: 1934. Pp. 103.

May, Henry F. *Protestant Churches and Industrial America.* New York: Harper Brothers, 1949. Pp. 297.

Mayer, F. E. *The Religious Bodies of America.* St. Louis: Concordia Publishing House, 1956, Pp. 591.

McPherson, Aimee Semple. *In the Service of the King.* New York: Boni and Liverwright, 1927. Pp. 316.

——. *The Story of My Life. In Memoriam.* Los Angeles: Echo Park Evangelistic Association, 1951. Pp. 246.

——. *This is That.* Los Angeles: Echo Park Evangelistic Association, 1923. Pp. 791.

——. *The Foursquare Gospel.* Los Angeles: Echo Park Evangelistic Association, 1946. Pp. 199.

——. *The Holy Spirit.* Los Angeles: Challpin Publishing Company, 1931. Pp. 287.

McWilliams, Carey, "Aimee Semple McPherson: 'Sunlight in my Soul,' " in Leighton, Isabel, ed. *The Aspirin Age, 1919-1941.* New York: Simon and Schuster, 1949. Pp. 50-80.

Mead, Frank S. *Handbook of Denominations in the United States.* Nashville: Abington Press, 1956. Pp. 255.

Mecklin, John M. *The Story of American Dissent.* New York: Harcourt, Brace and Co., [1934]. Pp. 381.

Melcher, Marguerite Fellows. *The Shaker Adventure.* Princeton: Princeton University Press, 1941. Pp. 319.

Mode, Peter C. *Source Book and Bibliographical Guide for American Church History.* Menasha, Wisc.: George Banta Publishing Co., 1921. Pp. 735.

Nelson, P. C. *Bible Doctrines, a Handbook of Pentecostal Theology Based on Scriptures and Following the Lines of the Statement of Fundamental Truths as Adopted by the General Council of the Assemblies of God.* Revised and enlarged edition. Enid, Oklahoma: Southwestern Press, 1936. Pp. 177.

Newman, Albert Henry. *A Manuel of Church History.* 2 vols. Philadelphia: American Baptist Publication Society, 1903.

Niebuhr, Helmut Richard. *The Social Sources of Denominationalism.* New York: H. Holt and Company, [1929]. Pp. 304.

Parham, Charles F. and Sarah E. *Selected Sermons of the Late Charles F. Parham and Sarah E. Parham.* Compiled by Robert L. Parham. n. p.: [Published by compiler], 1941. Pp. 135.

Parham, Sarah E. *The Life of Charles F. Parham, Founder of the Apostolic Faith Movement.* Joplin, Mo.: Tri-State Printing Company, 1930. Pp. 452.

Persons, Stow, ed. *Evolutionary Thought in America.* New Haven: Yale University Press, 1950. Pp. 462.

Pearlman, Myer. *Knowing the Doctrines of the Bible.* Springfield, Mo.: Gospel Publishing House, 1937. Pp. 394.

Redford, M. E. *The Rise of the Church of the Nazarene.* Kansas City, Mo.: Nazarene Publishing House, 1948. Pp. 223.

Russell, Elbert. *The History of Quakerism.* New York: Macmillan Company, 1942. Pp. 586.

Schaff, Philip. *History of the Apostolic Church.* New York: Charles Scribner Company, 1853. Pp. 684.

——. *History of the Christian Church.* Reprint, 8 vols. Grand Rapids, Mich.: Wm. B. Eerdman Publishing Company, 1949-50.

Schenck, Lewis Bevens. *The Presbyterian Doctrine of Children in the Covenant, an Historical Study of the Significance of Infant Baptism in the Presbyterian Church in America.* New Haven: Yale University Press, 1940. Pp. 188.

Schlesinger, Arthur Meier. *The Rise of the City, 1878-98.* Vol. X of *A History of American Life.* Edited by Dixon R. Fox & Arthur M. Schlesinger. 13 vols. New York: Macmillan Company, 1927-48.

Shaw, P. E. *The Catholic Apostolic Church, Sometimes Called Irvingite; a Historical Study.* New York: King's Crown Press, 1946. Pp. 264.

Shuler, R. P. *McPhersonism, a Study of Healing Cults and Modern Day Tongues Movements, Containing Summary of Facts as to Disappearance and Re-appearance of Aimee Semple McPherson.* Los Angeles: R. P. Shuler, n. d. Pp. 128.

Simmons, E. L. *History of the Church of God.* Cleveland, Tenn.: Church of God Publishing House, 1938. Pp. 157.

Sweet, William Warren. *The American Churches, an Interpretation.* Nashville: Abingdon-Cokesbury Press, 1947. Pp. 153.

——. *Religion in the Development of American Culture, 1765-1840.* New York: Charles Scribner's Sons, 1952. Pp. 338.

——. *The Story of Religion in America.* New York: Harper & Brothers, 1939. Pp. 656.

U. S. Bureau of the Census. *Religious Bodies: 1936.* 2 vols. Washington: Government Printing Office, 1941.

Wilson, Elizabeth A. Galley. *Making Many Rich.* Springfield: Gospel Publishing House, 1955. Pp. 257.

Winchester, Olive May. *Crisis Experiences in the Greek New Testament; an Investigation of the Evidences for the Definite, Miraculous Experiences of Regeneration and Sanctification as Found in the Greek New Testament, Especially in the figures Emphasized and in the uses of the Aorist Tense.* Final chapter and appendix by Ross E. Price. Kansas City, Mo.: Nazarene Publishing House, 1953. Pp. 110.

PAMPHLETS AND BROCHURES

Assemblies of God. *Workers Together.* Springfield, Mo.: Gospel Publishing House, n. d. Pp. 64.

Assemblies of God Home Missions. Springfield, Mo.: National Home Missions Department, Assemblies of God, 1953. 28 unnumbered pages.

A Brief Sketch of the Life and Labors of Florence L. Crawford. Portland, Oregon: Apostolic Faith Mission, n. d. Pp. 23.

Burr, Murray E. *The Hair Question.* St. Louis: Home Missionary Department, United Pentecostal Church, n. d. Pp. 16.

Educational Institutions of the Assemblies of God. Springfield, Mo.: Educational Department, Assemblies of God, [1951]. Pp. 16.

Facts and Figures. Springfield, Mo.: Foreign Missions Department, Assemblies of God, [1953]. Pp. 4.

232 *The Promise Fulfilled*

Gardiner, Gordon P. *The Origin of Glad Tidings Tabernacle.* New York: n. p., 1955. Pp. 47.

Idea Book. Springfield, Mo.: Home Missions Department, Assemblies of God, [1955]. Pp. 48.

McPherson, Aimee Semple. *Declaration of Faith.* Los Angeles: International Church of the Foursquare Gospel, n. d. Pp. 30.

National Association of Evangelicals. *Progress.* Chicago: National Association of Evangelicals, 1945. Pp. 67.

——. *United in the Faith.* Chicago: National Association of Evangelicals, 1948. Pp. 48.

The New Gospel Publishing House. Brochure published by the Assemblies of God, [1949].

The Origin and Development of the Assemblies of God. Springfield, Mo.: Gospel Publishing House, 1948. Pp. 24.

Pentecostal Young People's Association. Kansas City, Mo.: Pentecostal Church of God, n. d. Pp. 32.

Report of Organization and Development, Women's Missionary Council, Assemblies of God; District of Texas and New Mexico. Houston: Women's Missionary Council, District of Texas and New Mexico, 1925. Pp. 12.

Sandgren, F. A. *One Sunday in August, 1906.* Tract printed by F. A. Sandgren in 1917 for circulation in his Chicago church.

Survey of Services, Supplies and Literature Available to Assemblies of God Sunday Schools, 1955-56. Springfield, Mo. Sunday School Department, Assemblies of God, [1956]. Pp. 62.

Tomlinson, A. J. *Answering the Call of God.* Cleveland, Tenn.: White Wing Publishing House, n. d. Pp. 24.

——. *The Church of God Marches On.* Cleveland, Tenn.: White Wing Publishing House, [1939]. Pp. 27.

Vouga, Oscar. *Our Gospel Message.* St. Louis: Pentecostal Publishing House, n. d. Pp. 31.

Workers' Training, Assemblies of God. Springfield, Mo.: National Sunday School Department, Assemblies of God, n. d. Pp. 7.

Index